# THE
# MARKETPLACE
# ANNOTATED
# BIBLIOGRAPHY

## *A Christian Guide to Books on Work, Business & Vocation*

Pete Hammond,
R. Paul Stevens
& Todd Svanoe

InterVarsity Press
Downers Grove, Illinois

*InterVarsity Press*
*P.O. Box 1400, Downers Grove, IL 60515-1426*
*World Wide Web: www.ivpress.com*
*E-mail: mail@ivpress.com*

*InterVarsity Press® is the book-publishing division of InterVarsity Christian Fellowship/USA®, a student movement active on campus at hundreds of universities, colleges and schools of nursing in the United States of America, and a member movement of the International Fellowship of Evangelical Students. For information about local and regional activities, write Public Relations Dept., InterVarsity Christian Fellowship/USA, 6400 Schroeder Rd., P.O. Box 7895, Madison, WI 53707-7895, or visit the IVCF website at <www.ivcf.org>.*

*ISBN 0-8308-2672-6*

*Printed in the United States of America* ∞

**Library of Congress Cataloging-in-Publication Data**

*Hammond, Pete, 1936-*
  *The marketplace annotated bibliography: a Christian guide to books on work, business & vocation/Pete Hammond, R. Paul Stevens & Todd Svanoe.*
    *p.;cm.*
  *Includes bibliographical references and index.*
  *ISBN 0-8308-2672-6 (pbk.: alk. paper)*
   *1. Work—Religious aspects—Christianity—Bibliography. 2. Business—Religious aspects—Christianity—Bibliography. 3. Vocation—Christianity—Bibliography. 4. Employees—Religious life—Bibliography. I. Stevens, R. Paul, 1937- II. Svanoe, Todd. III. Title.*

*Z7854.H35 2002*
*[BV4593]*
*016.2618'5—dc21*

                                                                          *2002019719*

| **P** | 17 | 16 | | 15 | 14 | 13 | 12 | 11 | 10 | 9 | 8 | 7 | 6 | 5 | 4 | 3 | 2 | 1 |
|---|---|---|---|---|---|---|---|---|---|---|---|---|---|---|---|---|---|---|
| **Y** | | 16 | 15 | 14 | 13 | 12 | 11 | 10 | 09 | 08 | 07 | 06 | 05 | 04 | 03 | 02 | | | |

*To four companions who typify everyday Christians*
*who live out their faith*
*in the workplaces of our culture:*

SHIRLEY HAMMOND
*wife, mother and educator*

BOB LAVELLE
*African American banker,*
*exemplar and community builder*

ED MOY
*Chinese American health care executive,*
*entrepreneur and White House staff*

KAREN MOY
*personal manager,*
*speaker and White House staff*

# CONTENTS

# Foreword

Over the last few decades the significance of the marketplace for Christians has come increasingly into focus. Some have stressed the importance of seeing work as a divine calling or vocation, or as a ministry or service of the kingdom. Others have emphasized the need for a more comprehensive theology and ethics of work in general and of workplace trends, pressures, dilemmas, challenges and opportunities in particular. More recently the role of work as a spiritual practice or discipline has come up for discussion. Alongside these is a continuing concern with appropriate ways of being a witness or sharing the gospel in the workplace. This growing interest among Christians in the marketplace has also resulted in the development of organizations to further its progress, publications to clarify its concerns and gatherings to network its key advocates.

In addition to more attentive and focused thought being given to this area, Christians who live out most of their lives in the marketplace require resources to help them fulfill their workplace responsibilities. One of the most effective resources to appear in recent years is the *Word in Life Study Bible,* which flags and comments on every reference to work, the city, economy, society and the environment as well as on every lay believer, including marketplace believers, identified in Scripture. This resource was the brainchild of Pete Hammond, who worked with a team of scholars over a number of years to produce it.

While he was still supervising this project, Pete envisioned a second resource for the working Christian, an annotated bibliography of the main writings on the subject.

This has been an ambitious project, and Pete was only intermittently able to find the help he needed to complete it. I have watched and cheered its progress from the sidelines, and now and then I have been involved in discussions about it. But at last the task is done and what a wonderful resource it will be.

The following pages include a carefully selected list of over seven hundred publications that feature much of the best writing on Christianity and work over the last several decades. The annotations contain a mixture of description and evaluation and are a model of economy and usefulness. The annotations are enhanced by the provision of indexes at the end of the volume, which will be of great help for personal Bible study, for small group leaders and researchers, and as an aid in sermon construction. Pete Hammond himself provides an introductory survey of writings and developments in the area of Christianity and work.

My hope is that this volume will find itself on the bookshelves of every thinking Christian whose main field of service to God is in the marketplace— every Christian who initiates or facilitates discussions in and around their workplace, every leader of Bible study groups consisting of significant numbers of marketplace believers, every Christian educator in local churches, every college and university student ministry staffer, and every pastor committed to equipping his or her people for their ministries of daily life.

I congratulate Pete Hammond and his team on another significant resource to assist the people of God to change our world God's way.

*Robert Banks*
*Director and Dean of Macquarie Christian Studies Institute,*
*Sydney, Australia*

# Preface

My journey into the marketplace-faith movement began when my wife, Shirley, our three teens (Scott, Leigh Anne and Layne Marie) and I returned to the United States in 1979 after a year of teaching and studying in Manila, Philippines. I had stepped away from InterVarsity Christian Fellowship/USA after serving in the southeastern region for fourteen years. It was a good and very educational break.

When we returned to the United States, we moved from Atlanta to InterVarsity's national headquarters in Madison, Wisconsin. We made that move in the fall before InterVarsity's 1979 Urbana Student Convention. It was a scramble as I joined the Urbana leadership team. During the countdown to Urbana, a surprise that would shape my next twenty years happened. Three InterVarsity leaders came into my office late one day, and vice-president Jim McLeish said, "Pete, we think we have a problem. We are hearing comments like, 'Urbana— that's where you go to become a career missionary or feel guilty the rest of your life!' Pete, we want you to figure out the problem and fix it."

That is the kind of assignment that really appeals to an entrepreneurial spirit, especially one who has just finished a year of refreshment away from the day-to-day job. I jumped at the chance. I began to reflect on my previous work of building campus ministry in the southeast. I reviewed what we had emphasized with young Christian college students and what I recalled hearing from alumni and former staff. My seminary studies in theology and church history kicked in alongside my undergraduate training in sociology.

The heart of the next seven years centered around what I thought would be a student conference that paralleled Urbana. We would call students together around the issues of serving God in their postcollege careers in North America. They would meet and be led by veteran marketplace Christians from across the country. I ended up coleading three national events with other InterVarsity leaders: Washington '80, with Black Campus Ministry director Elward Ellis; San Francisco '83, with regional director Geri Rodman; and Marketplace '86 in Chicago, with regional director Jim Lundgren. Each convention was a laboratory for us as we engaged urban and ethnic problems in America, city church struggles, and career callings for young Christians. The Chicago event theme was "Marketplace: Jesus' Call to Service, Witness and Righteousness." Almost 200 everyday Christian professionals gave themselves to the 1,400 collegians and staff. During the Christmas-break conference we ran nine thematic schools across the city in offices, factories, health care centers and urban churches. We helped students deal with theological and ethical issues. And we sought to refresh the biblical call to all Christians to serve Christ as ministers who see work as inherent to their makeup as persons "created in the image and likeness of God" (Gen 1:27-31).

This seven-year learning process led to the launching of a Marketplace Ministry department within InterVarsity. Under interim president Tom Dunkerton I built a team: Robert Peitscher, Scott Young, Denyse Stoneman and later DeAnn Franklin. We started *Networks/Métier,* a bimonthly newszine; *Marketplace Voices,* a daily radio program; and a network of marketplace associates among staff and alumni across the country. We also began another seven-year research, writing and publishing venture that led to the *Word In Life Study Bible* (Thomas Nelson). Bill Hendricks, who had previously coauthored the important book *Your Work Matters to God* (NavPress), was my coleader.

One enriching piece of this twenty-year journey was when Scott Young and I were drawn into the launch of the Coalition for Ministry in Daily Life led by steel executive, author and Lutheran layman, Bill Diehl. In 1991 he called together Christian marketplace ministry leaders to connect with and encourage one another. It was like an oasis for lonely pioneers and prophets. Scott also made a connection with Australian Robert Banks, who had moved into the new position of professor of laity at Fuller Theological Seminary. This led to a ten-year partnership before Robert moved back to Sydney. His scholarly skills and international networking added to our growing awareness. It was also through the Coalition that we linked up with coauthor Paul Stevens from Regent College in Vancouver.

This book began in the spring of 1990. Todd Svanoe, a Madison journalist, and his wife, Vicki, were interested in doing some integrative studies on faith and work. Instead of encouraging him to move away to study, I asked if he would like to do some guided reading and reviews of books I had begun to collect in the field. Before long he was doing the initial work on an annotated marketplace bibliography. Within that year Todd reviewed over two hundred volumes, and the process that would lead to this book was on its way. After InterVarsity Press agreed in 1999 to publish the book, Todd rejoined the project and reviewed dozens of the newer books in my collection.

In 1995 Robert Cooley, then president of Gordon-Conwell Theological Seminary (GCTS), called. Bob wanted me to launch a center for faith in the workplace at GCTS. Joanna Mockler was funding the center to honor her late husband's practice of faith-based ethics at work while he served as president of Gillette. Bob's invitation led to a three-year commute between Madison and GCTS on Boston's North Shore. I worked with Walter Kaiser, who was Distinguished Mockler Professor of Old Testament and Ethics at the time but would eventually succeed Bob as president. Pastor Harry Heintz of Brunswick Presbyterian Church in Troy, New York, signed on to be my Mockler Associate and provide mentoring for our scholarship students. He and associate pastor Kate Kotfila had invested several years applying marketplace theology to the life of that congregation and had much to offer future pastors and professionals studying at the seminary. The Mockler Center is now under the capable leadership of director Will Messenger.

Now Paul, Todd and I offer this collection of reviews of books covering seven decades in the twentieth century. We hope it will encourage much more work on changing the North American church into a movement of confident and competent witnesses in everyday life.

*Soli Deo Gloria!*
*Pete Hammond*

# America's Change
## A Seedbed for Marketplace Ministry

**I** am intrigued by the increased interest in the workplace ministry of everyday believers, often referred to as "the marketplace ministry." Since 1979 I have been studying, networking, consulting and teaching in this area of faith. Today there is a new and broad-based grassroots movement among Christians in Western nations, especially in America. Two phrases are frequently used to describe this movement: "a lay renaissance" and "the second reformation." I use "the agitated pew" as a description of Christians who are asking questions about taking their faith beyond the walls of church buildings and into their jobs, community life and family responsibilities. This process is illustrated by questions I repeatedly hear across the country.

☐ Where is the church on Tuesday?

☐ What does the lordship of Jesus Christ mean in the workplace?

☐ What does biblical justice look like in government, education, finance, health care, agriculture, manufacturing and sales?

☐ What does the Holy Spirit have to do with the building trades, food service, communications, transportation, law or the arts?

☐ Does the Christian laity have any more to do in building the kingdom of God than just praying, paying and obeying church leaders?

☐ Is evangelism the special responsibility of those who are gifted or called into it as a profession, or is it the calling and privilege of every believer?

☐ Is work a result of the Fall, destined to be consumed by fire as chaff, or just a necessary evil?

☐ Is there a difference between the ministry of the laity and the clergy?

☐ Is biblical witness more than a few gospel-tractlike formulas or "button-holing" my work associates?

The increase of books exploring these questions reveals the growing appetite for practical spirituality. I have thirteen hundred in my library. Some are poorly researched and written, but many of the newest releases reflect historical, biblical and theological scholarship in the field. How did this movement develop in the twentieth century?

**Early Marketplace-Faith Initiatives: 1930-1950**
The earliest books on faith and daily life I have found were published in the 1930s. Max Weber contributed *The Protestant Ethic and the Spirit of Capitalism,* and Roland Allen added *The Case for Voluntary Clergy.* John R. Mott, international pioneer of the YMCA and the Student Volunteer Movement, released *Liberating the Lay Forces of Christianity* in 1932. German theologian Emil Brunner wrote *The Divine Imperative: A Study in Christian Ethics.* Rowland Hogbe published *Vocation* for Britain's Inter-Varsity Press. Episcopal bishop Francis McConnell added *Christian Materialism* in 1936. These authors were the first modern prophetic voices about practical, public faith. Other pioneers followed throughout the 1940s and 1950s.[1] The earliest faith-based biography of an American business leader I found is Richard Day Ellsworth's *A Christian in Big Business,* released in 1946. It told the story of Henry Parsons Crowell, who led the Quaker Oats Company and partnered with evangelist Dwight L. Moody.

Two authors were very influential as the movement gained visibility. Quaker professor Elton Trueblood was an early voice. He wrote *Signs of Hope in a Century of Despair* in 1950 and *Your Other Vocation* in 1952. Trueblood traveled and lectured extensively, giving new insight on what Scripture teaches about modern dilemmas. Hendrick Kraemer released his pivotal book *A Theology of the Laity* in 1958. It became a benchmark work and is still referred to today.[2] His was an informed but popular plea for the significance of lay ministry and mission.

Three British voices, sometimes referred to as the "mere Christians," joined the cry for faith that engaged modern needs. C. S. Lewis's writings captured the hearts of many wanting spiritual help in real life. Popular novelist Dorothy Sayers's *Creed or Chaos* (1949) moved into the gap between personal and public

---

[1]For more information on marketplace books and authors, see the chart at <www.ivmdl.org>.
[2]At the time Kraemer was the Fosdick Visiting Professor at Union Theological Seminary in New York City. He first served with the Dutch Bible Society in India, then as professor of the history and phenomenology of religion at Leiden, and as the first director of the Ecumenical Institute at Bossey.

faith. Popular poet, novelist, editor, columnist and social critic G. K. Chesterton added his acerbic wit and wisdom into the mix.[3] These three voices gained American readers because of their passion, clarity and humor.

But authors were not the only marketplace-faith change agents in the decades before the 1960s. A variety of networks and movements focused on faith in daily life. To empower the poor and combat racism, Southerner Clarence Jordan launched his Christian communal experiment, Koinonia Farms, in rural Georgia in 1942. Reverend Martin Luther King Jr. and his associates pioneered the Civil Rights movement in Georgia, Alabama, Mississippi and Tennessee. In the North Dorothy Day, a Catholic activist who called for justice among workers, women and the poor, launched the *Daily Worker* newspaper.[4] The emerging prayer breakfast movement was catapulted into visibility when U.S. president Dwight D. Eisenhower attended in 1953.[5] The same year *Fortune* magazine noted the revival among businessmen, asking, "Is this a superficial, merely utilitarian movement, or is it a genuinely spiritual awakening?"[6] The German *Kirchentag Movement* focused on faith and the rebuilding of the nation after World War II. (It still sponsors evangelical academies for laity and convenes a major event every few years, often attracting more than 25,000.) The second assembly of the World Council of Churches (WCC) met in Evanston, Illinois, in 1956.[7] And Protestant author Keith Miller's work led to the founding of the Faith at Work movement in 1957. (It publishes the oldest extant journal on marketplace-faith topics.)

## A Decade of National Change: The 1960s

A cultural crossroads for Americans occurred in the 1960s. Life as they had

---

[3]See Joseph Pearce, *Wisdom and Innocence: A Life of G. K. Chesterton* (San Francisco: Ignatius Press, 1976).

[4]Her autobiography, *Long Loneliness: The Autobiography of Dorothy Day,* was first published by Harper Collins in 1952. See also Jim Forest's *Love Is the Measure: A Biography of Dorothy Day* (New York: Paulist, 1986).

[5]Founder Abraham Vereide was an entrepreneurial businessman from Washington State. He moved to Washington, D.C., to work among government leaders because spirituality was being acknowledged among elected national leaders. See the review of Norman Grubb's biography of him, *Modern Viking,* this volume.

[6]Quoted by Marc Gunther, "God & Business," *Fortune,* July 9, 2001, p. 78.

[7]It issued a report, *The Laity: The Christian in His Vocation,* which declared, "The real battles of faith today are being fought in factories, shops, offices, and farms, in political parties and government agencies, in countless homes, in the press, radio, and television, in the relationship of nations. Very often it is said that the church should 'go into these spheres'; but the fact is that the church is already in these spheres in the persons of the laity."

known it since World War II ended, and a "new wind was blowing" for the nation and the church. Social critic, lawyer and theologian William Stringfellow declared, "Since the climax of America's glorification as a nation—in the ostensible American victory in World War II, most lucidly and aptly symbolized in Hiroshima—Americans have become so beleaguered by anxiety and fatigue, so bemused and intimidated, so beset by a sense of impotence and intuitions of calamity, that they have . . . become consigned to despair."[8]

During the 1960s the long-standing Sunday blue laws began to fall,[9] and the U.S. Supreme Court banned prayer and Bible reading in public schools. The seeds of sexual revolution were planted as the "pill" was released in 1960, restrictive laws were removed and the Kinsey report on *Human Sexuality* worked its way into the lives of many citizens.[10] The growing debate about sexual morality is exemplified by Leo Pyle's book *The Pill and Birth Regulation: The Catholic Debate.*[11]

In 1968 Theodore Rozak coined the term *counterculture,* suggesting that something big was happening in North America. The American Dream of a good job, financial security, home ownership, a forty-hour work week, and paid vacations was found wanting among the children of the middle and upper classes. Personal dissonance, broad unrest, growing mistrust of institutions and a rising youth culture shook the suburban serenity of the WASP majority.

Home ownership and suburban communities mushroomed after World War II.[12] The baby boom created exponential population growth.[13] Consumerism

---

[8]William Stringfellow, *An Ethic for Christians and Other Aliens in a Strange Land* (Dallas: Word, 1973), pp. 19-20.

[9]"One type of numerous extremely rigorous laws designed to regulate morals and conduct in colonial New England [that were] statute[s] regulating work, commerce and amusements on Sunday" (*Webster's Ninth New Collegiate Dictionary,* Miriam-Webster, 1990).

[10]Alfred Kinsey released his study *Sexual Behavior in the Human Male* in 1948, followed by his highly anticipated sequel *Sexual Behavior in the Human Female* in 1953.

[11]Baltimore: Helicon, 1964.

[12]"The suburban population doubled in one decade [1950s] from thirty-six million to seventy-two million" (Ruth Rosen, *The World Split Open: How the Modern Women's Movement Changed America* [New York: Viking, 2000], p. 9). The widespread appetite for comfort, safety and pleasure moved to the forefront of the rising middle class. Owning a home was made more possible with the "suburbs" when Levittown was created for young families on Long Island. It included 17,400 homes packed into a 4,000 acre farmland. Prices started at $8,000.

[13]One result was the massive increase in college students. Before World War II only 14 percent of college-age Americans enrolled, but by 1970 over 50 percent attended posthigh-school education. Another change during the sixties was an increase from 3 percent black students to 9 percent (David Burner, *Making Peace with the 60s* [Princeton, N.J.: Princeton University Press, 1996], p. 136).

expanded with the first significant use of credit cards in the 1960s. Black Americans challenged racism; women spoke about their prolonged subjugation and pain as second-class citizens; and America's role as world policeman was questioned as young Americans suffered and died in Vietnam.[14] This pivotal decade also launched the first Earth Day, which rallied many to concerns about pollution, consumption and diminishing natural resources.

Television's gross annual revenues bypassed radio's in 1954, and it was becoming very significant in the daily life of America. People began to have family meals while watching its news, entertainment and sports. The Federal Communications Commission reduced the legal requirements for free public-service air time and allowed networks to begin charging for it. Few religious organizations could absorb the increased costs and religious programming declined significantly.[15]

Possibly the most galvanizing shock of the decade was a series of highly visible assassinations: African American civil rights leader Medgar Evers (June 12, 1963); four young African American girls (September 15, 1963); President John F. Kennedy (November 22, 1963); civil rights workers Andrew Goodman, Michael Schwerner and James Chaney (June 1964); Malcolm X (February 21, 1965); Martin Luther King Jr. (April 4, 1968); Robert Kennedy (June 5, 1968); and four Kent State collegians (1970). These brutal deaths jolted the national psyche, raising deep questions about our nation and its values. Extensive media coverage of these movements produced anxiety, fear and anger in many citizens. The faith community was also inalterably affected by the tremendous violence.

Studying the youth culture of the 1970s, author and cultural analyst Arthur Levine captured the change in social fabric and values brought on by the events of the previous decade: "I was disturbed by the overwhelming sense of meism. . . . Today's meism grows out of a generalized cynicism, lack of trust and fear."[16] This translated into national insecurity, and concerns beyond the here-and-now began to surface. A more full-blown manifestation of this inner craving for deeper realities is evident in the growth of New Age spirituality and the marketplace faith movement.[17]

---

[14]For more on these issues see Taylor Branch's multivolume history of the Civil Rights Movement(*America in the King Years,* 2 vols. (New York: Simon & Shuster, 1988, 1998), and Rosen's *World Split Open.*

[15]Coalter, Mulder and Weeks, p. 6.

[16]Arthur Levine, *When Dreams and Heroes Died: A Portrait of Today's College Student* (San Francisco: Jossey-Bass, 1981), pp. xvii-xviii.

[17]For a much more extensive analysis of this era of change in our nation, read *A History of the Marketplace Movement in the 20th Century* <www.ivmdl.org>.

As America struggled with deep changes in the 1960s, the church had to face the fact that "business as usual" was no longer viable—it had tied itself to a culture that was coming to an end. The Christian faith could no longer be confined to church buildings and Sunday-only involvement. The laity had to wrestle with the integration and application of their beliefs into everyday responsibilities. Sunday worship needed to connect with Monday's challenging workplace realities in creative new ways.

## The Church's Response to the 1960s

*Europe.* In 1959 Dietrich Bonhoeffer's book *The Cost of Discipleship,* a critique of "cheap grace," was released posthumously. Frenchman Andre Bieler wrote *The Social Humanism of John Calvin,* describing Calvin's application of faith to daily life in Reformation-era Geneva. Anglican bishop John A. T. Robinson published *The Laymen's Church,* adding his *New Reformation* soon after. In 1963 WCC leaders Stephen Neill and Hans Ruedi-Weber released *The Layman in Christian History,* the first, and still the only, church-history textbook featuring the faith of professionals working outside of the church.[18] These works signaled a new understanding of the church as the body of Christ called to develop the kingdom of God in every sector of society. Ruedi-Weber also released his *Salty Christians* that same year, applying to modern culture what he learned from his understanding of church history.

Britain's popular author C. S. Lewis's impact on American Christianity was gaining momentum in the 1960s. Layman Mark Gibbs and pastor T. Ralph Morton released *God's Frozen People.* Mid-decade, Michael Green added his *Called to Serve.* Cardinal Stefan Wyszynski published *The Deeds of Faith,* describing Catholic faith of the people in communist-dominated Poland. Alfons Auer wrote *Open to the World: An Analysis of Lay Spirituality,* and Jacques Ellul released *The Presence of the Kingdom* in 1967. John R. W. Stott of London's All Souls Church described the church as a people in everyday life in *One People.* Sir Frederick Catherwood's *The Christian Citizen* was also published. This very productive decade ended with Gibbs and Morton's second work, *God's Lively People,* which added to their earlier plea for more faith-community impact on society.

A very different worldwide Christian dynamic began as popular British col-

---

[18]A major agenda item of the WCC's 1948 assembly (Evanston, Illinois) was "The Laity: The Christian in His Vocation." Ruedi-Weber and Neill's book was one of the fruit of that assembly. New images about the church as everyday people were introduced as they told the stories of the little people of God throughout church history.

umnist, world traveler and social critic Malcolm Muggeridge professed faith and began to use the media as a pulpit. He described his discovery of Jesus as the only figure of hope in his 1969 book *Jesus Rediscovered.*[19] That same year, his new faith was broadcast in the BBC film *Something Beautiful for God.* This film also introduced Mother Teresa to a worldwide audience. Over the next three decades she would challenge the Christian church to take the plight of the poor and dying seriously.

*America.* The *New York Times* reviewed William Stringfellow's 1966 book, *Dissenter in a Great Society,* saying, "This book hurts. . . . Stringfellow's strength lies in his acute perception of the pretensions, evasions and barbarities of our supposedly Christian, enlightened nation." Stringfellow added *A Private and Public Faith* and *An Ethic for Christians & Other Aliens in a Strange Land.*

Almost two dozen American authors added to the marketplace cause in the 1960s. D. Elton Trueblood and Peter Berger helped the people of God find their voice in the public square. Norman Grubb wrote about the rising impact of faith amid government leaders. Edmund C. Morgan told of a cultural precedent among early American settlers. Howard Grimes, Georgia Harkness, Francis O. Ayers and R. L. Oechslin wrote about the faith and ministry of the laity. Business leader John Mitchell, missionary Roland Allen, and Joseph C. McLelland added important works to the mix.

As the decade hit mid-point, more impetus for change appeared. In 1966 W. M. Abbott delivered the revolutionary Vatican II materials. George W. Forell and Notre Dame professors Oliver Williams and John Houck probed Christian ethics, illustrating how to sort out intricate ethical dilemmas from the perspective of faith. Several other key writers affirmed the church's need to mobilize every believer. These include Presbyterian pastor Richard Halverson, business leaders R. G. LeTourneau, Stanley Tam and Herbert J. Taylor. Elton Trueblood continued to be a major voice with three books at the end of the decade. The floodgates were opening wider as many wrestled with practical applications of faith to workplace, economic and cultural issues.

On the electronic front, the growing television industry included a few Christians. Through *Mr. Rogers' Neighborhood* Fred Rogers, an ordained Presbyterian, gained a prominent place in American homes as he taught Christian

---

[19]See his story and those of other marketplace Christians like Charles Colson, C. S. Lewis, Dorothy Day and Ethel Waters in Hugh T. Kerr and John M. Mulder, *Conversions* (Grand Rapids, Mich.: Eerdmans, 1983), pp. 251-54.

values to children in a low-key, entertaining style. In 1961 Pat Robertson launched what would become the Christian Broadcasting Network.

## Major Worldwide Gatherings

Pope John XXIII convened the Second Vatican Council in Rome (1962-1965) to "give the Church the possibility to contribute more efficaciously to the solution of the problems of the modern age."[20] Vatican II had a troubling but mobilizing effect on Roman Catholics worldwide as its leaders sought to modernize the faith. Some of the agenda had been shaped at the 1951 First World Congress of the Lay Apostolate in Rome, which aimed to mobilize laity. Vatican II developed several major papers, including one on the functions of the laity and another on the church in the modern world. These and other related papers are still being interpreted and debated today. One perspective asserts, "Vatican II refocused the church from institution to people . . . further expanding the role of the laity from spectators to participants. . . . The church has been returned to the people."[21] When Pope Paul VI released his encyclical *Humanae Vitae* (1968), affirming the spiritual life of both the unborn and all baptized believers, many laypersons took a more active role in church matters. New lay initiatives began, including several Vatican-sanctioned lay ministries in the 1970s.[22]

The Cursillo Movement ("little workshops in living Christianity"), focusing on personal faith experiences, originated in Spain in 1949 and broke onto the international scene first in Latin America and then in Great Britain. It came to the United States in 1961. Many of its early leaders would later be pioneers of the charismatic movement, which emerged in the 1960s and 1970s and eventually gained recognition from the Catholic establishment and elsewhere.[23] The World Congress of the Lay Apostolate reconvened in 1957, 1967 and 1975. The National Association of Laymen (NAL) was formed in St. Paul, Minnesota, in 1967. Issues like racism, nuclear arms and women's rights gained energy and visibility. Chicago Catholics called together a national gathering in 1975 to

---

[20]Walter Abbott, *The Documents of Vatican II* (New York: Guild, 1966), p. 705. The "Decree on the Apostolate of the Laity" "affirmed that the Protestant concept of the priesthood of all believers had authentic biblical and Catholic roots" (Avery Dulles, obituary of Congar, *America*, July 15, 1995).

[21]Mary Faulkner and Bob O' Gorman, *U.S. Catholic,* February 2001, p. 37.

[22]For a survey of writings about laity among Roman Catholics, see Leonard Doohan, *The Laity: A Bibliography* (Wilmington, Del.:Michael Glazier, 1987).

[23]*The Almanac of the Christian World,* 1991-1992 (Wheaton, Ill.: Tyndale House, 1990), p. 327.

focus on public justice, ethics and integration of faith in the workplace. Belgian Jan Grootaers described the changes: "Those who speak thus are no longer Catholics of the Constantinian era, engaged in claiming 'rights' which 'the others' must yield to them; they are Catholics who recognize that they themselves have 'duties' and that they cannot afford much longer to fail to fulfill these duties."[24]

Another major gathering was a 1961 ecumenical assembly that met in New Delhi, India. At that meeting the International Missionary Council was integrated into the WCC, and the newly expanded WCC began to wrestle with the place of the laity. In 1968 the fourth WCC Assembly met in Uppsala, Sweden. Leader D. T. Niles declared, "Our part in evangelism might be described as bringing about the occasion for men's response to Jesus Christ" and further stated that, "there is widespread defeatism in the churches about the work of evangelism and world mission."

In the late 1970s businessman Howard E. Butt and Christian Men, Inc., convened the North American Congress of the Laity in Los Angeles. It included eight hundred lay leaders. Along with several internationally known figures (e.g., business guru Peter F. Drucker, Gerald R. Ford, Ugandan bishop Festo Kivengere, British columnist Malcolm Muggeridge, Harvard professor of psychiatry Armand M. Nicholi and national columnist James Reston), they wrestled with what it means for a Christian to *be in the world*. The 1960s exploration into marketplace faith was beginning to bear fruit as the issue gained visibility and momentum.[25]

In 1966 evangelist Billy Graham was instrumental in leading the Berlin Congress on World Evangelization and in 1974 Graham convened 2,700 evangelicals from 150 nations in Lausanne, Switzerland. In the "Lausanne Covenant" evangelicals repented for their failures, committed themselves to preach the whole gospel and declared their willingness to work with all believers for world evangelization.[26]

### The African American Church

One of the most pervasive sources of change in terms of cultural impact was the Southern Christian Leadership Conference (SCLC), which was formed in

---

[24]Ruedi-Weber and Neill, *Layman in Christian History,* p. 329.
[25]Howard Butt, with Elliott Wright, *At the Edge of Hope* (New York: Seabury, 1978).
[26]The primary author was John R. W. Stott, whose influence was becoming worldwide by this time. For a survey of his writings, see Timothy Dudley-Smith, *John Stott: A Comprehensive Bibliography,* 2 vols. (Downers Grove, Ill.: InterVarsity Press, 1995).

Atlanta, Georgia, in 1957. Black leaders rallied around the emerging leadership of Baptist pastor Martin Luther King Jr. to actively engage southern racial discrimination. This new movement began to affect Anglo Christians when King led the 1955 Montgomery, Alabama, bus boycott. This expanded into nonviolent campaigns against racism throughout the South. The black church called the white church and national political leaders to accountability.

When the Ku Klux Klan and other white supremacists reacted with beatings, lynchings, imprisonment and legal maneuvering, all of America was exposed to racism via media coverage. King's challenge of America's entrenched racism resulted in new national legislation under President Lyndon B. Johnson.[27] King's example is a very significant model of applying faith to the deepest needs and problems within a culture.

Theologian William Bentley and former gang member Tom Skinner were the moving forces behind the establishment of the National Black Evangelical Association in 1963 at Fuller Theological Seminary. They were concerned about growing urban challenges and failure of white evangelicals to face social issues.

## American Mainline Protestants

In the 1960s conservative and evangelical members and pastors launched renewal movements in the Episcopal, United Methodist, Presbyterian and United Church of Christ denominations.[28] They were weary of the steady stream of political pronouncements by their leaders and deeply concerned about eroding theological convictions. Through these renewal movements many laypeople found a new voice in the affairs of their congregations and national denominational administrations.

In 1976 Lutheran layman William Diehl wrote *Christianity and Real Life*. After a career in the steel industry, Diehl spoke out about the loneliness he experienced as a Christian in the workplace and the lack of understanding and support he received from his church. As a result the Evangelical Lutheran

---

[27]Johnson signed the Civil Rights Act on July 2, 1964. It was the most sweeping civil rights legislation since Reconstruction. On September 24, 1965, the president issued an executive order enforcing the Act.

[28]The Presbyterians launched the Covenant Fellowship of Presbyterians in the southeast while Presbyterians United for Biblical Concerns grew in the northeast and west coast. Episcopalian evangelicals gathered together under the Episcopalian Renewal Movement umbrella. United Methodist leaders connected with each other nationally through the Good News Movement.

Church in America now has the longest-surviving department focused on the ministry of the laity at work. Diehl wrote several more excellent books in the field and founded the Coalition for Ministry in Daily Life among mainline Protestants and Roman Catholics.

Two other emerging cultural struggles surfaced in mainline churches: women in ministry and sexuality. These triggered major discussions of feminist, gay, lesbian, bisexual and transgender issues. Application of faith to modern needs and issues gained more momentum.

## Pentecostals and Charismatics

Pentecostalism was born of humble origins in the early twentieth century. Its impact on the marketplace-faith movement was strongly felt in 1953 when Demos Shakarian, a southern California dairyman, founded the Full Gospel Businessmen's Fellowship International.[29] In 1960 Assemblies of God pastor Loren Cunningham launched Youth With A Mission, which now ministers in over 100 countries with 6,000 workers.

The Charismatic movement is a popular interdenominational grassroots experience of the Holy Spirit's gifts borrowed from Pentecostalism. It burst on the American scene in the 1960s and 1970s. Charismatic Christianity caught on with youth in the Jesus Movement of the 1960s and 1970s.[30] Spiritual songwriting and street evangelism flourished in the youth movements. Spirituality now meant connecting faith with everyday personal life, and marketplace ministry advanced.

## Summary and Conclusion

The church faced massive change during the middle of the twentieth century. Old ways of being and doing church would not last. No longer could its leaders preach growth and continue to resist change. I delight in this ongoing crisis, painful as it might be. It is akin to prolonged labor pains. A highly institutionalized "churchianity" wrestles with declining numbers, loss of loyalty,

---

[29]H. D. Hunter, "Charismatic Movement," in *Dictionary of Christianity in America,* ed. Daniel Reid et al. (Downers Grove, Ill.: InterVarsity Press, 1990), p. 242

[30]"In 1900 there were, at most, a bare handful of Christians who were experiencing special gifts of the Holy Spirit similar to those recorded in the New Testament. By the end of the century, as many as 500 million . . . could be identified as Pentecostal or Charismatic" (Mark A. Noll, *Turning Points: Decisive Moments in the History of Christianity* [Grand Rapids, Mich.: Baker, 1997], p. 299). By 1970 it was estimated that 10 percent of all clergy and a million laypeople were involved in the charismatic movement.

declining social authority and some growing hostility.

As we enter the new millennium, this marketplace movement keeps growing.[31] *Fortune* magazine reluctantly acknowledged the growth of spirituality in the business world again in the summer of 2001, declaring: "These executives [Chicago Catholics] are in the vanguard of a diverse, mostly unorganized mass of believers—a counterculture bubbling up all over corporate America—who want to bridge the traditional divide between spirituality and work. Historically, such folk operated below the radar, on their own or in small workplace groups where they prayed or studied the Bible. But now they are getting organized and going public for change."[32]

I see the marketplace-faith movement as an encouraging but still youthful and awkward response to America's deepest needs. In it there's hope for a more vital practice of the kingdom of God. May the books, movements, new-wineskin experimentation and resources continue to multiply.[33]

*Pete Hammond*

---

[31]For a survey of the current activities, see my article "Marketplace Stirrings" <www.ivmdl.org>.

[32]Marc Gunther, "God & Business," *Fortune*, July 9, 2001, p. 60.

[33]For a much more extensive analysis of this era of change in our nation, read my expanded piece, "Marketplace Stirrings," about other dimensions of the movement by this title, at <www.ivmdl.org>.

# Annotated Reviews

**ADDINGTON, THOMAS, & STEPHEN GRAVES,** BUSINESS CONSULTANTS ■
*The Cornerstones for Life at Work,* Cornerstone Alliance, 1997. *Four books, each
60 pages.*
It is disheartening that this boxed set applies only to men. (Most women work—
including Christian women.) Aside from this irritation the books do a basic job of
helping men invite God into their working lives. Dealing with calling, serving, skill
and character in turn, each book serves as a workbook/devotional/meditation.
While the books are not in-depth, they would be appropriate as a jumping-off
point for a Promise Keepers-type Bible study or group.

**ALDERSON, WAYNE T., & NANCY ALDERSON McDONNELL,**
SEMINAR LEADERS ■ *Theory R Management: How to Utilize Value of the Person—
Leadership Principles of Love, Dignity and Respect.* Thomas Nelson, 1994.
*239 pages, hard.*
Alderson is experienced in applying biblical relational principles of reconciliation to
management-labor challenges and conflicts. As the manager of the failing Pittron
Steel Foundry, he turned it around only to be "outplaced" when the company was
bought out. That opened the door to his new career as a peacemaker in businesses.
Here he tells about the process, its foundations and some of the challenges that can
be expected. He has found a way to treat workers and managers in light of the
image of God they bear. This is an excellent model for applying core Christian principles in the marketplace without preaching or proselytizing.

**ALLAN, TOM,** RECTOR ■ *The Face of My Parish.* Loudoun, 1984. *117 pages.*
Allan tells the story of his parish church moving from an irrelevant institution to an
active congregation. He honestly relates the struggles and conflicts that he and his

church went through. His chapter "The Place of the Layman" is particularly helpful in showing the challenges that arise with lay involvement.

**ALLEGRETTI, JOSEPH G.,** PROFESSOR ■ *The Lawyer's Calling: Christian Faith and Legal Practice.* Paulist, 1996. *141 pages.*
This excellent, insightful book is based on philosophical and theological principles that can be easily transferred to other professions. Allegretti analyzes Niebuhr's *Christ and Culture,* transferring Niebuhr's categories to individuals who have attempted to integrate faith and work. His insights into professionalism and the concept of covenant is not just for lawyers but anyone interested in grappling with the integration of faith and work.

**ALLEN, ROLAND,** MISSIONARY ■ *The Case for Voluntary Clergy.* Eyre & Spottiswoode, 1930. *275 pages.*
Although Allen's comments are directed toward the Church of England, his criticisms can be applied to any tradition. His basic argument is that the qualifications required for ministry today are not those used by the apostles. Allen contends that if we want to see expansion of the church, then the clergy should earn their own livelihood in secular employment.

*Missionary Methods: St. Paul's or Ours?* 1912. Reprint, Eerdmans, 1962. *231 pages.*
Allen calls us to reexamine our missionary methods in light of Paul's methods. He notes the many differences between New Testament and present missionary methods—the goal of establishing self-supporting and self-governing churches, laying down simple but strong theological foundations, and an emphasis on being led by the Spirit rather than the enforcement of moral law.

*The Spontaneous Expansion of the Church.* Eerdmans, 1962. *157 pages.*
Drawing on his experience of missionary work in China, Allen argues for a change in missionary strategy so that spontaneous expansion of the church can take place. Such expansion occurs not under the foreign control of missionaries but from national Christians spontaneously sharing with others what they themselves have found.

**ANDERSON, JAMES D., & ELSA A. PORTER,** PRIEST; WRITER ■ *The Project on Moral Character and Development at Work.* Cathedral College of the Laity, 1989. *17 pages.*
This booklet reports the findings of a project sponsored by the Cathedral College of the Laity, whose basic mission is "to ask and answer practical questions

concerning the integration of religion and public life." The year-long project involved seventeen executives who addressed the following questions: What is the impact of the marketplace today on the development of moral character? What policies and practices bring out the best in people? What brings out the worst? What can leaders do to design organizations that bring out the best in people morally, socially and economically? Though brief, their conclusions are interesting. An important model for faith-work research.

**ANDERSON, JAMES D., & EZRA E. JONES,** CHURCH MANAGEMENT PROFESSIONALS ■ *Ministry of the Laity.* Harper & Row, 1986. *224 pages.*
The authors assert that real lay ministry springs from strong, moral character developed not just through church activities but also through everyday life. "This book aims to help laypeople see themselves as subjects who can act in ministry, not as objects who are ministered to. It explores practical exercise of faith in the settings of family, neighborhood, church, work, and society" (dustcover flap). An insightful perspective needed by clergy.

**ANDERSON, RAY S.,** PROFESSOR ■ *Minding God's Business.* Eerdmans, 1986. *143 pages.*
"This volume presents 'a biblical and theological basis for understanding the unique characteristics of Christian organizations and what it means to manage such organizations in a Christian way.' Included are parachurch organizations as well as congregations. Anderson explores the theological basis for such organizations, starting with an analysis of God's work in this world, moving through a discussion of management methods towards an appraisal of what it means to be a Christian leader" (introduction).

*On Being Human: Essays in Theological Anthropology.* Eerdmans, 1982. *226 pages.*
Inspired by Barth's remark that "theology has become anthropology since God became man," Anderson defines what it means to be human. Not merely philosophical, the book builds a foundation for contemporary issues facing the church (e.g., marriage and family, abortion) and brings fresh light to the pastoral ministry.

**ARMBRUSTER, WALLY,** ADVERTISING EXECUTIVE ■ *Let Me Out! I'm a Prisoner in a Stained Glass Jail.* Multnomah Press, 1985. *126 pages.*
Armbruster, a forty-four-year veteran of one of the world's largest advertising agencies, creatively imagines what God might say if he took the pulpit next Sunday. Fully illustrated, the book is designed to be read in an hour. It poses a highly provocative and honest challenge to religious conventions and platitudes that fail to

touch our workaday lives. An original and helpful articulation of marketplace concerns.

**ARMSTRONG, KAREN,** WRITER ■ *The Gospel According to Woman: Christianity's Creation of the Sex War in the West.* Doubleday, 1986. *366 pages.*
This is a historical survey of Western women's mixed experience in the male-dominated spiritual and secular cultures. Feminist Armstrong avoids none of the church's failures toward women, but she does not abandon her faith. She confronts and details painful subjects like sexual abuse, martyrdom, witchcraft trials, marginalized and subjugated womanhood.

**ASH, MARY KAY,** BUSINESS ENTREPRENEUR ■ *Mary Kay: The Success Story of America's Most Dynamic Businesswoman.* Harper & Row, 1987. *200 pages.*
Ash begins by admitting that work was her life. She feared retirement. The book is her retirement review of the "beauty consultants" company she founded. She recounts taking her company public and twenty years later taking it private again in order to focus on the golden rule and open opportunities for women to own their own business units. Ash is a very quotable cheerleader for a cultural rather than a distinctly biblical Christian way of life and work. The book is a warm and personal tale with interesting vignettes from her family and work life. She engages the prevalent sexism and male bias in the business world, but does not offer much on faith implications for work.

**ASHCROFT, JOHN,** U.S. ATTORNEY GENERAL ■ *Lessons from a Father to His Son.* Thomas Nelson, 1998. *222 pages.*
Ashcroft writes in a winsome style with instructive anecdotes, touching memories and very wise insights. It includes refreshing perspectives on the dangers of fame and power, and the rampant sickness of racism. There are many quotable principles for life, relationships, parenting and following Christ. For example, "In my father's view—and I think he was right in this—the factory floor in Detroit can be holy ground; the stock market exchange on Wall Street can be holy ground; the local elementary school; the fire hall; the Elks Lodge; even the chew-'em-up-and-spit-'em-out halls of Washington, DC" (p. 208). Recommended for parents, leaders and pastors.

**AUER, ALFONS,** PROFESSOR ■ *Open to the World: An Analysis of Lay Spirituality.* Trans. Dennis Doherty and Carmel Callaghan. Helicon, 1966. *337 pages.*
Auer has written one of the few books on lay spirituality appropriate for a secular milieu. He writes: "Our chief concern is to show that man and the world are intelli-

gible not in themselves but only insofar as they are seen to be intimately bound up with the mysteries of creation and salvation." He begins with a historical review of lay spirituality, followed by a theological basis for a lay spirituality today. Auer concludes with practical applications for technology, marriage and politics.

**AYLWARD, GLADYS, WITH CHRISTINE HUNTER,** MISSIONARY ENTREPRENEUR ■ *Gladys Aylward: The Little Woman.* Moody Press, 1974. *153 pages.*
This is a moving tale of faith. Aylward was rejected as a missionary candidate, became a maid, saved scrupulously, and then paid her own way from England to China. She and another female Christian expatriate managed an inn as a place of Christian hospitality and witness for mule drivers. Aylward became a Chinese citizen and adopted Chinese customs. She was contracted by the government to unbind the feet of Chinese women when that practice was prohibited. When she returned to England, she was deeply concerned about its worship of celebrities rather than God. Sadly, Alyward has been perceived as a professional missionary when she really is a crosscultural entrepreneur.

**AYRES, FRANCIS O.** ■ *The Ministry of the Laity: A Biblical Exposition.* Westminster Press, 1962. *136 pages.*
Along with Hendrick Kraemer's *A Theology of the Laity* (see reviews), this book has served as a foundation for much of the discussion on the laity. Ayres argues that ministry is the responsibility of every Christian. He even defines maturity in terms of fulfilling one's ministry. The first half of the book discusses the calling, freedom, commission and gifting of the minister; the second half outlines how ministry can be fulfilled by every Christian.

**BADCOCK, GARY D.,** THEOLOGIAN ■ *The Way of Life.* Eerdmans, 1998. *147 pages.*
Gary Badcock is concerned with the theological underpinnings of the Christian idea of vocation. He makes it quite clear that for God there is no real distinction between work, ministry and daily life. The book is a refreshing change from the usual how-to marketplace book, digging deeper into the foundation on which such practical books ought to be based. Badcock introduces concepts from Karl Barth (see review) and Hans Urs von Balthasar (see review) and then draws a conclusion that follows Jesus' own: what is required is to love God and your neighbor as yourself.

**BAKER, JAMES**, PROFESSOR ■ *Brooks Hays.* Mercer University Press, 1989. *218 pages.*

Hays, a lawyer and congressman from Arkansas, viewed his career in government as his parish. With refreshing candor, he discusses the hard things in his life. Hays also served as the president of the Southern Baptist Convention in the 1950s-1960s. Unlike many others of that time, his faith was not compartmentalized. As early as 1918 he was trying to get his college peers to engage "the Negro question of the South." The author does a good job weaving together family, politics, government and faith.

**BAKKE, RAY**, URBANOLOGIST, PROFESSOR ■ *A Theology As Big as the City.* InterVarsity Press, 1997. *221 pages.*

While urban dwellers grew from 8 to 50 percent of the world's population during the twentieth century, the white Christian church fled to the suburbs. Christians ready to reenter the urban world will find the story of Bakke's own journey and thirty-year urban ministry enlightening. Bakke guides us through the Old and New Testaments, introducing us to Brother Moses, Sister Ruth and other biblical urban leaders. An international urban expert, Bakke says, the Bible is a "map God used to get me into the city." He ends with a chapter on the first-to-twentieth-century saints who etched "the soul of the city."

**BAKKE, RAY, WITH JIM HART**, PROFESSOR ■ *The Urban Christian.* InterVarsity Press, 1987. *198 pages.*

The author makes a fresh call for Christian response to the cries of the city. Bakke's groundbreaking sense of mission is born of twenty years of life and work in Chicago. He tells stories of people's life experiences in the city and describes his own struggle to be faithful in that setting. This book is a valuable resource to those working, living or rearing a family in the city, and for those interested in learning how to view urban life in the light of the Scriptures.

**BALDA, WESLEY D.**, EDITOR, POLICEMAN, RESEARCHER, WRITER ■ *Heirs of the Same Promise.* Mission Advanced Research and Communication, 1984. *109 pages.*

This book is an excellent resource for beginning a study of ethnic evangelism in America. The first third of the book uses Acts as a Bible study guide to ethnic outreach. The last two-thirds contains readings in ethnic evangelism, including chapters on work with Hispanic, Native American, Jewish, Chinese American and South Asian people. It also includes two readings on urban evangelism.

**BALDWIN, STANLEY C.,** WRITER ■ *Take This Job & Love It.* InterVarsity Press, 1988. *144 pages.*
Baldwin encourages Christians to seek renewal in a wide range of work-related areas, suggesting that even cleaning floors can bring God glory. He gives biblical and practical advice on getting along with the boss, making a boring job interesting and overcoming work-related stress. Other chapters address problems of moral compromise and the challenge of changing careers. Discussion questions follow each chapter.

**BANKS, ROBERT, J.,** LAY ADVOCATE, PROFESSOR ■ *All the Business of Life: Bringing Theology Down to Earth.* Albatross, 1987. *176 pages.*
Banks practices what he preaches in this book on lay theology. Telling stories and experiences that have shaped his own thinking, he encourages readers to think for themselves and to develop a biblical theology that integrates their vocation with other areas of life. As a clergyman Banks learned through his own mistakes that unless the church serves the everyday needs of the ordinary Christian, it remains aloof from its own members and inhibits their growth.

*Faith Goes to Work: Reflections from the Marketplace.* Alban Institute, 1993. *189 pages.*
Fourteen authors reflect on how they minister to God, God's people and the world through their occupations. The profiles include "A Business Owner's Mission: Working as a Christian in a Car Sales Firm," "The Teacher as Revealer and Role Model: Education as a Reflection of the Incarnation," and "High-Technology Work and the New Creation: Dealing with Intangibles, Ambiguities, and Consequences." This is a great addition to the marketplace movement because it presents real people in real situations.

*God the Worker: Journeys into the Mind, Heart and Imagination of God.* Judson Press, 1994. *292 pages.*
As the church gropes for new wineskins amid a culture that is exploring all kinds of spirituality, Banks helpfully explores the images that God offers of himself: composer and performer, metalworker and potter, garment maker and dresser, gardener and orchardist, farmer and winemaker, shepherd and pastoralist, tentmaker and camper, and builder and architect. Knowing God in his work leads us to discover how we were designed and what we can become—fellow workers with God. This is very helpful for pastoring congregations who struggle with workplace identity, ethics and witness.

*Redeeming the Routines: Bringing Theology to Life.* Victor, 1993. *196 pages.*
Banks, in his very readable style, addresses the priority of and need for a theology that relates the practical and mundane to God and his purposes. But don't expect this book to give easy "answers" on specific subjects of daily living. Instead, Banks defines what a theology of everyday life would look like and how it could be developed in community. Two appendixes are also very helpful. The first appendix is a brief overview of lay theological education since 1945, and the second lists currently available resources for lay theological education.

*Theology Of, By and For the People.* Fuller Theological Seminary, 1989. *14 pages.*
Banks asserts from the start that "the people of God" must be the "main reference point" for biblical interpretation and exposition. The Bible is essentially a people's book and not merely a book for religious professionals or learned scholars. Therefore, the church's applications of God's Word to everyday life, its efforts to educate and its communal agenda must be decided or made with the help of the layperson. The goal is not to usurp the pastor's role, but rather the pastor's role should be to serve and assist the layperson.

*The Tyranny of Time: When 24 Hours Is Not Enough.* InterVarsity Press, 1985. *265 pages.*
This book is an extremely well-researched and penetrating analysis of the modern view of time in the West and its effect on our lives. Banks shows how the pressure of time has affected the social, political and religious fabric of the Western world, as well as each person's sense of well-being within it. Placing the notions of our "wristwatch society" in historical and biblical perspective, Banks holds out hope of liberation from its oppressive effects.

**BANKS, ROBERT, & KIMBERLY POWELL, EDS.,** PROFESSOR; MEDICAL CHAPLAIN ■ *Faith in Leadership: How Leaders Live Out Their Faith in Their Work and Why It Matters.* Jossey-Bass, 2000. *244 pages.*
Powell and Banks brought together fourteen essays by credible business people such as Joseph Maciarello of ServiceMaster and academicians such as Shirley Roels, dean of academic administration at Calvin College, along with a foreword by Max De Pree. Topics include the usual subjects but also cover some unexpected and sensitive ground. For instance, Roels examines vulnerability at work. Janet Hagberg, codirector of the Silent Witness National Initiative, addresses how sharing power can be an extension of faith. Winston Gooden of Fuller Theological Seminary's School of Psychology suggests that faith supports risk-taking. Though at times a bit opaque, the book provides interesting food for thought for any Christian executive.

**BANKS, ROBERT J., & R. PAUL STEVENS,** PROFESSORS ■ *The Complete Book of Everyday Christianity:An A-to-Z Guide to Following Christ in Every Aspect of Life.* InterVarsity Press, 1997. *1,166 pages.*

Banks and Stevens recruited experienced leaders from across the church to write succinct, practical and biblically informed articles on issues such as adoption, automobiles, chocolate, craftsmanship, debt, divorce, entertainment, gardening, gossip, partying, sex, shopping malls, storytelling, taxes, tourism and several hundred more of our day-to-day responsibilities and rhythms. It will help laypeople to connect faith with all of life, and serves as a quick but substantive reference for pastors and teachers as they build bridges between the Bible and life. Helpful indexes are included.

**BANKSON, MARJORY ZOET,** WRITER, SPEAKER, RETREAT LEADER ■ *The Call to the Soul.* Innisfree, 1999. *191 pages.*

Bankson, former president of Faith at Work and a retreat leader, lays out a six-stage "soulcycle" for monitoring and evaluating the reception of and response to God's call. She believes people receive and release several calls—to jobs, to child rearing, to care for the terminally ill and the like—from God in a lifetime. Ultimately, she says, we seek to answer four questions: Who am I? What is my work? What is my gift? and What is my legacy? While some treatments of "calling" are objective and systematic, Bankson's is subjective and personal. She uses analogies, metaphors, images and archetypes that are fertile guides to reflection, but they can be frustrating for those who prefer more objective methods.

**BARBER, ELIZABETH WAYLAND,** PROFESSOR ■ *Women's Work:The First 20,000 Years.* W. W. Norton, 1994. *334 pages.*

This book looks at the range of women's work in the last 20,000 years. The author, a doctor of linguistics and archaeology, makes the most of recent archaeological techniques. Since much of women's contribution came through items such as food and clothing, Barber follows (and uncovers) the contribution women have made to society via the art of textiles. The book is well-written and accessible, filling a historical gap that has until now been pretty much ignored by historians and archaeologists. This is not a "Christian" book, but in it readers should find a valuable and unusual contribution to the history of women through the ages.

**BARCIAUSKAS, ROSEMARY C., & DEBRA B. HULL,** PROFESSORS ■ *Am I My Sister's Keeper?* Meyer-Stone, 1989. *256 pages.*

In this well-researched book the authors surveyed three-hundred professional women and interviewed forty more who are trying to combine career and family.

They systematically reflect on this data from religious, cultural and historical perspectives, and conclude that the dichotomy between loving and working is not women's but society's problem. The authors note that self-sacrificial caring, the ethic of our mostly feminine home and private lives, has been separated from individual achievement, the primary ethic of our mostly masculine work and public lives. The Christian ideal of agape love can restore the balance in all our public and private relationships. Though drawing heavily from their own biblical tradition, the authors seek unity among women of all persuasions.

*Loving and Working: Reweaving Women's Public and Private Lives.* Meyer, Stone, 1989. *217 pages.*

This book explores the reweaving of women's public and private lives by developing the idea of Christian vocation. Even in evangelical and Roman Catholic circles the tide has turned: women's public vocation is no longer being denied. Yet such affirmations mean little if women's traditional domestic responsibilities remain exactly the same—that is, if some of those responsibilities are not assumed by men. "When women are denied work and when men are denied intimacy, both women and men fail to achieve their full human potential and all of us are diminished." The answer is to rediscover a view of vocation that provides for both loving and working.

**BARNES, CRAIG M.,** PASTOR ■ *When God Interrupts: Finding New Life Through Unwanted Change.* InterVarsity Press, 1996. *160 pages.*

This excellent study may be one of the most refreshing modern works on the problem of suffering. Barnes pulls no punches: suffering and failure are at the heart of spiritual maturity. Barnes's writing is extremely personal and full of stories that go beyond an intellectual treatise on the subject. The reader will come away with a deeper understanding of the centrality of suffering in spirituality and a deeper understanding of the Christian faith.

**BARNES, GEOFFREY** ■ *The Forgotten Factor: The Story of Lay People in the Church.* Uniting Church Press, 1991. *62 pages.*

Barnes addresses church history's usual preoccupation with the professional clergy. Starting with the New Testament church, Barnes discusses the position and role of the laity from the monastic movement to European Christendom (chap. 1) and through more recent historical movements (chap. 2). Chapter three is devoted to laywomen in the church. Barnes's fourth chapter deals with how the church might be made whole.

**BARNETTE, HENLEE H.**, PROFESSOR ■ *Clarence Jordan: Turning Dreams into Deeds.* Smyth & Helwys, 1992. *107 pages.*
This tribute to Jordan suffers from unevenness. Jordan is known and respected for his Cotton Patch Version of the New Testament and the founding of the experimental interracial Koinonia Farms community, which gave birth to Habitat For Humanity. The author obviously admires Jordan, but the collection of materials is too eclectic: two Jordan lectures, some correspondence, several personal reflections by several friends and an all-too-brief sketch of the subject's life. Jordan's rich faith and life as a pioneer in economic stewardship and racial reconciliation is addressed only minimally.

**BARTH, KARL,** PROFESSOR ■ *Church Dogmatics* III/4, *The Doctrine of Creation.* ed. G. W. Bromiley & T. F. Torrance. T & T Clark, 1961.
Barth's theology of work is integrated with the fundamental themes of theology and Scripture. He rejects cocreationism or any view that elevates human culture, warning that we should neither overspiritualize nor elevate work to the level of worship. He vigorously disputes the way human dominion over creation has been used to provide a rationale for capitalism, the development of technology and the work ethic. Barth offers five criteria for defining proper work: (1) objectivity: setting ends and devoting one's self to them, (2) worth: is it honest, constructive work? (3) humanity: the social and cooperative dimension of work, (4) reflectivity: the person must be the active subject and not just passive object of work, and there must be room for reflection, and (5) limitation: work must not become an absolute; rest is also commanded. Barth broadens the concept of vocation to go beyond the job and to include the work of caring for children, the sick, the elderly, the unemployed, and the work of mothers and housewives.

**BECK, ROY HOWARD,** JOURNALIST ■ *Prophets & Politics: Handbook on the Washington Offices of U.S. Churches.* Institute on Religion and Democracy, 1994. *193 pages.*
Designed to serve as a guide to how religious leaders and their groups function in national government, this book is data rich with people, addresses, budgets, charts and schedules. It offers practical helps on contacting these people. Beck recommends ideas, policies and networking preferences, and also gives his assessment of lobbying activities and priorities.

**BECKETT, JOHN D.,** BUSINESS OWNER ■ *Loving Monday: Succeeding in Business Without Selling Your Soul.* InterVarsity Press, 1998. *176 pages.*
Beckett has faced the daily challenges of growing a small, family business into a

major one in the turbulent 1990s, yet he loves his work. This book is a refreshing blend of personal story, theological and philosophical reflection, and practical application. Beckett is one of a few marketplace authors who is not a professor or pastor but a lifelong businessperson. With facility, he discusses and rejects the dualistic worldview that so often divides life into sacred and secular realms. Reflecting his own holistic understanding of life and faith, Beckett moves the reader easily between the worlds of family, employee development, theology and profitability.

**BELMONTE, KEVIN,** COMPILER, PROFESSOR ■ *Choice Treasures: A Wilberforce Anthology.* Riven Oak, 1999. *204 pages.*
This is a collection of thoughts and convictions from the great British reformer William Wilberforce (1759-1833). Wilberforce served in the British parliament and was a strong follower of Jesus Christ. He worked for twenty years to abolish slave trade (accomplished in 1807) and slavery throughout the British Empire (1833). He was active in at least sixty-nine philanthropic ventures serving the poor, children, factory workers and conducting scientific research. Wilberforce demonstrated the call to carry the Christian faith into every sphere of life.

*Selected Spiritual Writings of William Wilberforce.* Riven Oak, 1999. *67 pages.*
This is a collection of 365 ideas, prayers and reflections from the work of William Wilberforce. Comments about faith, family, politics, friends, social ills, Scripture and God reflect the diligent and disciplined way that Wilberforce sought to be an obedient servant of God in all that he did. This collection can be used as a devotional for busy people.

**BENJAMIN, PAUL,** RELIGIOUS EXECUTIVE ■ *The Equipping Ministry.* Standard, 1978. *71 pages.*
In this basic text on the equipping ministry, Benjamin shows Jesus and Paul as examples of equippers. He is honest about the practical difficulties of implementing an equipping program in a traditional "one minister" church but argues that the liberating effect for all those involved is worth the struggle.

**BENNE, ROBERT,** PROFESSOR ■ *Ordinary Saints: An Introduction to the Christian Life.* Fortress, 1988. *214 pages.*
Benne wrote this book in response to "the need often articulated by [my] students for a straightforward and comprehensive account of the Christian life." It is an excellent manual for anyone trying to sort out competing responsibilities to self, family, vocation, church and society. Benne discusses these issues in the context of

moral and mental development, and a sense of Christian calling before God. Helpful reading suggestions follow each chapter.

**BENTZ, RON,** REAL ESTATE BROKER ■ *God, Money and You: How to Be Financially Free.* Sheed & Ward, 1989. *151 pages.*
A Catholic layman combines his business sense with biblical insights and Catholic Church teachings to offer a no-nonsense approach to financial management. Practical advice includes "get out of debt and stay out; live on a practical, easy-to-use budget; make logical purchasing decisions; teach your children to be good money managers; plan for the future with sound investments," (back cover copy) and still do something to help the poor.

**BERNBAUM, JOHN A., & SIMON M. STEER,** TEACHERS AND RESEARCHERS ■ *Why Work? Careers and Employment in Biblical Perspective.* Baker, 1986. *101 pages.*
Why should we work? To find fulfillment, gain status or become prosperous? The authors help answer these questions as they summarize essential biblical teaching, survey the primary views of work in the history of Western civilization and interview six contemporary Christians. The virtues of this book are (1) its easy accessibility, (2) its realism (challenges cultural as well as Christian misconceptions about work without oversimplification), and (3) its usefulness (includes biblical passages, discussion questions, an annotated bibliography and a list of thirty-two Christian professional/academic associations). Highly recommended.

**BERRY, JO,** WRITER, SPEAKER ■ *Making Your Life a Ministry.* Zondervan, 1984. *176 pages.*
Berry encourages women to live like Priscilla, who "made her whole life [an] outcropping of her Christianity" wherever she was. Berry states that this most zealous and effective Christian woman in the New Testament was marked by her servant heart and receptivity to God's Spirit. The book is valuable for its magnification of an important biblical heroine and worker, but it is shallow in its applications to the issues of working women.

**BIELER, ANDRE,** CLERGYMAN, LECTURER ■ *The Social Humanism of Calvin.* John Knox Press, 1961. *79 pages.*
The author expands Calvin's thought beyond the popular stereotypes. Calvin's obsession with the glory of God is connected to his concern for the restoration of the human person and the society in which he lives. Bieler reclaims Calvin's views of money as an instrument of God, of the work of man as the work of God and of

commerce as a sign of the interdependence of God's creatures. Bieler finally critiques Calvin's writings, presenting his own view of a "universal Christian humanism."

**BLAMIRES, HARRY,** PROFESSOR ■ *The Christian Mind: How Should a Christian Think?* Servant, 1978. *191 pages.*
In this Christian classic Blamires seeks to reform Christian thinking. "Except in the area of personal conduct," says Blamires, "Christians have lost their saltiness intellectually. Thus we have retreated from society and have been trodden underfoot by secularism" (introduction). What should characterize the Christian mind? Blamires discusses six qualities: its supernatural orientation, its awareness of evil, its conception of truth, its acceptance of authority, its concern for the person and its sacramental cast.

*Where Do We Stand? An Examination of the Christian's Position in the Modern World.* Servant, 1980. *158 pages.*
Blamires "seeks to locate the often concealed frontier between faithful Christian witness and the faulty, barren doctrines of secularism." According to him, this is both a diagnosis and a prescription for the church in 1980. Where do we stand, asks Blamires, with regard to secularism, denigration of authority, worldliness, current idolatries and irrationalism? The author discusses far-reaching themes with which the church must wrestle to the end of the twentieth century.

**BLANCHARD, KEN,** BUSINESS CONSULTANT ■ *We Are the Beloved: A Spiritual Journey.* Zondervan, 1994. *95 pages.*
Blanchard uses the same warm conversational writing style that made his *One Minute Manager* an international bestseller. This is a very personal plea for readers to rediscover their faith in God, or at least hear Ken declare that they are loved! Each of the three chapters—"My Journey," "Staying on Course" and "Destinations"—is built on a verse from one New Testament letter. This book is a helpful peek into the soul of one of the hot consultants and speakers in modern American business circles.

**BLANCHARD, KEN, WITH BILL HYBELS & PHIL HODGES,** EXECUTIVE; PASTOR; WRITER ■ *Leadership by the Book: Tools to Transform Your Workplace.* William Morrow, 1999. *220 pages.*
In Blanchard's most overtly Christian book yet, the management guru teams up with coauthors Bill Hybels and Phil Hodges to tell the story of a professor and a minister who train a young professional in management skills and ethics. Citing

Jesus as a source for practical lessons in effective leadership, they explore the concept of servant leadership and offer simple strategies for bringing vision and values to any organization. What this breezily written book lacks in depth it makes up for with spirit and readability.

**BLOMBERG, CRAIG L.,** PROFESSOR ■ *Neither Poverty nor Riches.* Eerdmans, 1999. *300 pages.*
This book presents a theological overview of the concepts of wealth and poverty. Blomberg examines both Old Testament and intertestamental examples before laying out what the New Testament has to say on the subject. He avoids the extremes on both ends of the wealth-poverty discussion, opting instead to give the reader a biblical base to make their own decisions regarding possessions. The work is quite scholarly, moving the reader along in a logical, historical progression of biblical thought on the subject. The book's extensive bibliography will be useful to anyone wishing further study.

**BLUE, RON,** ACCOUNTANT ■ *Master Your Money.* Thomas Nelson, 1986. *236 pages.*
A thorough, clear and well-illustrated guide to personal finance written by an experienced certified public accountant. Blue discusses our attitudes toward money from a Christian perspective, giving practical guidelines for avoiding debt, watching inflation and doing taxes. The book integrates biblical principles of faith and giving with modern principles of wise investment; it also includes charts, worksheets and a glossary of money terms.

**BOA, KENNETH, & GAIL BURNETT,** WRITER; EDITOR ■ *Wisdom at Work: A Biblical Approach to the Workplace.* NavPress, 2000. *142 pages.*
Boa and Burnett have created a helpful devotional book organized in five 5-day units. The book takes the reader through different approaches to work, including the value and purpose of work, choosing work, work and identity, wealth, and character. The units are "daily excursions" on the journey to discover the place of work in the reader's life. Unusual for a devotional, the book calls for specific action commitments on the part of the reader. Also unique is its businesslike approach to "calling" and other potentially ethereal subjects. Although at first glance it seems as if Boa and Burnett wrote something very close to a Word in Life study, the book has its own unique and useful approach to the issue of work. This devotional easily could be used as a personal or group study guide.

**BOLLES, RICHARD NELSON,** CLERGYMAN, GUIDANCE COUNSELOR ■ *The New Quick Job-Hunting Map.* Ten Speed, 1979. *57 pages.*
Bolles has been widely recognized as a leading authority in his field since his *What Color Is Your Parachute?* first appeared in 1972. Bolles consistently leads the industry of career guidance without any denial of his faith values. This revised and updated "map" from that book helps the reader determine what their skills are and where they might like to use them. An excellent resource, this booklet is filled with warm, insightful and humorous vocational counsel.

*What Color Is Your Parachute? A Practical Manual for Job-Hunters & Career-Changers.* Ten Speed, 1972. 343 pages.
This work has been one of the longest-running top-ten books for years. Rooted in Bolles's Christian faith and the training he received as an Episcopal priest, this book is an example of how people of faith can serve others without giving offense. Lacking neither realism nor practicality, Bolles uses a wonderful blend of values, humor, wise guidance, exercises and resources that make this valuable for everyone. Excellent for group use or as a gift to friends just beginning their careers or in change. A new edition appears almost every year.

**BOOHER, DIANNA,** BUSINESS CONSULTANT, WRITER ■ *First Thing Monday Morning: Keeping Your Appointment with God.* New Leaf, 1998. *224 pages.*
Designed to encourage the Christian businessperson, this book contains a veritable gold mine of practical, biblical advice, written as fifty-two "business briefs" to be read over breakfast. With an expert grasp on the demands of both the corporate business culture and the Scriptures, Booher, a communication consultant to Fortune 500 companies, offers a fresh perspective on integrated, uncompromised Christian living. Good-humored and well written.

**BORMAN, KATHRYN, & JANE REISMAN,** EDS. ■ *Becoming a Worker.* Ablex, 1986. *296 pages.*
A sociology of work not necessarily from a Christian perspective, this book is a collection of original papers examining the challenges and constraints on youth entering the U.S. labor market. The authors explore the relative merit of academic learning and part-time employment in preparing youth; discuss the transfer of education to work; and examine the effects of race, class and community on work opportunities. The book also discusses how people become workers and how modern institutions work with or against that process.

**BOSCH, DAVID,** PROFESSOR ■ *Transforming Mission.* Orbis, 1991. *587 pages.*
Bosch argues that we desperately need a theology of the laity—something of which only the first rudiments are emerging: "Their ministry (or perhaps we should say their 'service,' for 'ministry' has become to be such a churchy word) is offered in the form of the ongoing life of the Christian community in shops, villages, farms, cities, classrooms, homes, law offices, in counseling, politics, state craft and recreation." This raises the question "who will do the theologizing?" Most of the theologies of work have been produced by academic theologians, but if mission and ministry belong to the whole people of God, then surely all God's people need to be appropriately equipped for this challenge. There is a need for a new level of partnership between missiologists, missionaries and the people among whom they labor.

**BRACKNEY, WILLIAM H., WITH RUBY J. BURKE, EDS.,** PROFESSOR; UNIVERSITY STAFF MEMBER ■ *Faith, Life and Witness: The Papers of the Study and Research Division of the Baptist World Alliance—1986-1990.* Samford University Press, 1990. *452 pages.*
These papers are part of an ongoing research collection for the international association of Baptist denominations. This particular volume covers research ranging from doctrine to history, human rights, ethics and pastoral leadership. Of particular interest to the marketplace-faith movement is "Commission on the Ministry of the Laity." Two of the six papers in this section are by George Peck, one of the early leaders of the mobilization of believers in the workplace. His opening piece is a very good biblical study on the foundation of the ministry of every believer. This is foundational work with excellent scriptural probing.

**BRADLEY, JOHN,** CAREER COUNSELOR ■ *Switching Tracks: Advancing Through Five Crucial Phases of Your Career.* Fleming Revell, 1984. *222 pages.*
This is not a Bible study tool. In fact, there's very little mention of Scripture, but the reader will find insight in each of the work's sections. The book prompts us to consider how the seasons of our lives and careers are different. Bradley defines the seasons as "passionate pursuit" (ages 20-30), "reevaluation" (early 30s), "confirmation" (35 to 45), "accelerated performance or devastation" (45-55) and "heightened performance or bitterness" (50s and up). A "talent definitions summary" is included in an appendix. One word of warning: the book seems to focus on worldly rather than spiritual definitions of success.

**BRAMLETT, JAMES,** EXECUTIVE PLACEMENT ■ *Finding Work: A Handbook.* Zondervan, 1986. *245 pages.*
A how-to handbook on job hunting, goal setting and discernment of vocational calling. This book is a good introduction for persons first entering the labor market. Written in a personable style it includes a helpful index of job descriptions and needed qualifications. However, the orientation of this book is contrary to marketplace thinking—it is geared toward the Christian seeking work in a Christian setting. It contains an extensive listing of Christian employers' addresses.

**BRILES, JUDITH,** WRITER, LECTURER ■ *Faith and Savvy, Too! The Christian Woman's Guide to Money.* Regal, 1988. *264 pages.*
Briles has an equipping ministry opening the world of finance to Christian women. She explains concepts of money management clearly and concisely. She includes practical advice about assets, debt, investment, taxes and annuities, and a chapter about how to pass money sense on to one's children. Terms are defined throughout.

**BRINER, BOB,** SPORTS AGENT, TELEVISION PRODUCER ■ *Business Basics from the Bible: More Ancient Wisdom for Modern Business.* Zondervan, 1996. *119 pages.*
Briner offers practical suggestions for living the Christian lifestyle in the fast-paced world of business. With firsthand knowledge of the temptations and difficulties that present themselves in the secular workplace, Briner's work is extremely relevant. He covers a variety of practical topics, including loneliness on business trips, firing employees and building relationships. Though not comprehensive, the book is a valuable entry packed with practical suggestions for Christian leaders in today's business world.

*Final Roar.* Broadman & Holman, 2000. *164 pages, hard.*
This posthumous volume is Briner's seventh and "final attempt to shake a sleepy church awake and to offer an apology to the many who are watching the Christian church out in the world" (from the foreword by Barry Landis). This work is blunt and forceful. Briner roars with rebukes and pleas to the American conservative church.

*Roaring Lambs: A Gentle Plan to Radically Change Our World.* Zondervan, 1993. *187 pages.*
This book offers Christians a rationale for becoming actively involved in shaping and reshaping American culture, particularly in the areas of media and communications. It's practical in that it outlines definite action steps Christians can take in areas

such as the arts, television, film and journalism. Evangelical in focus, Briner assumes (1) American culture was at one time a Christian culture and (2) that a return to that state of affairs is a desirable goal. There is a basic naiveté to these assumptions that may put off a nonevangelical or a more sophisticated evangelical thinker, especially artists and writers. Thus the whole approach is questionable.

*The Management Methods of Jesus: Ancient Wisdom for Modern Business.* Thomas Nelson, 1996. *114 pages.*

Briner lived in the funky world of professional sports entertainment. His faith was tested by glitz, fame and greed, and here he provides insight into how he survived. This is a short but pithy treatment on the personal and relational, not the organizational and systemic, sides of life. The applications are challenging. This easily read book is a good gift for those who are new to the faith or for those who have made little or no connection between faith and workplace leadership.

BRINER, BOB, & RAY PRITCHARD, SPORTS AGENT, TELEVISION PRODUCER; PASTOR ■ *Squeeze Play: Practical Insights for Men Caught Between Work & Home.* Zondervan, 1994. *141 pages.*

This book is a down-to-earth personal story of lessons on faith, work and family. Briner gives men some basic advice on personal faith applied to matters like loneliness during business travel, communication, family involvement and business relationships. But it is cast in the narrow world of a traveling executive, and this might limit its appeal to other workers. It is a quick read and would be very helpful to believers who have given little thought to faith beyond church life.

*More Leadership Lessons of Jesus.* Broadman & Holman, 1998. *172 pages.*

This book is a commentary on the Gospel of Mark (chaps. 7-10). It is a versatile guide with principles relevant to leadership at home, work, church or community. However, the devotional observations are generalized and undeveloped. As a guide to scriptural meditation, the book has great potential, but those seeking deep commentary may be disappointed.

BROWN, ROBERT MCAFEE, WRITER, PROFESSOR ■ *Saying Yes and Saying No: On Rendering to God and Caesar.* Westminster Press, 1986. *143 pages.*

Brown confronts the problem of official government policies clashing with ideas about God's kingdom of peace and justice. In respective chapters Brown criticizes American foreign policy toward Grenada, Nicaragua, South Africa and Poland. He devotes other chapters to domestic issues such as the sanctuary movement and national security. Discussion questions follow each chapter.

*Spirituality and Liberation: Overcoming the Great Fallacy.* Westminster Press, 1988. *153 pages.*

Brown "intends to offer an alternative to ongoing attempts to compartmentalize life into, roughly, the 'sacred' and the 'secular' (the former being 'good' and the latter 'evil')." By examining the issues of liberation and spirituality he seeks to bring some resolution to the dichotomy that persists between the spiritual and the temporal, between prayer and social action.

**BRUSO, DICK,** GUIDANCE MINISTER ■ *Bible Promises: Help and Hope for Your Finances.* Here's Life, 1985. *156 pages.*

*Bible Promises* contains topically arranged Bible verses to guide financial decision-making. Subjects include counsel, righteousness, budgeting and partnerships. Bruso is founder of Faithful Steward Ministries of Colorado, which shares these principles of stewardship through a daily syndicated radio program. Carefully written.

**BUFORD, BOB,** TELEVISION EXECUTIVE ■ *Game Plan: Winning Strategies for the Second Half of Your Life.* Zondervan, 1997. *170 pages.*

While Buford's *Halftime* put into words what men feel at midlife, *Game Plan* charts a strategic response: how to disengage; reflect on what you've accomplished; clear your plate; identify your truest, God-given self; envision a new or continuing mission; and emerge from the football locker room for "a runaway third quarter (in) the game of life." Though a business entrepreneur, Buford is a very accessible writer and is broadly empathetic. This is well-researched, rich in literary references and interdisciplinary in scope. Also available on audio cassette.

*Half Time: Changing Your Game Plan from Success to Significance.* Zondervan, 1994. *175 pages.*

The death of Buford's adult son shook his world and he began a journey toward a practical faith. He invites other men to weigh carefully what drives them and what it will amount to in eternity. The book comes from a mind honed in building a successful business and then applied to the broader issues of all of life. *Half Time* includes an intriguing introduction from Peter Drucker. It lacks help for those who are wrestling with values and priorities long before they reach their own midpoint.

**BURKETT, LARRY,** FINANCIAL CONSULTANT, WRITER ■ *Business by the Book: The Complete Guide of Biblical Principles for Business Men and Women.* Thomas Nelson, 1990. *242 pages.*

A book titled "the complete guide" is immediately suspect. No book can be that comprehensive. However, Burkett's classic work is still a wonderful source of information. He pulls no punches. Clear, easy to follow and very practical, this work is an important tool for managers, business owners and entrepreneurs. Burkett grabs the reader right away with "Basic Bible Minimums" and never lets go. Though Burkett's material is soundly reasoned, readers may not agree with all his recommendations.

**BUSHA, MARY C.,** WRITER, PUBLISHER, BUSINESSWOMAN ■ *Proverbs for Busy Women.* Broadman & Holman, 1995. *123 pages.*
Busha has pulled together a great set of short daily devotions from Proverbs and the insights, wisdom and wit of busy women who find their callings in both the marketplace and home. Written by fifty-four women from a variety of vocations, the brief daily reflections of this book form the first of a three-part series. The other two books in the series are *Devotions to Build Up Your Relationships* and *Devotions to Strengthen Your Walk with God.* Good insights from real people.

**BUSINESS EXECUTIVES FOR ECONOMIC JUSTICE,** CATHOLIC BUSINESS LEADERS ■ *On the Firing Line.* ACTA, 1990. *39 pages.*
This is a position paper responding to the U.S. Catholic bishops' letter on economic justice. It came out of a series of dialogues on the specific issue of the manager's roles and responsibilities in terminations and layoffs. The paper presents ten ideas to prevent or ameliorate the effects of terminations and layoffs, suggests cautions in carrying out specific programs, and includes personal testimony from business and professional managers on the relationship between their faith and work. This business "affinity group" exhibits the tremendous potential of shared Christian discernment in every vocational track.

**BUTH, LENORE,** WRITER ■ *The Employed Wife: Earning a Living, Making a Home.* Concordia, 1986. *183 pages.*
Buth neither condones nor condemns the two-paycheck family lifestyle; she simply discusses the stress it creates in marriages and suggests ways to cope. Her central purpose is to assist the Christian woman in assessing her roles as wife, parent and worker. She offers helpful biblical counsel on every major domestic issue, including financial responsibility, having children and household division of labor. Based on Buth's interviews of working couples.

**BUTT, HOWARD,** EXECUTIVE ■ *The Velvet Covered Brick.* Harper & Row, 1973. *186 pages.*
Though this book has a dated look, don't be fooled. It takes up the issues of authority and submission and shows in clear terms that one cannot truly exist with-

out the other. Drawing from his own experience with power struggles, Butt leads us from focusing on ourselves to the exemplary servanthood of Christ. Humility is never outdated. In an age of superegos and extreme competition, here is a refreshing look at leadership that applies to the truck driver as much as the CEO. This book retains its relevancy in spite of the rampant pace of technology.

**BUTT, HOWARD, WITH ELLIOTT WRIGHT,** AUTHORS ■ *At the Edge of Hope: Christian Laity in Paradox.* Seabury Press, 1978. *211 pages.*
This is a summary of the 1978 North American Congress on the Laity held in Los Angeles. A distinguished cross-section of Christian laypeople, including Malcolm Muggeridge, Gerald R. Ford, Peter Berger and James Reston, engage in "a mind-stretching, soul-stirring exchange on Christian hope and despair" in twentieth-century North America. A wide range of interesting topics and dialogue.

**BUZZARD, LYNN R., & LAURENCE ECK,** PROFESSORS, LAWYERS ■ *Tell It to the Church: Reconciling Out of Court.* Cook, 1982. *154 pages.*
Lawyers Buzzard and Eck show how the church can follow Christ's command to settle disputes between believers. The authors represent a commendable integration of business and church concerns, making lay expertise a resource for the church. Thorough and well written, the book contains helpful, Bible-based and legally specific advice, including suggested procedures for legal arbitration within the church.

**CAHILL, THOMAS,** PROFESSOR ■ *How the Irish Saved Civilization: The Untold Story of Ireland's Heroic Role from the Fall of Rome to the Rise of Medieval Europe.* Doubleday, 1995. *246 pages.*
A refreshingly honest historian openly tells of his biases and notes his interpretations amid other options, opinions or choices. He has crafted an interesting probe into one of the seams of history—the period between the decline of the Roman Empire and the rise of Medieval Europe. His view is that the Christian mission and monastic movement in Ireland preserved the most important documents of the Greeks, Romans, Hebrews and Christians because of their commitment to learning, reading and instructing their converts. He probes the Celtic movement and two of its great leaders, St. Patrick and Columba (Columcille). The work is well researched and even provides readers with a discerning guide to what he considers the best additional resources for further study.

**CALIAN, CARNEGIE S.,** PROFESSOR ■ *Today's Pastor in Tomorrow's World.* Rev. Fortress, 1982. *147 pages.*

After evaluating several current models of ministry, Calian presents the "grass-roots theologian" model of the pastor. He takes seriously the responsibility of clergy to relate theology to real life; this leads him into a discussion of the roles of both laity and clergy. Included is a thoughtful chapter on women and men in ministry.

**CAMPOLO, ANTHONY,** PROFESSOR, LECTURER, WRITER ■ *Partly Right.* Jarrell, 1985. *222 pages.*

Tony Campolo is no coward. He fields the attacks of Marx, Kierkegaard, Nietzsche, Freud and other major thinkers against middle-class "bourgeois Christianity." And in part, he agrees with them. Campolo helps the reader sort out the validity from the shortcomings in their claims from a Christian perspective. Academic in tone.

*The Power Delusion: A Serious Call to Consider Jesus' Approach to Power.* Victor, 1983. *165 pages.*

Campolo exposes the many ways Christians confuse kingdom-building with taking control. Christ emptied himself and became our servant; we fill ourselves and seek power. This error is exhibited in male-female relationships, in solo-clergy leadership, in demands that God fix the world's evils and in nuclear defense. Campolo reminds us that Jesus chose to win us from a position of weakness—the cross. From Jesus we learn that in all our relationships, when power is relinquished, love triumphs. This is a broad, very readable analysis with important implications. Highly recommended.

*The Success Fantasy.* Victor, 1980. *144 pages.*

Campolo discusses modern American ideas of success as they are experienced by teenagers, singles and midlife men and women. He then compares those ideas to biblical ideas of success. He explodes the fantasy of the American dream and takes us further into kingdom values. Written with Campolo's characteristic touch of humor and blend of sociological, prophetic and practical insight.

*Who Switched the Price Tags?* Word, 1986. *200 pages.*

"This book is about having fun," writes Campolo. "Without fun," he says, "marriages don't work, jobs become intolerable and dehumanizing, children are heartbreaking, and church becomes a drag. . . . When life is not fun, it is hard to be spiritual." In his candid, warm and witty way Campolo urges Christians to clarify their values at home, work and church, and to begin enjoying life the way God intended. The medium matches the message; his anecdotes are personal, creative and contagious. (Also comes as a video series.)

**CAPON, ROBERT FARRAR,** CLERGY ■ *The Astonished Heart: Reclaiming the Good News from the Lost-and-Found of Church History.* Eerdmans, 1996. *122 pages.*

Capon has an ability to hone in on religious realities with a surprising and refreshingly angular approach. His analysis of the splintered and internally competitive church is very helpful. It includes a brief but insightful analysis of the intricate history and the broad sweep of 4,000 years. He also provides some stimulating critique of both the mainline focus on social issues and the evangelical appetite for seekers. He attacks the all-too-glib view of America as being founded as a Christian nation. It may be easy to argue with Capon but hard to forget or ignore his critique and intense appeal for change away from doing church as usual. Capon appeals for a recovery of the astonishing dimension of the gospel and its graciousness toward all sinners.

**CAREY, GEORGE,** ARCHBISHOP ■ *The Church in the Marketplace.* Morehouse, 1984, 1989. *154 pages.*

Here is an intriguing and quite personal story of a moribund parish brought from near death to renewed life. When the young vicar arrived in new inner-city parish in Durham, England, death seemed inevitable. Carey, now the archbishop of Canterbury, tells the difficult journey that he and the parish members faced as he introduced change. He also recounts their struggle as they grew during his seven years there. This story is just painful enough to be on target. He is candid about his own needs and what spiritual renewal means for a parson and for a congregation. The second edition is shaped for study by any congregation or pastor that want to be fruitful in this postmodern and post-Christian time.

**CARSON, BEN, WITH GREGG LEWIS,** PEDIATRIC SURGEON ■ *The Big Picture.* Zondervan, 1999. *271 pages.*

In three sections Carson (1) tells the story of the second and third head-separation surgeries he performed on African Siamese twins, (2) calls for goal-oriented preparation of youth and adults for school and parenting, and (3) offers his perspective on the issues of education, health care and racial prejudice. "Education can turn dreams to reality," says Carson, who has become a role model to African American youth. Carson's hopeful, faith-based perspective includes, in two separate chapters, "Seeing Hardship as Advantage" and "Moving Beyond a Victim Mentality." Also available in audiocassette.

CARSON, CLAYBORNE, ED., HISTORIAN ■ *The Autobiography of Martin Luther King Jr.* Intellectual Properties Management, 1999. *400 pages.*
This is a special work resulting from thousands of hours by a team from Stanford University and the M. L. King Center for Change. It is well-documented and meticulously written. King's own writing is supplemented by key dates at the beginning of each of the thirty-two chapters. Extensive use was made of King's books and the many papers, sermons, news interviews, letters and comments in various documents. This provides readers with a rich collection of King's thoughts, convictions and reflections on major events, and a narrative of his growth as a Christian student and scholar, family man, and social critic. This is truly a faith-in-everyday-life classic.

CARTER, JIMMY, FORMER U.S. PRESIDENT ■ *Keeping Faith: Memoirs of a President.* University of Arkansas Press, 1982, 1983, 1995. *633 pages.*
Carter declares in the introduction, "This is a not a history of my administration but a highly personal report of my own experiences. . . . Any . . . defects in the book are my own, and may even be helpful to the reader in giving a more accurate picture of the kind of person I am" (p. xiv). Carter includes personal entries from his dairy, discusses his own foibles, and shares family anecdotes and struggles. Carter also details much of his international work with leaders of communist nations and other world powers.

*Living Faith.* Times Books, 1996. *257 pages.*
This is probably the most personal book by our former president. It grew out of his Sunday school teaching experience and presents how he applies his Christian faith to life. The reader is invited into the feelings, hopes, fears and agonies of this very private person. His roots in rural depression-ridden Georgia meant having to deal with racism, small town dynamics, courtship and close family ties. He describes how his public responsibilities as a naval officer, governor, president, Habitat for Humanity spokesman and peacemaking diplomat tested his faith. This is a moving look into the life of a committed Christian who occupied the White House.

*Sources of Strength: Meditations on Scripture for a Living Faith.* Waterbrook, 1997. *254 pages.*
This volume is a collection of fifty-two of Carter's favorite Bible lessons selected from the more than fifteen hundred he has taught as a Sunday school teacher. He views this volume as a companion to his personal memoir *Living Faith.* But these are more than Bible lessons. Each one includes personal anecdotes from and applications to his life. He never avoids the radical implications of a text. This is a great companion book for thoughtful, real-world reflection on faith in daily life, family and work.

*The Virtues of Aging.* Ballantine, 1998. *143 pages.*
Written in his mid-70s, Carter reflects on his life as a senior citizen. It is especially poignant because his three siblings and dad all died in their middle years. In his well-established candor, he writes of personal fears and discoveries, difficulties in marriage and family life, mentors in his journey, the near loss of the family business under his watch, as well as national issues regarding legislation and social security of the United States. Included is a well-crafted postscript on the place of his Christian faith in his career. Once again, the strength of faithfulness to Christ shines through in this book.

**CASSIDY, RICHARD J.,** PRIEST, PROFESSOR ■ *Society and Politics in the Acts of the Apostles.* Orbis, 1987. *256 pages.*
This respected priest and New Testament scholar follows his earlier work, *Jesus, Politics, and Society: A Study of Luke's Gospel,* with this analysis of Luke's other New Testament book, the Acts of the Apostles. Like Cassidy's first, this book describes the social and political setting of first-century Christianity and discusses how the apostles interacted with it. This book lays important groundwork for any person contemplating what it means to be loyal to Christ in conduct and to witness within one's sociopolitical context.

**CATHERWOOD, CHRISTOPHER,** PROFESSOR ■ *Crash Course in Church History.* Hodder & Stoughton, 1998. *188 pages.*
Catherwood combines good historical knowledge with an ecumenical spirit and refreshing candor. He helps readers face their own biases by regularly acknowledging his own. Catherwood goes beyond the all-to-frequent Euro-American centrism of much religious history and storytelling, taking his readers into China, Mongolia and Africa, and engaging the Orthodox and charismatic movements. Catherwood clearly identifies his own interpretations and opinions. Surprisingly, he also includes the International Fellowship of Evangelical Students movement in the last half of the twentieth century. Unfortunately there are no indexes.

*Why the Nations Rage: Killing in the Name of God.* Hodder & Stoughton, 1997. *271 pages.*
This is a well-crafted analysis of the terrible realities of ethnic cleansing, mass murder and religious wars of today. Catherwood helps the newcomer to this very confusing, even frightening, reality with personal illustrations of his difficult experiences in modern Bosnia, Britain and America. He avoids oversimplifying nationalism, religion and ethnicity, including thoughtful treatments of each as well

as the complex interplay between them. His scholarship sometimes demands careful reading. The bibliography is very extensive.

**CATHERWOOD, H. F. R.,** BRITISH PARLIAMENTARIAN ■ *The Christian Citizen.* Hodder & Stoughton, 1969. *191 pages.*
A British statesman confronts Protestant pietism "which regards the world as wicked, a place in which the righteous have no part" and "to encourage more Christian laymen, who are entitled to take their place in public affairs, to come out of their protective isolation and do their public duty." This book is written to "all who are concerned with the basis of ethics in society and its relation to law, to government and to the quality of personal relationships."

*The Christian in Contemporary Society.* Evangelical Press, undated. *14 pages.*
The result of discussions among twelve British businessmen, this book discusses the Christian attitude toward work, wealth, economics, politics, big business, trade unions, taxation, trading and the stock exchange. Catherwood writes: "The main concern of this book is in setting standards for the Christian by applying Christian doctrine to behavior in society today."

*On the Job: The Christian 9 to 5.* Zondervan, 1983. *185 pages.*
Catherwood's purpose in writing is "to see what obedience to Christ means in some major aspects of industrial society today." The book is born out of discussions in the early 1960s between "a dozen Christians concerned with industry and commerce." As such, it is of notable breadth, calling Christians to apply their faith to their views of work, income, politics, labor relations, competition, the stock market and taxation. The material is dated in places despite revisions made for the present edition. However, Catherwood's rare combination as a Christian scholar and member of the European Parliament gives this text timeless value.

**CATHEY, TRUETT,** CEO ■ *It's Easier to Succeed Than to Fail.* Thomas Nelson, 1989. *192 pages.*
Cathey was "born to sell" and founded the Chic-Fil-A fast-food company out of grit, hard work and determination. The fact that his Baptist pastor wrote the foreword is symptomatic of who you will meet in this personal rehearsal. His story is a bootstrap tale that lifts up the lessons that can only come from disappointment, trial and error. He learned that bad decisions refine one's character. Cathey also includes story after story of other men who made it under his influence.

**CERILLO, AUGUSTUS, JR., & MURRAY DEMPSTER,** PROFESSORS ■ *Salt and Light: Evangelical Political Thought in America.* Baker, 1990. *175 pages.*
"The authors identify four perspectives on the political spectrum: evangelical radical right, evangelical liberal, evangelical conservative and fundamentalist new right. Though evangelicals in America have emerged as a potent political force, they have not reached a consensus [as] their approaches to politics vary considerably. Here 16 proponents engage in lively and informed debate. Essayists include Carl Henry, Lewis Smedes, Nicholas Wolterstorff, Isaac Rottenberg, George DeVries Jr., Richard Quebedeaux, Jim Wallis, Jerry Falwell, and Ed Hindson" (dustcover flap).

**CHAPMAN, JOHN C.,** PASTOR ■ *Know and Tell the Gospel.* NavPress, 1985. *192 pages.*
This book was written for people who tremble at the thought of telling others about their faith in Jesus Christ. Chapman identifies with that fear. He says that there were times when fear caused him to doubt his faith, but God converted his weakness into a strength. This is, in part, a record of his discovery that "once we know why we should share the gospel and what the content of the good news really is, we can learn how to present it to non-believers by choosing methods that are naturally suited to our individual personalities and gifts." Chapman is the director of Evangelism for the Sydney Diocese of the Anglican Church in Australia.

**CHENU, M. D.,** PROFESSOR ■ *Theology of Work: An Exploration.* Trans. Lilian Soiron. Gill & Son, 1963. *114 pages.*
Chenu gave impetus to the doctrine of cocreation that dominated the theology of work in both Catholic and Protestant traditions for the last half of the twentieth century. Chenu begins by emphasizing the discontinuity of the "machine age" with all previous periods. As a result "the traditional images of potter, blacksmith and peasant with which the Bible furnished the old theologians are not only inadequate, but also lead to resentment against the new technology." Chenu holds a high view of both human work and modern technology. People transform history into eternity through their work. According to Chenu, earlier Catholic and Eastern theologians provide a more helpful "discussion of man's place in the universe. They observe the substantial connection of his human nature with material nature."

**CHERNOV, RON,** WRITER, JOURNALIST ■ *TITAN: The Life of John D. Rockefeller, Sr.* Random House, 1998. *774 pages.*
This is an award-winning biography of John D. Rockefeller Sr., who grew up with deep-seated control tendencies in his family life, work, church membership and charitable giving. Rockefeller began each day with readings from a devotional and

ended each day with other religious readings. Meanwhile, he devoured competitors as he built the first big American monopoly, Standard Oil, in the late 1800s. He was driven to become the world's richest man. Here is a classic case of compartmentalized Christianity.

**CHERVOKAS, JOHN V.,** ADVERTISING EXECUTIVE ■ *How to Keep God Alive from 9 to 5.* Berkeley, 1986. *115 pages.*
This is a profoundly empathetic book written to people who find it difficult to think of God while on the job. Chervokas writes, "We do not, and will not, assume that you accept, adore, or even tolerate God in any specific way. This book makes three assumptions: (1) There is a God, and (2) He is not George Burns, and (3) God works where we work." He then takes us on a journey through the business day, from waking up to the rush-hour commute home. Thirty-seven snippets, such as "Annoying Phone Calls" and "Lunch Alone," are sprinkled throughout with realistic and inspirational prayers. Lighthearted and human.

**CHEWNING, RICHARD C.,** PROFESSOR ■ *Biblical Principles & Business,* vol. 2: *The Foundations.* NavPress, 1989. *304 pages.*
This book is part of a series that addresses questions relating to how Christians should function in certain career situations. Fairly theoretical, this volume discusses the nature of biblical commands, covenant ethics, the distribution of wealth, eschatology and business ethics.

*Biblical Principles & Business,* vol. 3: *The Practice.* NavPress, 1990. *280 pages.*
This book is a strong resource for relating principles to practice. There is much to be gleaned on a wide range of topics from this compilation of writings by practitioners and professors. Some of the contributors are outside the marketplace looking in, thus business people might dismiss their thoughts more readily. The book seems best suited as a textbook. Without study questions, small group use is probably minimal, but creative leaders could build study material with a mix-and-match approach. Probably best suited for thinkers and not action-oriented individuals.

*Biblical Principles & Economics,* vol. 1: *The Foundations.* NavPress, 1989. *315 pages.*
Chewning successfully brings together scholars, economists, theologians and business people to lead us into biblical thinking. "While Scripture does not address or endorse particular economic systems as such, it does have a great deal to say about the attitudes, values, and ambitions that should govern a person's involvement in such systems. The purpose of this book is to examine which Scriptures should be

brought to bear on the complex economies of our modern society" and to deter-mine which economic systems "best take into account both the constructive ele-ments of human nature as well as the harmful or negative elements" (publisher's comments).

**CHEWNING, RICHARD C., ET AL.,** PROFESSOR ■ *Business Through the Eyes of Faith.* HarperSanFrancisco, 1990. *266 pages.*
Ever know someone who would like to go into business but also feels nudged to "ministry"? They can do both! The authors show in compelling terms how the world of business can be an arena for Christian service. The book is enriched with case studies, vignettes, biblical passages and commentaries from business theorists and practitioners. This is part of a series of career books commissioned by the Christian College Coalition.

*Christian History* Magazine, *131 Christians Everyone Should Know.* Holman, 2000. *384 pages.*
This book puts faces on the dates, events and movements of church history. Each profile includes a time line, a historical glimpse of the period and a one- to two-page summary of the life and work of the subject. Surprisingly, amid the usual col-lection of theologians, clergy, pastors and priests, and missionaries we find activists, rulers, scholars and scientists, and musicians. Unfortunately, politicians, business leaders, social activists and other workplace Christians are missing. This work dem-onstrates the ingenuity, sacrifice and diligence of our predecessors. A helpful index provides topical entries alongside the names of people and movements.

**CLARK, JAMES KELLEY, ED.,** PROFESSOR ■ *Philosophers Who Believe:The Spiritual Journeys of 11 Leading Thinkers.* InterVarsity Press, 1993. *284 pages.*
A change is taking place in higher education circles. In this book, academic leaders explore, and some even adopt, the possibility that God exists. Clark has invited sev-eral key thinkers to describe their Christian faith. He includes respected professors from such diverse places as Yale, Oxford, Maryland, Claremont, Cambridge and the University of Calgary. The book's personal and even confessional style is both mov-ing and encouraging. Clark adds a very helpful overview of trends in his introduc-tion.

**CLARK, STEPHEN** ■ *Building Christian Communities.* Ave Maria, 1972. *185 pages.*
Clark calls Christians to look beyond issues concerning institutions and programs to see the need for the establishment of "vital Christian communities." We need a

holistic vision of the church which will produce direction and priorities for building the church. His discussion on the importance of creating a Christian environment rather than an institution is very helpful.

**CLINTON, J. ROBERT,** PROFESSOR ■ *The Making of a Leader.* NavPress, 1988. *272 pages.*
Robert Clinton reviewed the lives of hundreds of leaders and discovered six common developmental phases. His book describes each phase and the specific tasks and conflicts unique to each. *The Making of a Leader* offers insight into today's Christian leaders, and uses them as a model for teaching others. Clinton defines leadership as "a dynamic process in which a man or woman with God-given capacity influences a specific group of God's people toward his purposes for the group." While most of his examples are from the clergy, the principles can be applied to lay leaders in the church as well. And though the examples are drawn mostly from the church, the principles are clearly applicable to today's leader in the business climate.

**CODDINGTON, DEAN, & DONALD ORVIS,** BUSINESS CONSULTANT; SEMINARY PROFESSOR ■ *Christianity in the Workplace: Your Faith on the Job.* Cook, 1989. *128 pages.*
This excellent study records twelve weekly gatherings of thirteen Christians who sought to relate their faith to the toughest issues of their careers. The book is intended to help launch other group discussions by providing format and focus. Each chapter begins with excerpts from those meetings. Authors provide extensive Bible study helps and questions for individual or group use. Topics include decision-making on the job, supervisor-employee relationships, two-paycheck marriages, changing careers, unemployment, ethical dilemmas and witnessing at work. Designed for twelve weeks of study, it is excellent for use in an adult education. A leader's guide is available. Highly recommended.

**COLLINS, DAVID R.,** WRITER ■ *Francis Scott Key: God's Courageous Composer.* Mott Media, 1982. *114 pages.*
This profile of the author of America's national anthem is one of a series written for children. It uses a first-person conversational style to help young readers enter into Key's childhood in a Christian family, a career as a lawyer, his rejection of slave ownership and his life-long pattern of writing poetry. The story culminates during his detainment by the invading British navy and its attack on Fort McHenry where he wrote what has become known as the "Star Spangled Banner." Included are all four stanzas, not just the first which is only what is traditionally sung. This is a good contribution to help children understand that faith is to be practiced in all walks of life.

*George Washington Carver: Man's Slave, God's Scientist.* Mott Media, 1981. *132 pages.*

Collins adds another Christian role model to the fascinating Sower series, nineteen biographies of history's great men and women written for children. The series, organized by vocation, places Carver next to scientists Isaac Newton, Samuel Morse, Johannes Kepler and the Wright brothers. Carver, born a slave, emerged as one of the greatest contributors to Southern agriculture through his chemical discoveries and progressive philosophy of farming. "Without my Savior, I am nothing," declared Carver. But with Jesus, Carver maintained, people can do an "uplifting work for humanity." One of America's great but unsung African American heroes is an inspiring example of Christian service.

**COLSON, CHARLES,** FOUNDER AND PRESIDENT OF PRISON FELLOWSHIP ■
*Dare to be Different, Dare to Be Christian: What It Means to Be a Christian in God's Holy Nation.* Victor, 1987. *48 pages, booklet.*
"Biblical Christianity demands our involvement and influence in every facet of society—from politics to education, from business to the media. But as believers we have an even higher calling, requiring total allegiance to our Heavenly King" (back cover). Former special counsel to Richard Nixon and subsequent convert to Christianity, Colson is uniquely qualified to address this subject. One of four booklets in Colson's Challenging the Church series.

*Presenting Belief in an Age of Unbelief.* Victor, 1986. *48 pages.*
"In a society which has relentlessly pursued pleasure, position, and power, we have become a self-absorbed, indifferent, and unthinking people" (back cover). In this booklet Colson challenges the church to reexamine its priorities and to begin to reach out boldly to our skeptical "me first" world. Clear and to the point, the booklet is full of effective anecdotes that reflect Colson's grasp of American culture. Part of Colson's Challenging the Church series.

**COLSON, CHARLES, & JACK ECKERD,** FOUNDER AND PRESIDENT OF PRISON FELLOWSHIP; CEO ■ *Why America Doesn't Work.* Word, 1991. *227 pages.*
Calling us back to our roots, this is a popular-level theology of work that examines the American work ethic. It places the loss of Judeo-Christian values and the corresponding work ethic at the center of America's problems. The book emphasizes pride of workmanship, competence and excellence, and its chapter "Restoring the Marketplace" contains helpful new material. Otherwise this book is a rehash of better organized material found in other books.

COLSON, CHARLES, & NANCY PEARCEY, FOUNDER AND PRESIDENT OF PRISON FELLOWSHIP; WRITER ■ *How Now Shall We Live?* Tyndale House, 1999. *400 pages.*

Colson and Pearcey use the metathemes of the Scriptures (creation, fall, redemption) as an outline to craft a work of immense importance and encouragement to Christians who believe they can shape their culture. Though not specifically written to marketplace issues, their chapter on work ("The Work of Our Hands"), particularly the latter part, is helpful. The book helps believers shift their worldview so they can be used by God to shape this world. Colson calls this his most important writing. A great work for any Christian, but especially for those of us actively hoping to influence the culture for Christ.

COMFORT, EARL V., PASTOR ■ *Living Stones: Involving Every Member in Ministry.* Standard, 1988. *160 pages.*

Comfort tells the success story of a suburban Lincolnville, New Jersey, church that has grown from 300 to 1,300 members during his term as its senior pastor. But this is not the story of a spiritual giant with a direct line to God. It is a humble confession. Comfort shares his realization that years of dynamic, do-it-all ministry at earlier churches had drawn an audience, but not a body of vital members. He outlines the ministry principles that have made Jacksonville Chapel a church of "living stones." This book is yet another in the long line of testimonies of revival through the Ephesians 4:12 model of lay-equipping ministry.

COMMENT, JEFFREY W., CEO ■ *Mission in the Marketplace: Perspectives for Life and Work.* Mission in the Marketplace, 1995. *146 pages.*

This book of marketplace reflections presents an integrated approach to marketplace themes using business rather than theological categories. Interspersed throughout are Comment's personal reflections and experience at Helzberg Diamonds and John Wanamaker Corporation. Comment divides his "lessons" into five major sections: "leadership," "doing business," "habits of daily living," "understanding mission" and "business from God's perspective." Presented by an insider with a commitment to integrity, it's an excellent introduction to major issues in today's business world. A good book for learning more about integrating work and faith.

COMMITTEE ON SOCIAL WITNESS POLICY OF THE GENERAL ASSEMBLY COUNCIL (PCUSA) ■ *God's Work in Our Hands: Employment, Community, and Christian Vocation.* The Office of the General Assembly, Presbyterian Church (USA), 1995. *62 pages.*

This booklet is a response to the recent large-scale changes to the place of work in human life, particularly in North America. Past and present policy of this denomination is discussed and presented in the light of a theology of work. "Principles of Vocation and Work" is included in several languages. Included is a vision for the future and case studies for group consideration.

**CONGER, JAY A., PROFESSOR** ■ *Spirit at Work.* Jossey-Bass, 1994. *222 pages.*
Conger has gathered a diverse group of individuals, including management experts, a Lilly Endowment program director and two Jesuit priests, to examine the role spirituality can play in the work environment. The basic premise is that in this day of increased isolation in people's personal lives, organizational leaders can make a spiritual impact in the workplace. Conger wants to "challenge and push us into thinking more deeply about the ways spirituality might play a role in workplace life and in its leadership." To that end, the essays cover topics such as "Leadership and Spirituality: A Quest for Reconciliation," "What Leaders Cannot Do Without: The Spiritual Dimensions of Leadership" and "Spirited Connections: Learning to Tap the Spiritual Resources of Our Lives and Work." Interesting and thought-provoking.

**CONGAR, YVES, THEOLOGIAN** ■ *Called to Life.* Crossroad, 1987. *148 pages.*
This is a wonderful book that examines the two sides of prayer: conversation with God and the revelation of God that makes up theology. Congar is a master of taking theological concepts such as sacraments, liturgy and preaching, and making them applicable to the reader's life. In fact, Congar seems to delight in bringing theology into the smallness of each human life and making it fly. The first third of the book looks deep into God's revelation of himself to us and our response to God's call. Congar does not over-explain concepts that should rightly remain a mystery. That makes this book a satisfying, stretching and soul-searching read.

*Lay People in the Church.* Christian Classics, 1985. *498 pages.*
This work is the only extensive theology of the laity currently available. Congar looks at Jesus as prophet, priest and king as a source of thinking on the roles of the laity in society. First published in 1953, this Christian classic helped lay the groundwork for reassessments of Catholic laity at Vatican II, where Congar was an expert witness and counsel. Exhaustive in its coverage, several reprints attest to its indispensability as the rallying cry of the Catholic lay movement. The lay movement needs more work like this if it is going to avoid being just another church fad.

**COOK, COLLEEN,** WRITER ■ *All That Glitters: A News-Person Explores the World of Television.* Moody Press, 1992. *267 pages.*

Cook gives readers an insider's view of television. Now a freelance writer, Cook was once a television news anchor and producer. Her chapter titles include "How and Why the Camera Lies," "Television Gone Tabloid," "The Prime Time Thief," and "Why Christ Came Before TV." Cook's insider experience can't be ignored or negated, but her attitude toward the medium of television does give one pause. Much like many conservative Christians, Cook is heavy on criticism and light on positive suggestions. Although well-written and well-researched, the book doesn't really offer the kind of creative and insightful suggestions needed for working with this powerful medium.

**COOK, JERRY, & STANLEY C. BALDWIN** ■ *Love, Acceptance and Forgiveness.* Regal, 1979. *128 pages.*

The authors' basic premise is that all Christians are to be ministers of love, acceptance and forgiveness to all people. Chapter three develops a helpful contrast between seeing the church as a field (i.e., as the place "where the people come to do the work of God") and seeing the church as a force (i.e., as the place where people are equipped to do the work of God in the world).

**COOPER, THOMAS,** CITY CHAPLAIN ■ *Crossings: Daily Paths to Faith in the Marketplace.* City in Focus, 1999. *72 pages.*

Cooper moved from ten years in business to executive director of City in Focus, a ministry in the marketplace of Vancouver. Over the past eleven years he has walked alongside the city's leaders as a partner, pastor and friend. *Crossings,* a devotional guide of daily readings, is the result of his musings and experiences. The thirty-one reflections are personal, practical and honest. Each includes a real-life vignette, Scripture, application ideas and a prayer. The contexts range from personal and family life to business and leadership. The reader is not put off by lofty spirituality, but rather is affirmed and honored by candor, humor and realism. The booklet is easily portable for use in all contexts of the pressured urban work world.

**COSTA, DONNA M.,** JOURNALIST ■ *The Ministry of All God's People.* Discipleship Resources, 1991. *52 pages.*

This study booklet, designed either for individual or group use, focuses on the calling, gifting, servanthood and covenantal relations of the laity. (Unfortunately, witness and justice were not included.) It affirms the significance of ministries in work, community and family—not just within the congregation. It includes introductory pieces on each theme; study exercises, including homework before each session; activities in the graphic arts; and liturgies to celebrate the discoveries. The booklet is very helpful in understanding the biblical ministry of the laity.

**COWAN, JOHN,** FORMER PRIEST, BUSINESSMAN ■ *The Common Table: Reflections and Meditations on Community and Spirituality in the Workplace.* HarperBusiness, 1993. *160 pages.*
John Cowan was a Catholic priest; now he is an Episcopalian businessman, sailor, husband and father. In this collection of short essays he seeks to humanize and spiritualize the life of work, covering topics like winning, losing, getting old and doing evil. He has a great knack for finding connections between free-floating aspects of life and weaving them together in a way that gives the reader a deeper understanding of spirituality and purpose.

**CRABTREE, DAVIDA FOY,** CLERGY ■ *The Empowering Church: How One Congregation Supports Lay People's Ministries in the World.* Alban Institute, 1989. *72 pages.*
Crabtree discovered that all her "Go Out into the World" sermons went nowhere. Then she realized that the congregational systems were all biased toward "inside the church spirituality." That began an adventure of change in her parish, Colchester Federated Church, in Connecticut. It lasted four years and led to her doctor of ministry thesis and this well-designed and easy-to-read tale. The approach is from more of a systems than a theological approach. It has good practical helps, but it needs rooting in Scripture. A study guide is also available. It would be helpful to have an update on the church now that Davida has been gone a while: this kind of change should be tested over decades. (See also Celia Hahn's *Learning to Share the Ministry* and Bill Diehl's *Ministry in Daily Life.*)

**CROSSON, RUSS,** FINANCIAL PLANNER ■ *A Life Well Spent.* Thomas Nelson, 1994. *246 pages.*
Christians blessed with material resources or career success should be the primary readers of this book, although all workplace Christians can benefit from it. They will be challenged, moved by important truths and forced to face questions they might wish to ignore. Crosson vividly describes the toll "success" can take on our families and ourselves, and he suggests practical remedies for those problems. What matters in his book are not dollars and cents, but daughters and sons and wives and posterity. This book is a thoughtful, life-altering conversation about what is truly important in our lives.

**CUNNINGHAM, GINNY,** PUBLIC RELATIONS, VIDEO PRODUCER ■ The
*Spirituality of Work series.* ACTA, 1996. *Booklets.*

These booklets published by the Catholic National Center for the Laity are a good
introduction to the "spirituality of work" for those struggling with faith issues in
their profession. Each booklet includes input from ten to twelve Christian business
practitioners. The booklets follow a question and answer format rather than a systematic treatment of each subject. The booklets are good discussion starters, and
the issues raised leave the reader aching for more. (See Droel, *Business People.*)

**D'ANTONIO, DAVIDSON, & WALLACE HOGE,** PROFESSOR; RESEARCHER ■
*American Catholic Laity in a Changing Church.* Sheed & Ward, 1989. *193 pages.*

"This book is about how American Catholics are continuing to respond to the
social, political and demographic changes of the 1960s, 1970s, and 1980s. American
Catholics now in their adult years began their lives in a church in which the laity's
prime role was to kneel, 'pray, pay, and obey.' Now, more and more of the laity
find that role unsatisfactory. The data for this book came from a 1987 survey of
American Catholic laity. The survey's focus was on whether or not the laity should
have the right to participate in Church decision making that affects their lives. This
book includes a chapter on women in the church. Its data and interpretation are
either disturbing or refreshing depending on your appetite for change" (introduction).

**DALE, ALZINA STONE,** WRITER ■ *Maker & Craftsman: The Story of Dorothy L.
Sayers.* Harold Shaw, rev. 1992. *158 pages.*

This is a very well done profile of one of Britain's best twentieth-century writers. It
is compact but well researched. The author explores Sayers's childhood, her
Oxford education, her experiences in advertising, publishing and radio, and her
poetry, articles, mysteries and plays. Dale counters the notion that Sayers bagged
her childhood faith during her university and premarriage experiences. She also
helps readers understand the quirkiness that characterizes so many gifted artists. A
very good contribution.

**DANKER, WILLIAM J.,** MISSIONS PROFESSOR ■ *Profit for the Lord.* Eerdmans,
1971. *183 pages.*

Danker makes a strong case for missionaries' calling and obligation to care for
natives' physical needs along with their spiritual needs. He does this by studying
the economic activities of two missions groups: the Moravians and the Basel Mission Trading Company. The economic impact of missions activities in Africa, Suri-
nam, Labrador and India are examined. Danker urges the Western church in

particular to take James's admonition to put faith into action. Though written from an unemotional historical perspective, the book is both readable and compelling. Good for those interested in church history, missions and tent-making.

**DAY, CECIL BURKE, JR.**, PROFESSOR ■ *Day by Day: The Story of Cecil B. Day & His Simple Formula for Success.* Jonathon David, 1990. *208 pages.*
This book is a son's profile of his father, Cecil B. Day, founder of Days Inns. Day Sr. believed in tenacity, fairness and business growth. One refreshing part of this somewhat predictable corporate tale is the company's commitment to disenfranchised people—the homeless, disabled and senior citizens. Even after its founder was long gone, Days Inns have a reputation for hospitality and service. This biography is a quick read.

**DAY, DOROTHY**, SOCIAL ACTIVIST ■ *The Long Loneliness: The Autobiography of Dorothy Day.* HarperCollins, 1997. *288 pages.*
This is the painful, graphic and very personal story of Day's journey through childhood, marriage, motherhood, separation and ministry to the poor. Her discovery of Christ moved her into serious study of the Sermon on the Mount and a lifelong passion to serve "the least among us." Day embraced a holistic gospel that led her to reject rugged individualism and the pietistic restriction of faith to the personal and private. There is much to learn from her open, thoughtful and practical commitment to justice. (See also Jim Forest's biography of her.)

**DAY, RICHARD ELLSWORTH**, WRITER ■ *A Christian in Big Business.* Moody Press, 1946. *317 pages.*
This is the story of Henry Parsons Crowell and the Quaker Oats Company. Crowell was friend and colaborer with evangelist D. L. Moody, helping start Moody Bible Institute. Of special interest to people working in the food industry.

**DAYTON, EDWARD R.**, PROFESSOR, ENGINEER ■ *What Ever Happened to Commitment?* Zondervan, 1984. *224 pages.*
This book is a constructive criticism of the American evangelical church's embrace of the values and mores of its culture. Dayton quotes de Tocqueville and other great social philosophers as he "gently nudges a select herd of sacred cows into a well-dug ditch" (Ted Ward). Dayton analyzes America's roots, comments on it disintegrating people, and calls Christians to community. This book deserves the attention of every serious Christian. It includes an extensive bibliography.

*Succeeding in Business Without Losing Your Faith.* Baker, 1992. *230 pages.*
This thoughtful book is designed to help the reader make a paradigm shift by clarifying biblical values that are at odds with Western cultural perspectives. The book begins with a reflections on success, business and faith, and then applies the results to society, church and workplace. Each chapter ends with reflection questions, and the appendix includes a helpful discussion guide. Though the book feels a bit shallow, it is a worthwhile resource for small groups studying the Christian cultural engagement.

**DAYTON, HOWARD L., JR.,** FINANCIAL ADVISER ■ *Your Money: Frustration or Freedom?* Tyndale House, 1979. *160 pages.*
This guide to earning, spending, investing and giving springs from Dayton's work as president of Crown Ministries, a firm training people to manage their resources. The author assimilates biblical insights nicely. Each chapter includes a small section contrasting what society says and what Scripture says, as well as a brief call to personal commitment or review questions in each area discussed. Geared toward personal finance, the book also contains a topical concordance of finance-related Scriptures. Well organized; very useful.

**DEEN, EDITH,** JOURNALIST, WRITER ■ *All the Women of the Bible.* Harper & Row, 1955. *409 pages.*
Deen gives us over three hundred concise biographical sketches of the women of Scripture, including many unnamed ones. This was the first of this genre by a woman, and it sets a precedent and serves as a model for the marketplace movement.

*Great Women of the Christian Faith.* Barbour, 1959. *410 pages.*
This is a classic in the field of profiles of church women from the second to the twentieth centuries. Preachers, mothers and wives of leaders, missionaries, movement founders, minority leaders, rulers, and saints are included. This book is beneficial as the church wrestles with the value and ministry of every believer. (It has some parallels to the work of Stephen Neill and Hans Ruedi-Weber's historical work on laity for the World Council of Churches.)

**DE PREE, MAX,** CEO, BUSINESSMAN ■ *Leadership Is an Art.* Michigan State University Press, 1987. *142 pages.*
Priceless reflections from the exceptional CEO of Herman Miller, Inc., a well-run and extremely successful office-furniture business in Michigan. De Pree writes about his corporation's tradition of servant leadership, encouraging interdepartmen-

tal criticism by employees, nurturing self-management and "abandoning oneself to the strengths of others." De Pree effectively translates biblical principles in everyday language. Unpretentious, witty, spirited and full of wisdom, this book is very highly recommended for leaders in any field of work.

*Leading Without Power: Finding Hope in Serving Community.* Jossey-Bass, 1997. *189 pages.*

De Pree believes the ground swell of America's nearly 1.5 million nonprofits holds golden insight into what makes for successful leadership in both the for-profit and nonprofit world. Nonprofit volunteers work for love and the common good, and find personal fulfillment doing something they believe in. Nonprofit leadership is rarely power-hungry but is built on shared values, commitment and moral purpose. Loyalty is won, not forced. De Pree shows why focusing on the human potential of the team, undistracted by bottom line motives, results in happy and more productive workers. Pithy musings from a forty-year corporate and nonprofit veteran.

**DENT, BARBARA,** WRITER ■ *The Gifts of Lay Ministry.* Ave Maria, 1989. *95 pages.*

Barbara Dent offers a homespun theology of lay ministry that combines biblical concepts of fellowship, service, witness and proclamation with post-Vatican II Roman Catholic concepts of liturgy and Eucharist. Most helpful is Dent's application and expansion of these concepts beyond the confines of the church. She makes a variety of suggestions for ministries at home and beyond, such as hospitality, peacemaking and listening. The author offers a unique perspective as a laywoman, Roman Catholic and New Zealander.

**DEVOS, DICK,** BUSINESS EXECUTIVE ■ *Rediscovering American Values: The Foundations of Our Freedom for the 21st Century.* Dutton, 1997. *306 pages.*

Amway Corporation's CEO DeVos, a self-confessed evangelical, has written a crossover book with minimal religious jargon or Bible references. DeVos focuses on eight values—honesty, reliability, fairness, compassion, courage, humility, reason and self-discipline. He does a good job affirming the value of work as a calling from God, and he defines stewardship as being responsible for everything we have as on loan from God. Nevertheless, this is an unreserved espousal of free enterprise and the possibility of everyone achieving the American dream.

**DE VRIES, PAUL, & BARRY GARDNER** ■ *The Taming of the Shrewd.* Thomas Nelson, 1992. *295 pages.*

Here's a book good not only for leaders in business but also lower-tier managers as well. In a take-no-prisoners approach to ethics and working, the authors mix theory and faith in an analysis of real-life circumstances. They follow it up with tough case studies for homework. The issues presented are very compelling. Although there is a minimal use of Scripture, scriptural principles run under this work. This is a great work on ethics and on faith at work.

**DEWITT, CALVIN B.,** PROFESSOR ■ *Earthwise.* CRC Publications, 1994. *86 pages.*
Most evangelicals have failed to address environmental issues—but not Cal DeWitt, who has been plugging away at it for years. Here he presents his understanding of the biblical call to all Christians to care for creation. He candidly describes the "dark recesses of creation's degradation" and appeals for commitment and action. This piece deserves broader circulation than it will receive as a small denominational publication. More can be gained from another of DeWitt's ventures—the Evangelical Environmental Network and its magazine, *Green Cross.*

**DIBACCO, THOMAS V.,** PROFESSOR ■ *Made in the U.S.A.: The History of American Business.* Harper & Row, 1987. *290 pages.*
"This comprehensive narrative history of 350 years of American business covers all of the major lives, events, and inventions of our country's economic past. Lively, anecdotal and informative, it captures the spirit of each age that led a struggling settlement of pilgrims to become the most prosperous nation in the world" (publisher). While not writing from an explicitly Christian perspective, DiBacco does not ignore the theological ideas or motivations that influenced both individual entrepreneurs and the general development of American business culture. (For more on this aspect see R. Lunden's *Business and Religion in the American 1920s.*) DiBacco's book is a primary resource, written by a respected historian. Includes a detailed index.

**DIDSBURY, HOWARD F., JR., ED.,** PROFESSOR ■ *The World of Work.* World Future Society, 1983. *338 pages.*
This collection of papers by thirty-nine authors was prepared in conjunction with the World Future Society's 1983 conference titled "Working Now and in the Future." It offers "insights into the problems associated with work and careers, employment and unemployment in a world that is being rapidly transformed by accelerating technological innovations" (preface). From a wide variety of academic disciplines and value orientations, the authors examine changes that emerged by 1983. They also discuss topics such as economic structural change, management, computers, work trends, education and lifestyle. The collection

offers an objective description and scientific analysis of the various tensions inherent in the working.

**DIEBOLD, JOHN,** MANAGEMENT CONSULTANT ■ *The Role of Business in Society.* American Management Associations, 1982. *134 pages.*
When this book was published, Diebold had become an internationally recognized expert in the fields of management and technology. His books *Automation* (1952) and *Beyond Automation* (1964) earned him a reputation as a pioneer. In these five speeches, Diebold (1) discusses threats of and solutions to regulatory pressures placed on private enterprise in the 1970s, (2) proposes adjustments in the traditional life pattern of education, full-time work and retirement to accommodate individual expression, (3) suggests a program by which private industry can deliver services traditionally provided by government, (4) pinpoints six new problems facing business and society, and recommends solutions, and (5) suggests ways society's most needed services can become the most profitable for business to deliver.

**DIEHL, WILLIAM E.,** RETIRED EXECUTIVE ■ *Christianity and Real Life.* Fortress, 1976. *120 pages.*
The most impressive quality of Diehl is not his profundity but his time-tested wisdom. Every word in this book is born of experience, and Diehl's experience has been exceptional. A courageous nonconformist, Diehl includes a rich smattering of stories about grass roots Christianity. He demands that his church be more than an institution, and helps to create the supportive community he desires. Diehl calls the reader to make faith relevant to the whole of life. Readers may not agree with all of his conclusions, but they'll respect the carefulness with which he arrived at them. See other titles by Diehl, one of the foremost lay leaders in the Lutheran church.

*In Search of Faithfulness: Lessons from the Christian Community.* Augsburg Fortress, 1987. *127 pages.*
Diehl conducted seventy interviews and surveyed 174 Lutheran business executives to discover how God's people think of and express faithfulness in daily life. The attributes which emerged are a sense of identity, growth, prayer/meditation, life in community, giving, a sense of justice and simplicity of lifestyle. Diehl concludes that the institutional church often severs the connection between faith and daily life. An excellent marketplace book, springing from Diehl's forty years of experience in business and tireless lay advocacy within the church.

*Ministry in Daily Life: A Practical Guide for Congregations.* Alban Institute, 1996. *107 pages.*

This is a very candid narrative of the attempts, struggles and successes to reorganize Diehl's church around commitment to the ministry of every member—at home, at work or in the community. In his own gentle but forceful way he poses hard questions for clergy and seminary leaders as well as decision makers in local parishes (he tells real stories of people, pastors, committees and programs). Practical and honest, this is a much-needed contribution. (See also Crabtree and Hahn for congregational case studies.)

*The Monday Connection: A Spirituality of Competence, Affirmation, and Support in the Workplace.* HarperCollins, 1991. *200 pages.*

A basic theology of work emphasizing the importance of Christian competence and competition, this book is laced with real-life stories and personal reflection. Diehl is a man who has struggled with issues of integrating work and faith on a daily basis, and he speaks as someone who has arrived at a highly developed sense of connection between the two. Filled with great quotes, anecdotes and a lifetime of learning, this book is a must-read.

*Thank God It's Monday.* Fortress, 1982. *196 pages.*

The author brings biblical concepts and images to bear on job-related issues such as competition, materialism and status. Using his forty years of business experience as a guide, Diehl suggests ways the gospel should inform the Christian's life at work. He establishes the book's exceptionally empathetic tone in the first chapter through a series of interviews with struggling Christian workers. He also includes a valuable discussion of the modern "principalities and powers" that can control our lives—ideology, security and institutions. The book offers an original and highly stimulating critique of modern life in America. An excellent autobiographical introduction to marketplace thinking and living.

**DITTES, JAMES E.,** PROFESSOR ■ *When Work Goes Sour.* Westminster Press, 1987. *117 pages.*

Dittes makes three observations about men's experience of work. (1) "Men's most intense love affairs are often with work." But work, like love affairs, often fail to meet expectations and to be adequately remunerated. (2) "Men's most intense religious commitment is often to work." But it does not bring the salvation we seek from it. (3) Men often derive their sense of self-worth from work. Dittes advises readers to "let work be work: no more, no less. . . . More important, let men be men, not (solely) workers." He adds that in order to restore a healthy view of work, we must remember that "love and God are both available to us without working for them," and that "we are more than workers." Short, readable, and to the point.

**DOLAN, JAY P. ET AL.,** PROFESSORS ■ *Transforming Parish Ministry:The Changing Roles of Catholic Clergy, Laity, and Women Religious.* Crossroad, 1989. *366 pages.*

This book offers a historical view of changes in the U.S. Roman Catholic Church between the years 1930 and 1980. There are four chapters, each an essay by one of the four authors. The heart of this book is three essays on the priest, the sister and the layperson. Each of these essays examines two major issues—the change that took place in the understanding and practice of ministry and how this altered the priest/sister/layperson's relationship with the parish. In part four Dolan attempts "to integrate the essays and some of their major points into a broader social context with a primary focus on the parish over the course of these fifty years" (p. viii).

**DONALDSON, THOMAS, & PATRICIA WERHANE,** PROFESSORS ■ *Ethical Issues in Business:A Philosophical Approach.* Prentice Hall, 1983. *392 pages.*

This is a business-ethics text that includes fifty-three traditional and contemporary essays or modern case studies on all aspects of business. It is divided into four parts: general issues in ethics (including ethical relativism, egoism and truth telling); morality and corporations; property, profit and justice; and contemporary business issues (including employee rights, affirmative action and environmental issues). Case studies include Three Mile Island, the Chrysler Corporation and the Nestle infant formula controversy. Both an illustrated second edition (paper, 1983) and an unillustrated third edition (paper, 1988) are available.

**DONER, COLONEL V.,** PROFESSOR ■ *The Samaritan Strategy:A New Agenda for Christian Activism.* Wolgemuth & Hyatt, 1988. *252 pages.*

Doner describes the political rise and fall of the "Christian right" in the 1980s and proposes an agenda for the 1990s that is more attuned to "the needs of our time." A sweeping critique and call to action that was up-to-date, well-researched and immersed in Scripture. While "Christian politics" is inescapably controversial, Doner's reasons for political involvement deserve a hearing. He offers a politically conservative view.

**DOOHAN, LEONARD,** PROFESSOR, LAY ADVOCATE ■ *The Laity:A Bibliography.* Michael Glazier, 1987. *159 pages.*

Volume three of a three-volume set titled Theological and Biblical Resources, this is a great source of bibliographic materials on the laity written from a Catholic perspective. This book list—without annotations—has almost 1,000 books organized into 41 categories. Doohan includes books, articles, Vatican papers and bulls, and academic theses grouped in helpful categories like "Official Documents," "Survey Works," "Laity in History," "Training of Laity for Ministry" and "Work."

*Laity's Mission in the Local Church.* Harper & Row, 1986. *144 pages.*
Doohan's mission is to bridge "the frequent gap between church teaching and lay hopes," which he does by telling the clergy stories of laity who are making a difference, and by providing a theological foundation for each aspect of lay life. He builds on his *Lay-Centered Church* (see below) by updating his analysis of the Catholic lay movement since Vatican II and examining four major components of lay life: work, family, social service and celebration. Historically based and visionary. An extensive bibliography is provided.

*The Lay-Centered Church.* Harper & Row, 1984. *175 pages.*
Doohan shows his unusual grasp of the history of lay movements within the Catholic Church, especially of theological trends since Vatican II. He offers a synthesis of modern lay activity and Vatican Council rulings as well as a rigorous assessment of how each has contributed to the mission of the Church. In the second half of the book, Doohan suggests the family as a particularly apt model for the lay-centered church, which he believed would continue to grow within all denominations through the 1990s. This is a thorough, incisive and accessible study. It includes a valuable bibliography on the laity, which was expanded and published as *The Laity: A Bibliography.*

**DORR, DONALD,** THEOLOGIAN ■ *Spirituality and Justice.* Orbis, 1984. *255 pages.*
Dorr writes to bring together two popular but clashing concerns. Those interested in social justice often criticize traditional spirituality for being individualistic and passive in the face of the world's evils. And those who stress the need for spirituality see the inability of many social activists to deal with frustration and anger. In attempting to resolve this dilemma Dorr touches on a number of diverse subjects: economics, politics, theology and prayer.

**DOSICK, WAYNE,** RABBI ■ *The Business Bible: 10 New Commandments for Bringing Spirituality and Ethical Values into the Workplace.* Jewish Lights, 2000. *176 pages.*
The Hebrew tradition is often overlooked as a source of insight on integrating worldviews. In this book, a rabbi who grew up waiting on customers in his father's

grocery stores applies ancient wisdom to the modern marketplace. Dosick takes a fresh look at the Decalogue, providing contemporary commandments for ethical business behavior. He shows why the *worth* ethic is as important as the *work* ethic, how business *ethics* lead to business *excellence,* and why *value* means more than net *worth*. Dosick's realism is rooted in ancient wisdom and a well-developed faith. His style makes his Jewish tradition accessible to people of any faith, and his use of real-life situations is very helpful. The bibliography ranges far beyond studies in Judaism.

**DOUD, GUY RICE,** TEACHER ■ *Molder of Dreams.* Focus on the Family, 1990. *192 pages.*
This is the personal story of a small-town boy in Minnesota who became national teacher of the year. His roots are similar to Garrison Keillor's Lake Wobegon. Doud tells the tale of his alcoholic family, poverty, childhood chubbiness, poor academic record and low expectations in a homespun style. He notes people who gave him love, hope and encouragement as he grew to be what he longed for—an affirmer and developer of students. Focus on the Family has also released a video of his story.

**DOWLEY, TIM,** PROFESSOR ■ *The Kregel Guide to EVERYDAY LIFE IN BIBLE TIMES.* Kregel, 1998. *32 pages.*
This is a very colorful look at everyday life among ancient Jews and Romans. Color sketches are supported by brief textual descriptions. Seventeen two-page topical chapters cover clothing, housing, family life, foods and their development, crafts, and travel. Occasional boxes describe single items in more detail (e.g., sandals, shopping, education, festivals). A helpful index makes for quick access. Illustrations are large enough for small group demonstration.

**DOWNEY, MICHAEL, ED.,** PROFESSOR ■ *That They Might Live: Power, Empowerment, and Leadership in the Church.* Crossroad, 1991. *222 pages.*
This volume is a collection of thirteen essays by authors addressing the theme of empowerment for leadership, particularly with respect to lay ministry and leadership in the Roman Catholic Church. These essays include feminist, historical, contemporary, church and theological-biblical perspectives.

**DOZIER, VERNA J.,** TEACHER ■ *The Authority of the Laity.* Alban Institute, 1982. *42 pages, booklet.*
Dozier addresses the problems of lay inferiority and clerical supremacy in the church. A no-nonsense lay theologian, Dozier combines her cultivated sensitivity

and astute grasp of Scripture to help laypeople reclaim their authority as agents of God's kingdom. She asserts that laypeople are morbidly concentrated on themselves and the church as an institution; therefore they need to be redirected into the service of the world.

*The Calling of the Laity.* Alban Institute, 1988. *149 pages.*
One of the premier female lay leaders of our day coordinates an anthology of twenty-five articles on lay ministry. Themes include ethics, living with the incomplete and educational support systems for the laity. A formidable survey of lay concerns, this book is highly recommended.

*Equipping the Saints: A Method of Self-Directed Bible Study for Lay Groups.* Alban Institute, 1981. *45 pages, booklet.*
Dozier declares, "The point of lay Bible study is to help lay people reclaim their authority as the people of God" (Celia Hahn in the preface). Hahn adds, "Laity are raised in a culture of dependence on authorities. We are taught to sit at the feet of experts, and not to trust the validity of our own wrestling." Dozier wants to help laypeople discover their call through Scripture. She provides guidelines for personal or small group Bible study and presents a dramatic narrative of her group wrestling with Scripture and its application. This is very helpful for beginners in Bible study not led by an expert.

**DROEL, WILLIAM L.,** PROFESSOR ■ The Spirituality of Work series. National Center for the Laity, 1989-1991. *Booklets.*
These booklets are designed to help people see their work as spiritual. Each booklet begins with a profile of the modern worker and discusses issues such as meaning in a changing environment, connections between God and nursing (for example), work environment and continuing the search. Droel mentions some issues (e.g., paperwork, pay, ethics, nursing shortage) without attempting to deal with them. But these booklets are ideal resources for witnessing or consciousness-raising with coworkers, acquaintances and friends. This excellent series is based entirely on interviews with practitioners in each field. Most highly recommended.

**DROEL, WILLIAM L., & GREGORY F. AUGUSTINE PIERCE,** PROFESSOR; PUBLISHER ■ *Confident and Competent: A Challenge for the Lay Church.* Ave Maria, 1987. *110 pages.*
According to the authors the church must remember that it is a means, not an end. An overemphasis on internal problems (such as membership and financing) has led to a neglect of lay spirituality based on work in the world. American Catholic lay-

persons have developed fantastic liturgies and lay ministry teams, but until this renewal spreads to the neighborhoods and social institutions, say the authors, it will be self-serving. With respectful and constructive criticism, the authors examine vocation, the spirituality of work and social teaching. Recommended for Protestant as well as Catholic readers.

**DROEL, WILLIAM L., & PATRICIA D. BERMAN,** PROFESSOR; WRITER ■ *Business People.* National Center for the Laity, 1991. *64 pages.*
This booklet quickly and efficiently communicates a spirituality of business work. Many business people contributed to this booklet covering five topics: "The Meaning of Business"; "God and Business"; "My Work Environment"; "Fitting Business into the Rest of My Life"; "Continuing My Search." (See also Ginny Cunningham's *The Spirituality of Work: Military Personnel.*)

**DYER, GEORGE J., ED.,** PRIEST, THEOLOGIAN ■ *Chicago Studies: Religion in the Marketplace.* Archdiocese of Chicago, 1989. *104 pages.*
Published three times a year, Chicago Studies is "for the continuing theological development of priests and other religious educators." The April 1989 issue contains seven compelling marketplace articles written by leading Catholic laypersons. It includes results from a key survey of business executives on the role of religion in their work. Also included are articles on women in business, a biblical theology of work and a spirituality that makes sense to the worker. Interesting and incisive.

**DYLONG, JOHN,** WRITER, PROFESSOR, GRAPHIC ARTIST ■ *The Spirituality of Work: Visual Artists.* National Center for the Laity, 1995. *37 pages, booklet.*
This booklet, part of a series of booklets on the spirituality of work, follows an interview format rather than a systematic treatment of the subject. This booklet is a good introduction for persons struggling with issues within the arts. (See Droel for others in the series)

**ECKER, RICHARD E.,** WRITER ■ *The Stress Myth.* InterVarsity Press, 1989. *132 pages.*
Ecker attempts to dislodge the popular assumption that stress is a necessary work hazard. But far from suggesting that stress is a figment of our imagination, Ecker suggests ways we may prevent stress in our lives and relationships. (See also *Staying Well* [InterVarsity, 1984], in which Ecker discusses diet, drugs, physical activity and stress. He also analyzes why "the good life" is so bad for our health.)

**ECKERD, JACK, WITH CHARLES PAUL CONN,** BUSINESSMAN; WRITER ■ *Eckerd.* Revell, 1987. *190 pages.*

Alongside rave reviews by Gerald Ford, Warren Burger and Billy Graham, Charles Colson writes, "This is the amazing, exciting story of one of the most remarkable men I've ever known. It is a gripping account; when you're finished, you will want to sing the doxology." Eckerd turned the New York drugstore he inherited into a billion-dollar chain through wise business practices. His self-service concept transformed retailing. But he writes this book "to show what changed a prosperous, tough-talking businessman's philosophy from beat the competition to living the Golden Rule." The author details how his religious conversion helped make sense of his life.

**EDGE, FINDLEY B.,** PROFESSOR, LAY LEADER ■ *The Doctrine of the Laity.* Convention Press, 1985. *156 pages.*

Edge discusses the role of the laity in God's mission to the world, the need for pastors to equip them, and how and where this mission should be expressed. He helps readers discover their gifts and encourages individual and corporate response. Each chapter ends with a personal learning activity. An introductory-level consciousness raiser.

**EDMUNDS, VINCENT, & C. GORDON SCORER,** DOCTORS ■ *On Being a Christian Medical Student.* InterVarsity Press, 1958. *72 pages.*

Two doctors have packed this little volume with wisdom, guidance and realism. They drew other doctors into the work with chapters from six peers. They probe topics like patient care, witnessing, pitfalls in medicine, faith healing misconceptions, marriage and calling. The content is rooted in a strong evangelical faith and thoughtful reflection about the industry. As a primer it is excellent, but it needs significant updating in light of the modern medical scene and its complications in ethical issues and legislation.

**EISENMAN, TOM L.,** PASTOR ■ *Everyday Evangelism.* InterVarsity Press, 1987. *180 pages.*

Eisenman suggests that taking the time to show kindness, concern and patience with neighbors, coworkers and strangers can transform many ordinary moments into opportunities to show the love of Jesus. Chapters with a marketplace emphasis include "The Witness of Working Women," "All Businesses Should Be Service Stations" and "Creative Excellence and Quality Products." Discussion questions follow each chapter.

**ELLIOTT, CHARLES** ■ *Praying the Kingdom: Towards a Political Spirituality.*
Darton, Longman & Todd, 1985. *150 pages.*
Elliott considers Jesus' instruction to pray "Thy kingdom come." The kingdom, according to Elliott, will neither be an entity replacing this world nor concerned only with internal or spiritual matters, but the "transformation of human society." Beginning with the predicament most people find themselves in, plagued by guilt and powerlessness, through story and myth he shows people how to pray effectively.

**ELLIS, LEE, & LARRY BURKETT,** CAREER COUNSELOR; FINANCIAL ADVISER ■ *Your Career in Changing Times.* Moody Press, 1993. *324 pages.*
This practical work is not for someone who may be in a work crisis. It should be read before a crisis comes. Ellis and Burkett explore how work world is changing, and provide practical steps for Christians to deal with that change. The authors drill home the importance of basing decisions on truth. Though not as strong as Mattson and Miller's classic *Finding a Job You Can Love*, it's still worth reading.

**ELLUL, JACQUES,** PROFESSOR ■ *The Ethics of Freedom.* Eerdmans, 1976. *517 pages.*
For Ellul, work does not have absolute value, but this does not mean it has no value. Work offers the possibility of sustaining life, upholding the world and continuing of history. And this is God's will. From Ellul's point of view, work should neither be despised nor idealized.

*Money and Power.* InterVarsity Press, 1984. *173 pages.*
Ellul is a consummate Christian thinker. In this updated 1954 classic he exposes the inability of socialism, capitalism and Marxism to ensure economic justice. Money is not neutral in any system, according to Ellul; it is a "power . . . that acts by itself." Jesus personifies mammon as a demanding god, an enemy of God's kingdom. After chapters on wealth in the Old Testament, teaching children about money, and the world's rich and poor, the author challenges Christians to live responsibly, by the law of grace and not by ideologies of this age.

*The Presence of the Kingdom.* Seabury, 1967. *153 pages.*
In this early work Ellul considers the problem of how to live as a Christian in the world—that is, in the domain of Satan. He is concerned for the layperson who, though salt and light, is a sheep in the midst of wolves.

**ELSDON, RON,** TEACHER ■ *Bent World: A Christian Response to the Environmental Crisis.* InterVarsity Press, 1981. *170 pages.*
Elsdon helps Christians make informed responses to current environmental concerns. Elsdon discerningly begins by justifying Christian involvement in ecological issues. He devotes a chapter each to the problems of global depletion of metal resources, large-scale energy consumption, rapid urbanization and world hunger. In the final chapters Elsdon examines the biblical metathemes of creation, fall and redemption and concludes with an interdisciplinary approach to possible solutions.

**EMERSON, ALLEN, & CHERYL FORBES,** TEACHER; WRITER ■ *The Invasion of the Computer Culture.* InterVarsity Press, 1989. *180 pages.*
On a scale from one to ten, this book gets an eleven. Emerson and Forbes have done Christians a tremendous service by explaining in simple terms "What You Need to Know About the New [Computer] World We Live In" (subtitle). They take a positive view of the "exciting and fascinating world of computers," while warning of the psychological and philosophical dangers it poses to the Christian worldview. The book provides a descriptive overview of the field of computers and a theoretical analysis of computer-brain comparisons. Prophetic; substantive and accessible. A must read.

**ENGSTROM, TED W., & DAVID J. JUROE,** WRITER, EXECUTIVE; COUNSELOR ■ *The Work Trap.* Revell, 1979. *222 pages.*
Engstrom and Juroe expose the common problem of overworking and examine its conditions, causes and cures. Their goal is to reorient our thinking about work and restore its pleasure and proper place among all of life's priorities. They describe the characteristics, attitudes and habits of people who overwork and explain why they become addicted: cultural conditioning, spiritual deficiencies or psychological factors. The authors take a biblical view of work and establish its inherent worth, and they propose practical strategies for escaping the work trap and restoring balance to one's life. The book provides important help for avoiding a major form of idolatry in our day. (See also *When Work Goes Sour* by James Dittes, a book on workaholism among male workers.)

**ENLOW, DAVID, & DOROTHY ENLOW,** BUSINESS PERSONS ■ *Saved from Bankruptcy: The Story of the Boat-Building Meloons.* Moody Press, 1975. *111 pages.*
This is a story about the boat-building business of the Meloon family, which began in 1945. In an emergency, the Meloons successfully supplied 300 storm boats to Allied troops for a military maneuver at Berlin. After years of financial loss, the Meloons had to declare bankruptcy. But they eventually recovered. Their story is an adventure that has become a testimony to the wisdom of biblical business prac-

tices. This book builds empathy with the financially stricken Christian. Foreword by Billy Graham.

**EVERIST, NORMA COOK, & NELVIN VOS,** PROFESSORS ■ *Where in the World Are You? Connecting Faith and Daily Life.* Alban Institute, 1996. *140 pages.*
This book is a helpful resource for individuals who want to slow down, get off the stress treadmill and reconnect faith to daily life. The book is framed by a series of fourteen weekly exercises for small groups. The goal is that people learn to develop disciplines that allow them to faithfully balance life's demands.

**FAIVRE, ALEXANDRE,** PROFESSOR ■ *The Emergence of the Laity in the Early Church.* Paulist, 1990. *242 pages.*
This compelling study of the first five centuries of Christianity adds significant data to modern dialogue on ecclesiology and clergy-laity distinctions. Faivre quotes extensively from both early church sources and current European research. While the book is primarily exegetical, Faivre presents this study as a measuring rod for post-Vatican II evaluations of the church. Finally, he offers guidance to those calling for a rediscovery of the role of the laity today. This book is a historical gold mine. Upper-level reading.

**FENHAGEN, JAMES C.,** PRIEST, SEMINARY DEAN ■ *Ministry and Solitude: The Ministry of the Laity and the Clergy in Church and Society.* Seabury, 1981. *90 pages.*
"Christian ministry is born in solitude, expressed through an active caring for the world and the people in it, and sustained by an openness to the presence of God in every aspect of human life." This statement represents the central focus of the book, but the author also touches on a variety of issues related to ministry, including ministry of clergy and laity, gift discernment, and spiritual disciplines.

*More Than Wanderers: Spiritual Disciplines for Christian Ministry.* Seabury, 1978. *100 pages.*
"One of the most critical tasks of the local church is to enable people to become 'journeyers' rather than 'wanderers.'" The journey that Fenhagen speaks of is not toward personal fulfillment but rather to increased participation in Christ's ministry to the world. But for this to be an authentic ministry we need an inner transformation so that Christ is seen through us. It is with this in view that he introduces spiritual disciplines.

*Mutual Ministry: New Vitality for the Local Church.* Harper & Row, 1977. *147 pages.*

"This book is written for those persons in the local church—clergy and laity— who are concerned about the vitality of [their] congregations. It is based on the assumption that [a serious evaluation of congregational vitality must include] four elements: the vision by which the church lives; the ministry through which the church acts; the structures by which the church is shaped; and the experience of faith in which the church is nourished. . . . My point of view has been shaped by my encounter with Holy Scripture, by what I have learned from the behavioral sciences, and from my own experience as an educator and parish priest" (introduction). Well written.

**FERGUSON, JOHN,** BRITISH CHURCH LEADER ■ *O My People: God's Call to Society.* Oliphants Outlook, 1977. *144 pages.*

Ferguson sees Scripture calling Christians to education, work, economic sharing, environmental conservation, political decentralization and nonviolence. "To say that [God] is Lord of our personal lives, but not of our corporate lives, Lord of the individual heart, but not of politics and economics, is to say that he is not God." Ferguson presents a refreshing blend of social and historical, literary, and theological perspectives from classic British literature. Includes questions for discussion and action.

**FEUCHT, OSCAR E.,** CHURCH WORKER ■ *Everyone a Minister.* Concordia, 1974. *160 pages.*

This book grew out of Feucht's twenty-five years of work as a denominational secretary of adult education. It is as good as or better than any other book explaining the concept of the priesthood of believers; it also suggests ways to implement the concept. This is a particularly good synthesis of literature from the lay movement in the 1950s and 1960s.

**FIELD, DAVID, & ELSPETH STEPHESON,** PROFESSOR; BROADCASTER ■ *Just the Job: Christians Talk About Work and Vocation.* InterVarsity Press, 1978. *127 pages.*

The authors conducted interviews with Christians in bricklaying, engineering, homemaking, church work, sales, surgical care, broadcasting, teaching, scientific research, social work, computers and art. Respective chapters are devoted to reflections on each vocation with an emphasis on the ways in which Christian convictions inform the life of the worker. Field introduces the book with a very helpful nineteen-page theology of work. (For information on a similar survey of marketplace testimonies see Gregory F. A. Pierce's *Of Human Hands.*)

**FINN, VIRGINIA SULLIVAN** ■ *Pilgrims in This World: A Lay Spirituality.* Paulist, 1990. *312 pages.*
This volume develops a theology of the ministry for laypeople of the American Catholic Church in the light of Vatican II and the Synod on the Laity. The tone is personal, detailed and thorough.

**FISH, SHARON, & JUDITH ALLEN SHELLY,** NURSES ■ *Spiritual Care: The Nurse's Role.* 3rd ed. InterVarsity Press, 1988. *188 pages.*
The authors walk through twenty-seven case studies of nurses and patients in a variety of settings, offering helpful principles of spiritual care. Respective chapters ask "What is human?" and "What are spiritual needs?" The authors discuss how to discern a patient's spiritual needs and suggest resources to help meet them. Separate chapters consider when and how to use Scripture and pray. The book features a helpful thirty-nine-page appendix titled "The Nurse's Personal Spiritual Resources." *Spiritual Care* is designed to be used individually or in a group (a "spiritual care workbook" is included in this edition). This is not an oversimplified how-to book; it is sensitive, empathetic and insightful. An excellent handbook for the Christian nurse.

**FLOOD, EDMUND,** PRIEST ■ *The Laity Today and Tomorrow.* Paulist Press, 1987. *112 pages.*
This British Benedictine priest reports "on the new consciousness of lay Catholics and how it might change the face of tomorrow's Church." The laity, once asked to be only helpers, are now partners in ministry, work and worship. Flood views this change as a rediscovery of community values of the past, and he suggests implications it will have in our views of social outreach, the role of priest, work in the marketplace and minority group enfolding.

**FOLEY, GERALD,** LAY ADVOCATE, PRIEST ■ *Empowering the Laity.* Sheed & Ward, 1986. *199 pages.*
The concerns of the "Monday church" in the shops, factories, schools and homes are quite different from those addressed in Sunday liturgies or Wednesday night church education programs, says Foley. This represents a crisis in the Roman Catholic Church; new theologies of work, leisure, marriage, family and civic involvement are sorely needed. In this book Foley clearly, honestly and helpfully provokes, explains, mediates and suggests. "I trust that it will raise more questions than it answers," he writes. The book is a worthy attempt to increase the Catholic Church's relevance to the life of its members. Non-Catholics will find it helpful too. Discussion questions follow each chapter.

**FORELL, GEORGE W.,** PROFESSOR ■ *Christian Social Teachings.* Augsburg
Fortress, 1966. *252 pages.*
Forell provides a panoramic view of 2,000 years of Christian teaching on subjects
such as political justice, peace, civil rights, family law and civil liberties. The chronologically arranged readings include everything from obscure pietistic to classic
Reformed literature. This book is a treasure house of history and is accessible to the
nonspecialist. Helpful introductory remarks and biographical information precede
each excerpt. (Also available through this publisher: *History of Christian Ethics:
From the New Testament to Augustine,* vol. 1, 1979.)

**FOREST, JIM,** ACTIVIST, WRITER ■ *Love Is the Measure: A Biography of
Dorothy Day.* Paulist, 1986. *224 pages.*
This is the intriguing story of one of the Catholic Church's greatest American lay
leaders. Day was one of the founders of the Catholic Workers Movement. She was
also a journalist, nurse, solo mom, socialist activist and author. Based on her childhood experiences with poverty, religion and social systems, she built a career of
prophetic work focused on the contradictions and injustices that offended her.
Besides her journalistic pioneering of the Catholic Worker newspaper, she founded
houses of hospitality for the poor. She willingly risked rejection, condemnation, jail
and opposition because of her spiritual convictions about justice for all. Forest
brings his friendship and shared experiences to the story of this radical Christian
who loved her church while calling it into accountability all the time. (See also
Day's autobiography.)

**FOSTER, RICHARD J.,** PROFESSOR, WRITER ■ *Celebration of Discipline: The
Path to Spiritual Growth.* Harper & Row, 1978. *171 pages.*
An invaluable rediscovery of the classical spiritual disciplines of meditation,
prayer, fasting, study, simplicity, solitude, submission, service, confession, worship, guidance and celebration. Avoiding the two dangers of legalism on the one
hand and antinomianism on the other, Foster presents the disciplines as a means
whereby God by his grace can change us. What makes this book stand out is
that it is meant not only for the mystic in a cloister but also the Christian in the
world.

*Money, Sex and Power* (retitled *The Challenge of the Disciplined Life*). Harper &
Row, 1985. *260 pages.*
Whereas Foster's classic *Celebration of Discipline* introduced the traditional Christian disciplines, this book deals with three contemporary secular gods and demonstrates the role of disciplines in keeping them at bay. A proper view of money, sex

and power requires vows of simplicity, fidelity and service. Written to help Christians face "the many ethical choices we face almost daily," the book combines Foster's knowledge of major thinkers through the ages with a fresh, well-informed and progressive Christian perspective. The author raises issues of profound importance for any marketplace Christian. A study guide is available.

**FOUNTAIN, WYN,** BUSINESS EXECUTIVE ■ *"The Kingdom Come ..." in the Other Hundred Hours.* Self-published, 1984. *126 pages.*
This book is unique in the faith-at-work material of the 1980s and 1990s. It is a complex story of a man who learned to live all his nonchurch waking hours (the other hundred hours) for God. Fountain tells his own journey of faith, family and business (including failures, breakthroughs and hard lessons along the way). Fountain "believes that the churches as now structured, will never enable the prayer—'Thy kingdom come, thy will be done on earth as it is in heaven'—to be answered because the church is too introspective, constantly devoted to their own growth and activity within themselves rather than being involved with the restoration of the kingdom of God where people live, and exercise their creativity" (author's page). This is challenging to read, but we have much to learn from Fountain.

**FOWLER, JAMES W.,** PROFESSOR ■ *Becoming Adult, Becoming Christian: Adult Development and Christian Faith.* Harper & Row, 1984. *147 pages.*
Fowler applies the discipline of developmental psychology to development in the Christian life. He argues for a view of vocation that sees us as participants in the redemptive-creative work God is doing in all sectors of human life. This is to be seen in contrast to the dominant view that destiny, or self-actualization, is the proper ultimate goal for human development. A very thought-provoking book.

*Faith Development and Pastoral Care.* Fortress, 1987. *120 pages.*
Fowler's interest is to set the stage for "the recovery of practical theology as a discipline." He draws on his work in the area of faith development to raise issues for pastoral care in the church. His overall goal is to see all Christians active in their respective vocations, which he defines as aligning "our efforts as responsible selves, as much as we can, with the purposes of God."

**FOX, MATTHEW,** PRIEST, EDUCATOR ■ *The Reinvention of Work: A New Vision of Livelihood for Our Time.* HarperCollins, 1994. *352 pages.*
Matthew Fox is best known for his controversial work on creation spirituality. Fox was dismissed from the Dominican Order in 1993 for his radical views. He contin-

ues to pursue the mystical creation tradition of spirituality with a special emphasis on the contribution of Meister Eckart, Hildegard of Bingen and Thomas Aquinas. Fox attempts to provide the outline for an emerging "post-modern systematic theology"—one based on creation spirituality rather than the "fall-redemption" ideologies that have so influenced Western theology in the modern era. In *The Reinvention of Work* he applies creation spirituality to the modern experience of work. Fox offers us a Green theology and spirituality applied to work.

FRANKE, MERLE G., PASTOR ■ *Lord, Where Are You? I'm Hip-Deep in Alligators.* C.S.S. Publications, 1985. *88 pages.*
This collection of prayer reflections was written by Franke as a form of intercession for his Christian friends in business, whom he interviewed. Franke says, "I was somewhat taken aback by the avalanche of concerns they expressed!" (foreword). Using remarkably fresh and realistic language, he expresses the tensions between Christian tenets of faith and common practices in the business world that oppose them. Poems in this book deal with issues such as competition, reputation, honesty, promotions, company closings and retirement concerns. Insightful and straightforward, this is ideal reading at coffee break, in transit, on elevators or at the beginning of the day.

FREY, BRADSHAW, ET AL., YOUTH WORKERS ■ *All of Life Redeemed at Work and Play: Biblical Insight for Daily Obedience.* Paideia, 1986. *111 pages.*
At the time of its publication, the four authors worked for the Coalition for Christian Outreach, a ministry to students on forty-three campuses in western Pennsylvania. As the title suggests, the authors link devotion to Jesus Christ with the whole of life, personal and cultural. Dr. J. I. Packer calls it "a lively mix of thoughts on what true faith requires in the way of a changed lifestyle. . . . This book will keep you awake, force you to think, build you up and make you wise." Contains a fine annotated bibliography arranged by academic discipline.

FULLER, MILLARD, LAWYER, BUILDER ■ *The Theology of the Hammer.* Smyth & Helwys, 1994. *154 pages.*
The founder and leader of Habitat for Humanity lays out his understanding of faith, poverty and homelessness, which now drives this worldwide home building ministry that he founded in 1976. He acknowledges his dependence on the Bible and the influences of Dorothy Day, Clarence Jordan, Thomas Merton, Henry Nouwen, Walter Rauschenbusch and Albert Schweitzer. His book is a combination of spiritual biography, Scripture, stories and organizational development. He acknowledges scores of people as he weaves his theology together. Pictures add to the variety and

richness. Appendixes include organizational values and principles, a covenant and guidelines. This is a wonderful story of Christian faith translated into action and service.

**GALLAGHER, SUSAN V., & ROGER LUNDIN,** PROFESSORS ■ *Literature Through the Eyes of Faith.* Harper & Row, 1989. *192 pages.*

This book helps Christians interpret literature on an introductory level. The authors argue that the reading and writing of literature are important forms of human action in God's world. They help students see literature "as a product of history as well as a participant in history" and recognize that "many modern assumptions about literature grew out of intellectual traditions that challenged the central beliefs of orthodox Christianity." The authors cite and excerpt numerous texts. Highly recommended.

**GARLOW, JAMES L.,** PASTOR ■ *LITE (Lay Institute to Equip) Manual.* Beacon Hill, 1980. *177 pages, spiral-bound.*

Garlow describes this manual as "a 'school' of lay ministry designed to assist pastors and laypersons to become 'partners in ministry.' " It's designed as a two- to three-month adult education course. Cartoon character Lonnie Layman guides the reader through four stages of training: a called people, a gifted people, a trained people and a sent people. This extremely useful fill-in-the blank manual for adult education is highly recommended. A leader's guide is also available.

*Partners in Ministry: Laity and Pastors Working Together.* Beacon Hill, 1981. *195 pages.*

A popularly written account of what "every Christian is a minister" means. Garlow believes that "we are on the verge of a meaningful reclaiming of the heritage that every believer is truly called to ministry."

**GARLOW, JAMES L., & MYRA SCHUBERT,** PASTOR; COMPOSER, PIANIST ■ *We "Laity" Are Ministers: A Musical Presentation of the Garlow Concepts of Lay Ministry Training.* Beacon Hill, 1983. *64 pages.*

This is a hidden treasure—a musical on training laity for ministry. Garlow, a Nazarene pastor, is passionate about lay ministry. Seventeen scores are included for instruments, actors, narrator and singers. The only known musical drama resource on lay ministry.

**GARRISON, JAYNE,** WRITER ■ *The Christian Working Mother's Handbook.* Tyndale House, 1986. *246 pages.*
Garrison offers practical help for the woman who is doing it all: finding a career niche, making the family's world beautiful, finding private time, staying organized and handling stress. Garrison offers creative ideas to conquer the morning blues, guide children's behavior, keep in touch with family and friends, plan nutritious meals, and more. Her own journal entries precede each of twenty chapters, including Scriptures as food for thought. Practical and unpretentious.

**GAY, CRAIG M.,** PROFESSOR ■ *With Liberty and Justice for Whom? The Recent Evangelical Debate over Capitalism.* Eerdmans, 1991. *276 pages.*
This book provides detailed analysis of the ways evangelical Christians, particularly in North America, have viewed capitalism. Providing an extensive bibliography, this volume is for students and scholars.

**GEANEY, DENNIS,** PRIEST, ADMINISTRATOR ■ *Full Church, Empty Rectory: Training Lay Ministers for Parishes Without Priests.* Fides/Claretian, 1980. *134 pages.*
Geaney sees recent changes in the Roman Catholic Church, including reduced numbers of ordained ministers, not as indicators of impending death but as opportunities for new life. Laypeople on fire with the love of Christ are asking to take part in church ministry. He writes, "This book is about the channeling and refining of these energies through programs of theological education and pastoral training." He addresses what the essential content of their training should be.

**GEORGE, DENISE,** WRITER ■ *The Christian as a Consumer.* Westminster Press, 1984. *114 pages.*
George offers "realistic suggestions for replacing an overly complicated, money-oriented life-style with a more Christian existence." In respective chapters, she (1) does a biblical analysis of money's proper place, (2) discusses the critical problems of deceitful advertising, (3) examines the compulsion to keep up with one's neighbor and (4) considers the needs of the underprivileged. Finally, she asks, "Are you called to a simpler lifestyle?" (See her *Faith for Everyday Stress.* Broadman, 1988.)

**GIBBS, EDDIE,** PROFESSOR ■ *ChurchNext: Quantum Changes in How We Do Ministry.* InterVarsity Press, 2000. *252 pages.*
Gibbs, a well-known church strategist and practitioner, both analyzes the new models of American churches and suggests changes needed to reach the world in the future. He takes a proactive approach to the future. This book is a piece of techni-

cal research and analysis, and thus reads in a dense, academic way. Gibbs poses questions that would make leaders of newer church models squirm. His purpose is to enable all churches to more effectively reach the lost.

**GIBBS, MARK,** LAY ADVOCACY MINISTER ■ *Christians with Secular Power.* Fortress, 1981. *123 pages.*
Gibbs argues for a lay ministry that takes place primarily in the world rather than in the church. He sees the clergy's as "educational advisers" rather than "educational monopolists." The last half of the book deals with the specific issues of politics, business, labor unions, police and military, and the media.

**GIBBS, MARK, & RALPH T. MORTON,** LAY ADVOCACY LEADERS ■ *God's Frozen People.* Westminster Press, 1964. *192 pages.*
This book helped spawn the present lay movement in the Western church. It addresses the life of the layperson in the church and in the world. Based on eight years of dialogue and discussion between the authors and their faith communities, it claims unusual depth and originality. Distinctly British, but broad in scope, it is written "for God's ordinary people inside and outside our Sunday congregations" (back cover copy).

*God's Lively People.* Westminster Press, 1970. *212 pages.*
In this sequel to *God's Frozen People* (1964), Gibbs and Morton continue their mission of lay advocacy. Writing about the vocation of God's people in tomorrow's world, the authors mourn the relatively slow emergence of the lay movement in Europe and the difficulty of reforming the vast machinery of the institutional church. They encourage Christian self-education and mobilization into secular society.

**GILL, ROBIN,** DEAN ■ *A Textbook of Christian Ethics.* T & T Clark, 1985. *571 pages.*
In this well-organized ethics text Gill excerpts text from Augustine, Aquinas and Luther consecutively on each of four subjects: methodology, politics and social justice, war and peace, and human life and interpersonal relationships. He adds extracts from modern ethicists on each subject, including Barth, Bonhoeffer and Fletcher. Gill then helps the reader navigate amid such diverse thought, identifying the tension between views as well as the context from which each emerged. "I will suggest that the unity of Christian ethics lies mainly in certain biblically consonant values held in tension" (preface). This is carefully tailored work, well worth its weight.

**GILLETT, RICHARD W.**, PRIEST, INDUSTRIAL MISSION SPECIALIST ■ *The Human Enterprise.* Leaven Press, 1985. *156 pages.*

In this wide-ranging book, Gillett examines a world shifting from a blue-collar work base to one dependent on information and service. Stressing the importance of an action-oriented theology, Gillett outlines the problems this economic revolution has brought about and how public policy can and should change our concept of work. In particular, Gillett calls for a new theology of work and an appropriate response to make it work. This book has the potential of disturbing Christians married to the Western idea that capitalism somehow has God's approval and blessing. Both compelling and unsettling.

**GLADWIN, JOHN**, PROFESSOR ■ *God's People in God's World: Biblical Motives for Social Involvement.* InterVarsity Press, 1979. *191 pages.*

This book was written as a foundational work on the theology of and motives for being active in the larger world community for the common good. Systematic in its approach, it debunks commonly held beliefs about social involvement. Readable and thorough, this book is recommended for those struggling with the biblical view of social action.

**GOETZ, JOSEPH W.**, PRIEST, PROFESSOR ■ *Mirrors of God.* St. Anthony Messenger, 1984. *93 pages.*

This is an intriguing collection of profiles and reflections of six women who are God's mirrors: Dorothy Day—the daily turning to the Lord in conversion *(metanoia)*; Anne Morrow Lindbergh—building community, not merely living in it *(koinonia)*; Simone Weil—proclaiming the good news of God's love *(kerygma)*; Dorothy Sayers—reasoning with all one's faculties about the faith *(theologia)*; Evelyn Underhill—worshiping God in the gathered body of Christ *(leiturgia)*; and Mother Teresa—reaching out to others in loving service *(diakonia)*. The profiles are not intended as eulogies but as an offering of role models portrayed in human weakness as well as strength.

**GONZÁLEZ, JUSTO L.**, PROFESSOR ■ *Faith and Wealth.* Harper & Row, 1990. *240 pages.*

This is a history of early Christian views on the origin, significance and use of money. González has exhaustively researched this vital marketplace topic largely ignored in Christian theology. He examines four centuries of Christian ideas about money, property, communal sharing, and the rights and obligations of the rich and poor. In the early church, wealth was invariably regarded as a theological issue. González asks why it is not so regarded today. Highly recommended. (For another patristic view of money, see "Money and Property" in A. Bieler's *The Social Humanism of Calvin.*)

**GOOD, LOU ANN** ■ *Bible Readings for Office Workers.* Augsburg, 1987. *109 pages.*
Somebody steals money from the lunchroom. A silly joke leads to flirting and worse. Another person's incompetence ruins your day. Sometimes ordinary jobs can be a cauldron of pressure and frustration. These Bible-based meditations aim to help workers remain sensitive to God's voice amid it all. Topics covered range from office politics and coping with boredom to time management and sexual harassment.

**GOOSEN, GIDEON,** LAY THEOLOGIAN ■ *The Theology of Work.* Clergy Book Service, 1974. *78 pages.*
Drawing from obscure European sources, this learned South African lay theologian condenses a history, sociology and theology of work into seventy-eight pages, leaving his reader with a positive biblical view. (Volume 22 in the Theology Today series.)

**GORDON, TERRENCE W.,** PROFESSOR ■ *Marshall McLuhan: Escape into Understanding.* Basic Books, 1997. *465 pages.*
This is an excellent biography of a very perceptive Canadian scholar, professor and social critic. Included in Gordon's carefully researched profile is a helpful presentation of McLuhan's childhood and his quiet, deep and little-known Christian faith. This is one of the better biographies about a true marketplace Christian who showed an ability to analyze culture and its sicknesses in the modern technologically dominated era of the late twentieth century. Very challenging personally, historically and intellectually.

**GOSSE, JOSEPH,** TRAINER ■ *The Spirituality of Work: Unemployed Worker.* National Center for the Laity, 1993. *41 pages, booklet.*
This is a good introduction to the spirituality of work for those who are struggling with being unemployed. It raises issues and provides answers for questions frequently asked by unemployed workers. Written from input and discussion with a dozen Christians who have been unemployed, the booklet follows a question-oriented format rather than a systematic treatment of each subject. It skims some of the issues raised by these experienced veterans, but also introduces the concept of a spiritual dynamic into the possibility of being unemployed.

**GRACNIK, PAT, & FRANK GRACNIK, EDS.** ■ *Family Values in the Marketplace.* Christian Family Movement, 1987. *168 pages.*
This is a response to the 1986 Catholic Bishops' Pastoral Letter *Economic Justice for All.* Members of the Christian Family Movement apply their "social inquiry method" (observe the facts, judge them in light of Christ's teachings, then act on your conclusions) to several problems of social and economic justice raised in the pastoral letter. A consciousness-raising tool designed for use in group discussion. The book raises issues of family spending, world hunger, employment opportunities, farming and the sanctuary movement.

**GRANBERG-MICHAELSON, WESLEY,** RELIGIOUS EXECUTIVE ■ *A Worldly Spirituality: The Call to Redeem Life on Earth.* Harper & Row, 1984. *203 pages.*
Granberg-Michaelson seeks to redirect our spirituality from being only concerned with self to being concerned with the world. He argues biblically that as God's creation the earth has been entrusted to our care. To appreciate this we must see Jesus as being much more than a "personal Savior"; his redemption is cosmic and leads to a new creation. From this perspective Granberg-Michaelson offers a number of constructive suggestions for Christian living.

**GRANT, GEORGE,** WRITER, LECTURER ■ *Bringing In the Sheaves: Transforming Poverty into Productivity.* Wolgemuth & Hyatt, 1988. *220 pages.*
"This book proposes a solution. It's a radical solution because the key component to its strategy is you. And your church. It proposes a way for you to actually do something. Right now" (back cover). The intellectual debates about "whether our responsibilities to the poor are to be discharged primarily by personal charitable action or through supporting the humanitarian policies of the state" are over. The abysmal failure of the war on poverty has made them defunct. Honest Christians simply need to see the unity between believing rightly and doing good. Few authors draw on such an enormous, historically diverse treasure of sources.

**GRAVES, STEPHEN R., & THOMAS G. ADDINGTON,** BUSINESS CONSULTANTS ■ *The Fourth Frontier.* Word, 2000. *207 pages.*
This book invites readers to ask, Does my work fill me with passion? Has it taken over my life? How is my faith integrated into my everyday work world? Does my work have any impact for God? If answering these questions leaves the reader feeling blank, troubled or confused, Graves and Addington suggest he or she go on a journey of self-discovery. This book purports to help that reader discover an individual path rather than outlining one single "method" for use by everyone. What is the fourth frontier? The world of work. Written in a clear, friendly style with plenty

of call-outs and lots of personal stories, *The Fourth Frontier* is a good way to introduce the uninitiated to marketplace ideas such as calling, witness, stewardship and integrating faith, work and home life.

**GREEN, MICHAEL,** ANGLICAN PRIEST, EVANGELIST ■ *Called to Serve.* Hodder & Stoughton, 1964. *95 pages.*
Taking the ministry and teaching of both Jesus and the early church as his cues, Green discusses the orders of ministers in Christ's church. He devotes a chapter each to the origins of the offices of deacon, priest and bishop, carefully sorting essential biblical conceptions from nonessential components. Green defends clerical ordination, for example, as having biblical precedent, but not as an absolute requisite to priestly service. Green discusses the two main issues of ministry which stand as barriers to reunification of the church: apostolic succession and sacrificial priesthood.

*Evangelism in the Early Church.* Hodder & Stoughton, 1970. *280 pages.*
A comprehensive treatment of the evangelistic mission of the early church up to about A.D. 250. Green makes history come alive in his attempt to understand afresh the gospel these early Christians preached, the methods they employed, the spiritual characteristics they displayed, the extent to which they were prepared to think their message through in the light of contemporary thought forms. One of the best theological works on evangelism.

**GREEN, THOMAS H.,** PRIEST, PROFESSOR ■ *Darkness in the Marketplace: The Christian at Prayer in the World.* Ave Maria, 1981. *128 pages.*
Green contemplates "the mysterious unity between prayer and a busy life in the world" (back cover). In part one Green uses Mary's sister Martha as an illustration of the active person whose fatigue and frustration need not be seen as obstacles to prayer but as the means God uses to purify and lead us to union with himself. In part two Green explores more fully the kinds of darkness experienced in the marketplace—any realm of activity outside one's place of contemplation. He maintains that "there is no need for spiritual schizophrenia in the life of the active contemplative."

**GREENE, MARK,** PROFESSOR ■ *Thank God It's Monday.* Scripture Union, 1994. *159 pages.*
Realistic "snapshots" of work tensions combined with personal insights and biblical connections. Greene lays a basic foundation for calling and ministry in the secular workplace. The book ends with some punchy and brief case studies that lend themselves to discussion. The style is fresh, lighthearted and easy to read. (Also in video.)

**GREENLEAF, ROBERT K.,** BUSINESS LEADER, CONSULTANT ■ *Servant Leadership:A Journey into the Nature of Legitimate Power and Greatness.* Paulist, 1977. *335 pages.*

This is a perceptive discussion of the kind of leadership that will produce a better society. Greenleaf argues that society's institutions need servant-leaders. He writes, "This is my thesis: caring for persons, the more able and the less able serving each other, is the rock upon which a good society is built." This is still referred to as a pace-setting work.

**GREENSLADE, PHILIP,** THEOLOGIAN ■ *Leadership, Greatness and Servanthood.* Bethany House, 1984. *201 pages.*

While promoting the traditional view of male leadership in the church, Greenslade makes a significant contribution by emphasizing the servant-role of the leader. Based in part by looking at Jesus' example of leadership, Greenslade contends that New Testament qualifications for leadership have more to do with character than gift.

**GREGG, SAMUEL, & GORDON PREECE,** SCHOLAR; PROFESSOR ■ *Christianity and Entrepreneurship.* Centre for Independent Studies, 1999. *113 pages.*

This monograph is a scholarly yet understandable study of entrepreneurship from both a Protestant (Preece) and a Catholic (Gregg) perspective. Among other things, both argue that Christians should not look at entrepreneurs with suspicion, for they too bear God's image and can be instrumental in fulfilling God's purposes in the marketplace.

**GRIFFITHS, BRIAN,** FINANCIER ■ *The Creation of Wealth.* InterVarsity Press, 1989. *160 pages.*

Griffiths presents a Christian case for capitalism by considering the economic, ethical, ideological and theological dimensions of creating wealth. He offers a helpful "practitioner's" perspective. Although from a British context, Griffiths has much to offer the cluttered American financial landscape. (For alternative views of economics, see *Wealth and Poverty: Four Views of Economics,* ed. Robert Clouse. InterVarsity Press, 1984.)

**GRIGG, VIV, ED.,** URBAN ACTIVIST ■ *Creating an Auckland Business Theology.* Urban Leadership Foundation, 2000. *68 pages.*

Grigg's urban experience on several continents has given him an appetite for faith that works in the world system. In this book Grigg and some Auckland theology students help eleven businesspeople tell their faith stories and connect them with major biblical themes. Then Grigg interprets these stories and puts them in the larger context of redemptive history. This kind of grassroots theological formation advances the gospel through the lives of everyday believers. A very good step toward developing theology at the working level of faith.

**GRIMES, HOWARD** ■ *The Rebirth of the Laity.* Abingdon, 1962. *171 pages.*
Though somewhat dated, this still is a good introduction to lay theology. With chapters on the laity in the Bible and history of the church, Grimes covers ground that few others do. His discussion of the lay and ordained ministry is clear and balanced. Grimes broadens our perspective by interacting with discussions in Protestant, Catholic and Orthodox circles.

**GROTE, JIM, & JOHN MCGEENEY,** CLERGY; LAWYER ■ *Clever as Serpents: Business Ethics and Office Politics.* Liturgical Press, 1997. *149 pages.*
Grote, a church worker, and McGeeney, a lawyer, take a shrewd, humorous and sometimes cynical look at some ethical aggravations faced daily in the marketplace. Their aim is to help Christian workers "interact shrewdly with other people and market conditions" while staying true to their values. The authors use cartoons and clever comments to keep things light.

**GRUBB, NORMAN,** RELIGIOUS LEADER ■ *Modern Viking—The Story of Abraham Vereide, Pioneer in Christian Leadership.* Zondervan, 1961. *207 pages.*
This is the story of a Norwegian immigrant to the United States who was the founder of International Christian Leadership, the legal name of what is popularly called The Fellowship, the origin of the Prayer Breakfast movement. While pastoring in Seattle, he also founded the first Good Will Industry. Vereide was a single-minded pre-World War II pioneer. The book is a narrative of meetings, people and letters as Vereide befriended government and business leaders in the name of Christ. He was a world-class leader whose legacy is thriving today on every continent.

**GRUBE, EDWARD,** CHURCH EDUCATOR ■ *Coffee Break Meditations: 260 Devotions for the Workplace.* Concordia, 1997. *260 pages.*
This is a spirited gift to harried Christians who can't make the connection between faith and work and who feel there is no time to do so either. Grube really believes the Father, Son and Holy Spirit are interested, available and want to be involved in the everyday stuff of the fast-paced workday. Each reflection has a catchy title, a short Scripture text and some helpful comments. Subjects

include personal integrity, labor problems, communications, success and upward mobility, wealth and debt, name-dropping and bragging, taxes and retirement. This is a very good work.

**GUDER, DARRELL L., ED.,** PROFESSOR ■ *Missional Church.* Eerdmans, 1998. *143 pages.*
Six scholars from the Gospel and Our Culture Network build on the work of Bishop Lesslie Newbigin. Atrophy is the natural end of churches focused on programmatic and institutional maintenance, they say. Instead, we must recapture the church's essential purpose as a "missional" agent to the world. Since the world is migrating to our cities and the unchurched are now our neighbors, we must update our concept of missions from "foreign" to "domestic." Then all Christians become missionaries and the entire congregational budget is designated to missions, in whatever creative form it takes. This is a call to and study of "the missionary encounter of the gospel with North American . . . perspectives, preferences and practices."

**GUINNESS, HOWARD,** CAMPUS PASTOR ■ *Sacrifice.* InterVarsity Press, 1975. *84 pages.*
This classic examination of the sacrifices called for in the course of a Christian life was first issued in Great Britain in 1936. Although the issues have changed somewhat, the concepts remain true to the Christian life. With clear, easy-to-access prose, Guinness examines how sacrifice impacts several areas of life, including love, power, discipline and poverty. While short, the book makes an excellent start for meditations on sacrifice and how it impacts every person's life.

**GUINNESS, OS,** SOCIOLOGIST ■ *The Call.* Word, 1999. *247 pages.*
This is a definitive text on calling. Calling (defined as a sense of God's summons to invest everything we are, do and have in his service), says Guinness, is bigger than our jobs, talents or a self-centered identity quest. It is not a matter of what we do or where we are so much as who we are and how we partner with God. With an unparalleled grasp on Western cultural perspectives, Guinness presents alternative views before presenting his own with unusual clarity. Probing and passionate, philosophical yet readable, this book provides no tests or techniques for evaluating one's calling. It simply peels away misconceptions and restores a sense of what it means to follow Christ.

*The Devil's Gauntlet.* InterVarsity Press, 1989. *32 pages, booklet.*
No critique of church and society in America today is more incisive than Guinness'. "Church and society is not just a large abstract topic," writes Guinness. "It is

the test-bed truth that reveals the character and health of all our truths. If we don't demonstrate Christian truths in the crucible of society, then, whatever we profess, they mean nothing." According to the author, the spiritual and social aspects of the gospel stand together; without either the other will fall. An excellent marketplace consciousness-raiser, this is a scathing exhortation to the evangelical church.

*Doubt.* Lion, 1976. *302 pages.*
The author systematically exhausts the subject of doubt: "Doubt is everyone's problem. But it is a special problem for Christians because of the premium placed on God's truthfulness." Doubt for the Christian is rooted in uncertainty about God's trustworthiness, says Guinness. He adds that ignoring or suppressing this uncertainty will get us nowhere; seeking to understand it may well be an expression of faith. He discusses seven causes of doubt and follows each section with suggestions for resolution. This is an unparalleled book on doubt.

**GUINNESS, OS, ED.,** SOCIOLOGIST ■ *Character Counts.* Baker, 1999. *160 pages.*
Through the lives of four people, Guinness demonstrates vividly the case for the importance of character in helping us to stand for truth. Guinness's extremely readable and quotable writing sets up the biographies so they become more than just good stories: they serve as templates for our own character formation. Written in delightful, page-turning prose, the sketches cover the lives of Alexander Solzhenitsyn, William Wilberforce, Abraham Lincoln and George Washington.

**GUSHEE, DAVID P., ED.,** PROFESSOR ■ *Toward a Just and Caring Society: Christian Responses to Society.* Baker, 1999. *576 pages.*
This collection of essays is technical, scholarly and daunting. This book includes treatises on poverty in a wealthy nation and challenges Christians to confront their own thinking on it. This book is not an argument for the Social Gospel but for compassionate Christianity.

**GUSTAFSON, GUS,** BUSINESSMAN ■ *Called to Be a Layman: Ever-expanding Circles of Christian Witness.* Bristol Books, 1989. *159 pages.*
Using his own and others' experiences and testimonies, Gustafson discusses Christian discipleship in terms of what it means to be called, guided, empowered and given victory by God. A heartwarming book of encouragement for those seeking to understand God's will and calling.

**HAAS, RICHARD C.,** JOURNALIST, BUSINESS MANAGER ■ *We All Have a Share: A Catholic Vision of Prosperity Through Productivity.* ACTA/Evangel Press, 1995. *188 pages.*

Haas creates a sacramental vision of America's free enterprise economy, showing that the market, the Christian home and the church community demand loving, serving relationships, and prosper when supplied with them. This vision takes us beyond self-interest (part one), grounds us as free yet responsible agents (part two) and convinces us that this love is the primary "value added" (part three). A rosy, ethnocentric yet compelling view of economic relationships, in which Haas believes "symbols of God's love abound."

**HAHN, CELIA A.,** LAY MINISTER ■ *Lay Voices in an Open Church.* Alban Institute, 1985. *62 pages.*

Hahn synthesizes early 1980s research in which North American laypeople were asked to assess the church. The emerging themes include (1) what laypeople need from their church, (2) connections between life at church and life in the world, (3) the difference between going to church and being religious, (4) the gap between vision and reality, and (5) the difference between the church as a world in itself and the church in the world. The book offers useful directions toward ecclesiastical health but alienates those churches it could help. Hahn's obvious bias against connectional churches seems to imply that such churches cannot be "open." Despite the lack of balance, the book offers concrete insights for control-prone clergy. It is ennobling for the disenfranchised layperson.

**HAHN, CELIA A. & JAMES R. ADAMS,** LAY MINISTERS ■ *Learning to Share the Ministry.* Alban Institute, 1975. *68 pages.*

This book is a case study of St. Mark's Church on Capitol Hill in Washington, D.C. The church uses the senior minister's six-month sabbatical to experiment with methods of shared ministry. Some worked, some didn't. The study includes excerpts of letters between pastor and congregation about the new opportunities for growth and the new perspectives each was gaining during the sabbatical. Includes a study guide. (See also Crabtree and Diehl's *Ministry in Daily Life.*)

**HAILLE, PHILIP P.,** PROFESSOR ■ *Lest Innocent Blood Be Shed.* Harper Colophon, 1979. *303 pages.*

This is a beautifully crafted story of a village in southern France that gave itself sacrificially to help Jews flee Nazi and Vichy persecution during World War II. At one level it is the story of the local Protestant pastor Andre Tocmé and his wife's leadership in the risky venture. At another level it is a report on one generation of Huguenot Christians living out their belief in Jesus Christ and his teachings. The book is rich in lessons about the church's witness amid war, hostility, persecution and danger. Haille bares his own soul as a Jew, World War II veteran and professor of ethics. Very well written. (For more see David Clyde Jones.)

**HALL, CAMERON P.,** SEMINARY PROFESSOR ■ *Lay Action—The Church's Third Force: A Strategy for Enabling Lay Ministry in Secular Institutions.* Friendship Press, 1974. *144 pages.*
Hall believes Christianity will influence secular institutions and social structures through the laity. Training the laity to do so should be the aim of adult education in the church. The final chapter presents the model of the clergy as enablers of the laity for their "in the world" ministry.

**HALL, DOUGLAS JOHN,** PROFESSOR OF THEOLOGY ■ *The Steward: A Biblical Symbol Come of Age.* Eerdmans, 1990. *258 pages.*
Hall defines a steward as one who is a caretaker *and* a servant of God. He contrasts this with the institutional, power-oriented role stewardship has played in the last sixteen centuries, to the detriment of both the church and the world. Hall posits that the church has failed in its stewardship, relinquishing the concept to secular movements such as environmentalism. He advocates bringing global stewardship back into the church's sphere of influence, elaborating on the World Council of Churches General Assembly theme of justice, peace and the integrity of creation. (See also R. Scott Rodin's *Stewards in the Kingdom*).

**HALL, EDDY, & GARY MORSCH** ■ *The Lay Ministry Revolution: How You Can Join.* Baker, 1995. *126 pages.*
This book seeks to educate Christians about lay ministry. The following key points represent chapters of the book: "[a] all Christians are called to be ministers; [b] ministry involves meeting all kinds of needs, not just spiritual needs; [c] most ministry takes place not when the church is gathered, but when it is scattered; [d] so-called secular work can be approached as and transformed into ministry; [e] you can identify your spiritual gifts and discern your calling." The authors use biblical texts and case studies.

**HALTEMAN, JAMES,** PROFESSOR ■ *The Clashing Worlds of Economics and Faith.* Herald, 1995. *224 pages.*
Halteman writes from an Anabaptist perspective and does an excellent job of developing a postmodern biblical economic theory from the biblical narrative. What makes this book worthwhile is Halteman's use of comparative graphics and figures.

His comparisons of historic worldviews and their economic ramifications is outstanding. The latter half of the book is devoted to developing Halteman's Anabaptist two kingdom model of economics. An overview of other models' strengths and weaknesses would have strengthened the book. An excellent resource.

**HALVERSON, RICHARD C.,** PASTOR, U.S. SENATE CHAPLAIN ■ *How I Changed My Mind About the Church.* Zondervan, 1972. *120 pages.*
Here is a classic work from an early pioneer in the American marketplace movement. Halverson tells of his own journey out of an institutional view of church and into a "people mobilized for ministry in daily life" view. He is very honest in confessing some traditional but nonbiblical perceptions he had of the roles of the pastor and congregation in his early days. He discusses two kinds of Christians: those "who are meeting-centered in their Christian experience, develop a kind of spiritual dyspepsia, a spiritual satiation and stagnancy" and "those who are always going [but] rarely have anything to offer when they get there. Their intentions are good but they lack spiritual resources to benefit those to whom they go under the duress of their incentive" (pp. 22-23). Halverson closes with a personal and practical "Where Do You Begin" for his pastoral peers.

*Relevance: The Role of Christianity in the Twentieth Century.* Word, 1968. *102 pages.*
Halverson declares, "The role of every Christian is to act redemptively in society" (dust jacket). Each chapter begins with a page of Scripture to be discussed. He probes politics and racial issues, and chastises pastors who feel "robbed" when work and civic responsibilities draw parishioners away from congregational activities. Halverson calls this a "blasphemous contradiction," and describes his own guilt of clinging to his parishioners instead of launching them into the world. Good stuff that deserves rereading.

*Walk with God Between Sundays.* Ronald N. Haynes, 1981. *138 pages.*
Halverson has penned a series of devotions urging ordinary people to walk with God during the week. As a long-time chaplain of the U.S. Senate, Halverson knows how to make pithy remarks that hit home. This book would make a wonderful desktop devotional, providing a quick calm-down break for the harried professional.

**HAMILTON, DON,** CORPORATE EXECUTIVE, MISSIONARY EQUIPPER ■
*Tentmakers Speak: Practical Advice from 400+ Missionaries.* TMQ Research, 1987. *99 pages.*
Because the world's rural population is moving to the city and other demographic

and political changes occur, traditional missionary methods are in a constant state of flux. Within this climate, Hamilton examines what makes effective missions work today. Responding to his survey (1985-1986), over 400 lay missionaries worldwide offer sobering advice: be a self-supporting tentmaker; be spiritually qualified; have a team for accountability; keep a proper perspective on job and ministry; and possess social and professional skills. Many of today's missionaries are training with stethoscopes and computers alongside their Bibles. Hamilton presents pioneering research, helping to create a new paradigm. Includes discussion questions.

**HAMMACK, MARY L.**, EDUCATOR, WRITER ■ *A Dictionary of Women in Church History.* Moody Press, 1984. *167 pages.*
The product of Hammack's extensive research, this invaluable reference book should be on the shelf of every church and school library. It catalogues the distinctive role of women in church history since the time of Christ in music, literature, medicine, ministry, education and politics. The nearly 1,000 biographical entries are arranged alphabetically, accompanied by a chronologically arranged chart. The book reads like a dictionary, factual and concise. A much needed resource.

**HAMMETT, EDWARD H.**, PROFESSOR, CHURCH EXECUTIVE ■ *The Gathered and Scattered Church: Equipping Believers for the 21st Century.* Smyth & Helwys, 1999. *104 pages.*
Hammett, the leadership-discipleship consultant for the Baptist State Convention of North Carolina, wants to move Christianity outside of church walls and into the daily lives of Christians. He concentrates on effectively equipping church members to minister to the secular world around them. The book is well organized and thoughtful. This slim volume is practical and applicable, and is an excellent place for church leaders to start on their journey to make an impact on the world outside their doors. The helpful resources in the back include organizations and books, and an outline for creating a "school of ministry."

*Making the Church Work.* Smyth & Helwys, 1997. *113 pages.*
Hammett reflects on two struggles on the organized church: the lack of real conversion (or depth of spiritual formation) and the misfocus on institutional survival. He believes churches can educate and empower true disciples and shape their ministries to the world's need in the workplace and community. This small, future-oriented book is uniquely designed as short reflections and questions for discussion, ideal for use as an evaluative tool in a church visioning process or in the context of a church retreat. Hammett's prescription for the twenty-first-century church is further elaborated in his sequel, *The Gathered and Scattered Church.*

**HAMMOND, PETE, ET AL.,** CONSULTANT ■ *The Word in Life Study Bible.*
Thomas Nelson, 1993, 1996.
This innovative study Bible is right on target for the marketplace/ministry in daily life movement. Unlike all other study Bibles, this one focuses on connecting the people, times and struggles of biblical people with their workplace, national and local politics, family life, economies, cities, and so on. Then it helps today's readers reflect on the principles and parallels for today. Other helps include personality profiles, seven indexes and a "Jobs and Occupations" listing of over 260 roles then and now. This study Bible is receiving high acclaim from both long-term Bible students and scholars as well as seekers and newcomers to faith. This must-have resource is a comprehensive Scripture study designed to help people relate in a practical, simple, yet profoundly biblical way to the spheres of the world in which they live.

*Living in a World of Wealth and Poverty.* Thomas Nelson, 1995. *184 pages.*
This study is divided into thirteen chapters that focus on different aspects of wealth and poverty, walking the fine line between concept and application. The questions sprinkled throughout the study challenge readers to stop looking outward and start looking inward to examine ways to apply the truths gleaned from each portion of Scripture presented. The sidebars are well-written, interesting and make good discussion starters in small groups or Bible studies. The study does not focus merely on monetary issues but moves on to examine societal structure, "classes" of people and even the family. Good for individuals or groups.

*Making Your Work Count for God: How to Find Meaning and Joy in Your Work.*
Thomas Nelson, 1994. *184 pages.*
This volume is a guided study into a theology of work and its applications. A wide variety of topics are covered, including God as worker, poverty, stress, biblical principles on handling money, and balancing commitment to work and family.

*Marketplace Networks.* InterVarsity Marketplace Department, 1986. *43 pages.*
This is a directory of ministries, affinity groups and organizations focused on faith in the workplace. It begins with "How to Start an Affinity Group" and lists about 40 groups, including, addresses, leaders' names and an organizational profile. Dated.

**HANSEL, TIM,** TEACHER, DIRECTOR OF WILDERNESS SURVIVAL ■ *When I Relax I Feel Guilty.* Cook, 1979. *147 pages.*
"When was the last time you woke up rested—really rested and exuberant and excited about meeting the day?" asks Hansel. "Chances are, it's been too long." Many American Christians, he maintains, believe they aren't serving God unless

they're miserably busy and exhausted. "This is not a treatise against work, but against overwork," writes Hansel. He suggests ways to reenthrone "the things in life that are truly important—my relationship to God, my health, my family, my personal growth, and my friends." Chapters offer a balanced perspective on leisure, thoughts about how to make and let life happen, a reminder to learn from children, and ideas for active rest and minivacations. A leader's kit is available.

**HARDY, LEE,** PROFESSOR ■ *The Fabric of This World: Inquiries into Calling, Career Choice and the Design of Human Work.* Eerdmans, 1990. *213 pages.*
"Lee Hardy's book . . . seeks to reintroduce neglected Reformed insights into work. It proceeds to do this by way of conversation with a number of classic [and modern] texts on work. Hardy's aim is 'to help revitalize the concept of work as vocation' (p. xv). . . . For me, the major value of the book lies in its emphasis upon the 'providential' character of work. . . . [It] includes discussions of conflict and strategy, the work of prayer, balancing commitments, people and profits, [and a detailed treatment of the factors involved in vocational choice]" (Robert Banks). This book was perhaps the most advanced synthesis of perspectives on work available when it was first released.

**HARKNESS, GEORGIA,** PROFESSOR, WRITER ■ *The Church and Its Laity.* Abingdon, 1962. *202 pages.*
Harkness argues that the recent rethinking of the nature of the church and the concern for the place of the laity need to be brought together. In describing the nature of the church she outlines the historical developments that have divided clergy from laity. Then in analyzing the current situation she shows how secular standards are influencing churches and, although somewhat dated now, describes some signs of hope for seeing lay involvement in the world.

*John Calvin: The Man and His Ethics.* Abingdon, 1958. *266 pages.*
Most attempts to understand Calvinism since its inception in the 1530s emphasize his doctrine at the expense of his moral ideas and have sidestepped the study of his life, says Harkness. This book was originally published to fill that vacuum. The author provides a short biography, reviews the major aspects of Calvinistic doctrine and considers the ethical obligations arising from the duty of glorifying God. Finally, Harkness deals with Calvin's social ethics related to family, economics and the state. She also provides largely overlooked material from Calvin's writings. Expensive reprints are available through AMS Press and Gordon Press.

**HARPER, MICHAEL** ■ *Let My People Grow: Ministry and Leadership in the Church.* Logos, 1977. *234 pages.*

"There are some other evidences of life, but growth is the most important and reliable one." Harper argues that if the church is to take seriously the ministry of every Christian, there will need to be an examination of traditional church structures. Building on the basis of seeing ministry in all of its forms as service, he pleads for much more flexibility among church leaders and a real dependence on the leading of the Holy Spirit.

**HARR, JOHN ENSOR, & PETER J. JOHNSON,** ROCKEFELLER FOUNDATION EMPLOYEES ■ *The Rockefeller Century.* Charles Scribner & Sons, 1988. *621 pages.*

This is a study of the three generations of Rockefellers, John D., John D. Jr. and John D. III, and how they lived with wealth. The authors do not gloss over the struggles and shortcomings of this wealthy industrial family of philanthropists. They probe the religious roots in John Sr.'s lifelong activity and loyalty to his Baptist faith. They present carefully documented histories of Standard Oil, the several foundations growing out of the massive accumulation of wealth. (It is a good complimentary volume to *Titan*, the story of John D. Rockefeller by Ron Chernov.)

**HARRIS, IRVING,** MAGAZINE EDITOR ■ *He Touched Me.* Abingdon, 1985. *156 pages.*

Here is a collection of brief and easy-to-read life stories of people impacted by personal encounters with Jesus Christ. Of particular interest for marketplace faith people are journalist Jack Rowles; James Bell Nicoll (M.D.); Millard Fuller, founder of Habitat for Humanity; Bill Wilson, founder of Alcoholics Anonymous; and Jewish businessman Joseph Klutch.

**HARRIS, JANIS LONG,** COMMUNICATIONS CONSULTANT ■ *Secrets of People Who Love Their Work.* InterVarsity Press, 1992. *167 pages.*

Harris has gleaned the common experiences of workers—from drywallers to artists to captains of industry. Her subjects have one thing in common: a passion for their work that amounts to a sense of calling. Harris covers a variety of diverse topics: making enough money, finding a balance between work and other areas of life, setting goals, and taking risks. She also reveals how to light the flame of passion within and know if that passion is from God. This book is both practical and visionary.

**HARRISON, PATRICIA, ED.,** BUSINESSWOMAN ■ *America's New Women Entrepreneurs: Tips, Tactics, and Techniques of Women Achievers in Business.* Acropolis, 1986. *224 pages.*
Biographical sketches of seventeen businesswomen who have made a difference, this book contains practical insights but lacks any focus on faith and work.

**HARRISVILLE, ROY A.,** PROFESSOR ■ *Ministry in Crisis: Changing Perspectives on Ordination and the Priesthood of All Believers.* Augsburg, 1987. *94 pages.*
In this small volume of lectures Harrisville asks, "Is the difference between clergy and laity one of essence? Does the laying on of hands in ordination give to the clergy a discrete and particular 'character'? Or is the difference one of function? Does ordination reflect a democratic choice? What is the origin of the doctrine of apostolic succession? Was the rise of the Christian hierarchy inevitable? Should the Church have bishops?" (back cover). A fresh and lively critique.

**HATCH, NATHAN O., ED.,** PROFESSOR ■ *The Professions in American History.* University of Notre Dame Press, 1988. *220 pages.*
This collection of essays by distinguished scholars provides histories of American higher education, law, medicine, church ministry, military service, science, engineering, journalism, government service, psychology and counseling, and management. "An important contribution to our understanding of the way professions shape, and are shaped by, American culture." (Dennis M. Campbell). A very helpful study showing how professions rise and fall. Each essay is followed by suggested books for further study.

**HATFIELD, MARK O.,** U.S. SENATOR ■ *Conflict and Conscience.* Word, 1971. *172 pages.*
Hatfield speaks openly about his belief that "the wisdom and compassion demanded to solve any of today's personal and societal problems cannot be found in any person or place other than in the power of God, working through a person." Thus he encourages the political involvement of every Christian. Secondly, he states that "our nation stands in need of a complete spiritual renaissance, faith in Jesus Christ."

**HAUERWAS, STANLEY, & WILLIAM H. WILLIMON,** PROFESSOR; CAMPUS PASTOR ■ *Resident Aliens.* Abingdon, 1989. *174 pages.*
The book is a reality check for the church. We no longer live in a Christian culture. Based on their years of service and worship in parish and campus life, and deeply informed by the Scriptures, these veteran leaders call Christians to be a countercul-

ture or "alien" people. They prophetically teach what it means to be disciples in a postmodern world. Hauerwas and Willimon offer clear and challenging commentary on the futility of doing church as usual.

**HAUGHEY, JOHN C.,** PRIEST, EDITOR, SENIOR RESEARCH FELLOW ■ *Converting 9 to 5: A Spirituality of Daily Work.* Crossroad, 1989. *180 pages.*
Roman Catholic scholar Haughey helps Christians develop their own theology of work. One of the lessons learned is that God is not a distant, contemplative being but a worker in the present tense, productive and industrious. Haughey moves beyond the view that God needs to be *brought* to work. Instead, God is *found* at work. Our spirituality will be nurtured and strengthened as we find that our productive work picks up where God left off. A bit heavy going in places but the persistent reader will find the effort rewarding.

*The Holy Use of Money: Personal Finances in Light of Christian Faith.* Crossroad, 1989. *288 pages.*
Haughey sees money as a simple tool with which to express God's love for others. He spends one chapter naming the illness that besets many in our culture: consumption, or greed. He goes on to outline that it is faith that can rescue money from its sinful role and make it into one more way God can move through his people to reach others. The thing that makes this book different is Haughey's lack of pretension and how-to directions. He is neutral about money itself, seeing it not as a weapon but as a tool. Although the book is scholarly, it is very accessible to the layperson.

**HEIDEBRECHT, PAUL H.,** NPO EXECUTIVE, PASTOR ■ *God's Man in the Marketplace: The Story of Herbert J. Taylor.* InterVarsity Press, 1990. *120 pages.*
This biography wrestles with how Taylor worked out his faith in the various corporate positions he held. He turned a failing company around during the Great Depression, led it into stability and then sold it to a friend. Based on the Sermon on the Mount, Taylor authored the Four-Way Test, a biblically based code of ethics for business and society. It became the foundational creed of Rotary International. Easy to read. (See also his own *Herbert J. Taylor Story.* InterVarsity Press, 1968.)

**HEIGES, DONALD R.,** SEMINARY PRESIDENT ■ *The Christian's Calling.* Fortress, 1984. *108 pages.*
In a secular age where the automation of industry and unemployment have deepened people's sense of meaninglessness and alienation, Heiges correctly points to the necessity of restoring a Christian sense of vocation. In a brief Old and New Tes-

tament survey, he highlights God's plan to call his people and provide them a destiny. Heiges discusses Luther's understanding of vocation and offers general principles to guide every person's sense of calling today. He also applies the principle of vocation to shared ministry within the church and includes a bibliography for further research on Christian vocation. Exceptionally well researched, the book is deeply sympathetic to the disillusioned worker.

**HEINTZMAN, PAUL, GLEN E. VAN ANDEL, & THOMAS L. VISKER, EDS.,** PROFESSORS ■ *Christianity and Leisure: Issues in a Pluralistic Society.* Dordt College Press, 1994. *251 pages.*
A complete Christian view of work must account for what God did on the seventh day, when "he rested from all his labors" (Genesis 2:2-3). In this book twenty-two educators, coaches, physical therapists and camp directors met for four years to formulate a biblical understanding of leisure. They discuss the implications of a theology of leisure for the New Age Movement, people with disabilities, contemplatives, and for humor and drama. Seven of twenty chapters are devoted to play, sports and athletics. This book is a healthy alternative view for those caught between work obsession and living for the weekends. Full of bibliographical references.

**HELLDORFER, MARTIN C.,** THERAPIST ■ *Work Trap: Rediscovering Leisure, Rediscovering Work.* Twenty-Third Publishers,1995. *105 pages.*
Written by a Catholic psychotherapist, this book peeks into the destructiveness of workaholism and offers suggestions for how to evade its traps. The book makes little or no reference to Scriptures or to Christ, but is an effective study guide for workers whose jobs are consuming them and their families. When used in small groups this book should be supported by Scriptures.

**HENDERSON, LOIS T.,** WRITER, LECTURER ■ *Lydia.* Harper & Row, 1979. *255 pages.*
A novel of particular interest to the marketplace Christian. Lydia, Paul's first Christian convert in Europe, was a successful businesswoman who sold purple cloth in the thriving Roman town of Philippi. The members of the Philippian church were first nurtured in Lydia's home. This book is fascinating and believable. Biblically and historically sensitive, it is highly recommended reading.

**HENRICHSEN, WALTER, & WILLIAM GARRISON,** LAY ADVOCATE; LAWYER ■ *Layman, Look Up! God Has a Place for You.* Vision Foundation, 1988. *142 pages.*
This book's explicit theme is disciple-making. The authors provide helpful descrip-

tions of the process of Christian growth, the church's mission, five classifications of Scripture, the role of clergy and laity, the functions of parachurch groups, and more. They describe the lack of marketplace concern in most churches but do little to address the problem. The book is well-conceived and easy to read, but it doesn't say enough.

**HENRY, CARL F. H.,** THEOLOGIAN ■ *The Christian Mindset in a Secular Society: Promoting Evangelical Renewal & National Righteousness.* Multnomah Press, 1984. *156 pages.*

Henry writes, "Incisive critics tell us that our culture is crumbling, not so much because of alien powers but because of our own moral compromises and spiritual hesitancies." Henry believes that only the involvement of Christians through the proclamation of the gospel and political action will arrest the drift of modernity.

*Twilight of a Great Civilization: Drift Toward Neo-Paganism.* Crossway, 1988. *192 pages.*

"A perceptive diagnosis of America's spiritual malaise. . . . Henry shows how the wider culture, and many within Christian circles, have accommodated to the Spirit of the Age. But beyond the careful diagnosis lies Henry's prescription and vision for recovery" (front flap). This is a clarion call to "march and sing our faith in the public arena, in the streets . . . [in] the mass media" or wherever God places us.

**HIEBERT, BRUCE** ■ *Good Work: How to Live Your Values in the Workplace.* Northstone, 1997. *192 pages.*

Most people spend more of their waking hours working (or preparing for it or recovering from it) than anything else. Few of us spend much time pondering our work or its impact on us. Hiebert shows how work can become our own personal carrier of beliefs and values. Done right, work can be our unique way of being creators and transformers. He urges workers to ask, "What am I trying to accomplish, not just today, but with this work situation?" There is plenty of helpful guidance but occasionally it gets preachy.

**HIGGINSON, RICHARD,** PROFESSOR ■ *Called to Account.* Eagle, 1993.

Higginson writes for business people who are struggling to relate their personal faith and values to business. He devotes each chapter of this book to exploring the theological and ethical implications of a portion of the Creed to the business world. Higginson's approach is that it develops the Bible story in a way that most Christians are familiar with. He emphasizes Luther's image is not of a God who *drives* us but who *calls* us to work. The foundation is an assurance of God's grace, not our achievements.

**HILFIKER, DAVID,** PHYSICIAN ■ *Healing the Wounds.* Penguin, 1985. *209 pages.*

"Drawing on his own experience in both rural and urban practice, Dr. Hilfiker tells what it really feels like to be a doctor: How do you face your mistakes? How do you tell a parent that his son has just died, or tell a longtime patient that he has cancer? How does money affect your choices? . . . a personal exploration of what frustrates doctors (and infuriates patients) and what might be done about it" (publisher). Hilfiker worked from 1975 to 1982 in a small town in rural Minnesota and now works in two health clinics in Washington, D.C., where he is a member of the inner city ministry Church of the Savior.

**HILL, ALEXANDER,** PROFESSOR, EXECUTIVE ■ *Just Business: Christian Ethics for the Marketplace.* InterVarsity Press, 1997. *232 pages.*

Hill bases his Christian framework for business ethics on "the changeless character of God." He explores concepts of holiness, justice and love as the keys to Christian business ethics, and shows how some common ethical responses fall short. Case studies are employed to illuminate specific topics such as employer-employee relations, discrimination and affirmative action, and the environment.

**HILLMAN, OS,** ADVERTISING EXECUTIVE ■ *Faith & Work: Do They Mix?* Family Christian Press, 2000. *128 pages.*

A business person's book from start to finish, it debunks the dualistic split between spirituality and work. Hillman advocates work as a calling and uses Joseph as a prime example of how to do it right (Genesis 39—50). The most intriguing and important aspect of Hillman's book is his examination of why the recent rise in workplace spirituality has not produced an equal rise in Christian impact on that workplace. His points are clear, easy to follow and practical. Hillman concludes by outlining the attributes of a modern "kingdom" business. An excellent presentation.

*TGIF: Today God Is First.* Destiny Image, 2000. *396 pages.*

Hillman understands the problems confronting those in the marketplace. This devotional has a Scripture reading and meditation for every day of the year. Diverse topics are covered, including the importance of a workplace mentor, jealousy toward those who do not believe and yet prosper, the importance of being salt on the job, humility with coworkers, and relational leadership. Written in the first person, Hillman uses his own experience to illustrate the concepts presented. A fine contribution to the marketplace faith movement.

**HIND, JAMES F.,** BUSINESS EXECUTIVE, CONSULTANT ■ *The Heart and Soul of Effective Management.* Victor, 1989. *132 pages.*
Hind insists that the best role model for management today is Jesus Christ. "In only 3 years He defined a mission and formed strategies and plans [such that Christianity] has grown to have 1.5 billion proponents today, is international in scope, and has branches in all the world's 223 countries." This extraordinary expansion was not based on a profit motive, but rather on sacrificial service and personal care. Hind discusses Christ's character in terms that relate to the modern businessperson. Finally, he offers eleven commandments of servant leadership. A wonderfully creative analysis, the book is both biblically sensitive and doggedly relevant.

**HOGBEN, ROWLAND,** MISSION EXECUTIVE ■ *Vocation.* Inter-Varsity Press, 1938. *86 pages.*
This book is an early entry in the recovery of God's call on every area of life. Hogben declares, "Others may regard my work as just a job; but to me it is my service for my Master—my vocation" (p. 16). "No Christian man or woman should think that because their path lies plainly in business circles or in other so-called mundane pursuits they are therefore without a true and vital vocation for God" (p. 17). He has brief but excellent chapters on calling, choice, motive and misfits. He stresses workplace integrity and excellence as gifts to God. Hogben is surprisingly sensitive to gender inclusion at this early date.

**HOLIFIELD, BROOKS E.,** PROFESSOR ■ *Health and Medicine in the Methodist Tradition: Journey Toward Wholeness.* Crossroad, 1986. *198 pages.*
This book explores the ways in which major religions in the West respond to questions of human well-being. It is organized around ten categories: well-being, sexuality, passages, morality, dignity, madness, healing, caring, suffering and dying. Recommended.

**HOLMES, ARTHUR F.,** PROFESSOR ■ *Contours of a World View.* InterVarsity Press, 1983. *240 pages.*
Regarded as a modern classic on Christian worldview development, this book contrasts secular and Christian ways of looking at the world and defends the Christian perspective as the strongest alternative. "In a world ravaged by dehumanizing barbarism and torn by ideological conflict we have an obligation to rekindle and disseminate the Christian vision of a unified world view" (back cover). Chapters include applications to work, play, science and technology, and human creativity. This is literature for the serious Christian thinker.

*Ethics:Approaching Moral Decisions.* InterVarsity Press, 1984. *132 pages.*
Holmes examines some of the major approaches to ethics, including cultural relativism, emotivism, ethical egoism and utilitarianism. He shows how they compare to a Christian approach, making application to four moral issues: human rights, criminal punishment, the legislation of morality and sexual behavior. Says author Peter Kreeft, "This book is a joy to read. It is utterly lucid—in thought organization and style."

**HOPKINS, C. HOWARD,** PROFESSOR ■ *John R. Mott: 1865-1955.* Eerdmans, 1979. *816 pages.*
This book is a well-balanced and detailed biography of Protestantism's leading ecumenical statesman for the first half of the twentieth century. An organizer, fundraiser, evangelist and diplomat, Mott built a worldwide fellowship of students and young people, and influenced governments in many countries. This mammoth text is the product of fifteen years of research. (See also Mott's *Liberating the Lay Forces of Christianity.*)

**HOPLER, THOM,** MISSIONARY, URBAN WORKER ■ *A World of Difference: Following Christ Beyond Your Cultural Walls.* InterVarsity Press, 1981. *223 pages.*
Hopler urges America's largely rural church to throw off its northern European blinders and to begin to follow Christ beyond its own cultural setting and customs. In part one Hopler presents a cultural survey of the Bible from Genesis through Acts. In parts two and three he develops concepts and strategies for crosscultural communication of the gospel. A group study guide is available.

**HORE-LACY, IAN,** BUSINESS MANAGER ■ *Creating Common Wealth:Aspects of Public Theology in Economics.* Albatross, 1985. *103 pages.*
Hore-Lacy, a middle-manager in Australia's mining industry, is a board member of the Zadok Centre, a think tank for the expression of Christianity in society. In this book he explores the meaning of wealth creation as a prelude to understanding capitalism and business from a Christian perspective.

**HORNER, BOB, RON RALSTON, & DAVID SUNDE,** CAMPUS MINISTRY STAFF ■ *Promise Keeper at Work.* Focus on the Family, 1996. *123 pages.*
This excellent study guide contains an approach used by Campus Crusade Staff in their Marketplace Connections ministry. Designed to be used in a men's Bible study small group, the book is divided into four parts: Walk, Work, Relationships and Ministry. Each of the 48 sessions has a warm up question, Scripture, Scripture background, interaction and wrap up section. This book, supplemented with other materials, is a good resource for any men's group.

**HOROWITZ, CAROL, & MICHELLE WEISSMAN,** JOURNALIST; WRITER ■ *A History of Women in America.* Bantam, 1978. *400 pages.*
This history of feminism in twentieth-century America was published in cooperation with the Anti-Defamation League of B'nai B'rith. The authors include African Americans, factory workers, authors, immigrants and activists. They are not friendly toward Christianity or the Bible, seeing both as major sources of abuse and discrimination toward women.

**HOUSTON, JAMES M.,** PROFESSOR, COUNSELOR ■ *I Believe in the Creator.* Eerdmans, 1980. *275 pages.*
Houston reminds us that how we integrate our Christian faith with life in the world is based on what we believe about God as Creator and about his creation. With great erudition he challenges popular worldviews with a radical Christian faith in God the Creator. He then draws out the implications of this faith for how we look at and live in the world.

**HOUTZ, ELSA,** NEWSCASTER, EDITOR, COPYWRITER, PUBLIC RELATIONS MANAGER ■ *Desktop Devotions for Working Women.* NavPress, 1991. *cloth.*
*Desktop Devotions* is a great gift book for working women, offering short scripturally grounded passages full of advice, counsel and reflection. This book helps readers reorient themselves as they reflect on what it means to be disciples in the workplace. This book is a good devotional counterpart to Horner's *Promise Keepers at Work.*

**HOWARD, J. GRANT,** PROFESSOR ■ *Balancing Life's Demands.* Cook, 1992.
Though Howard's book has only a small section about balancing work with life's other demands, he is so thorough in his discussion that readers will find it a valuable tool for marketplace Christians. Howard proposes that our priorities are a circle rather than a list, and the way he deals with each of the areas is an encouraging paradigm. An easy read filled with practical wisdom.

**HUDNUT, WILLIAM, III, WITH JUDY KEENE,** MINISTER, MAYOR OF INDIANAPOLIS; WRITER ■ *Minister/Mayor.* Westminster Press, 1987. *184 pages.*
Hudnut has shown that "politics at best is a ministry, and that ministry is inescapably political" (Donald Shriver). The former Presbyterian preacher explains how his biblical understanding has been useful in countless aspects of public service: tough decision making, serving as leader, responding to social injustice and dealing with personal loss. Recommended reading.

**HUMPHREYS, FISHER, & THOMAS A. KINCHEN, EDS.,** SEMINARY PROFESSOR; WRITER ■ *Laos: All the People of God.* New Orleans Baptist Theological Seminary, 1984. *131 pages.*

Ironically, the authors of this collection of nine articles, first presented at a convocation whose stated purpose was to develop a "theology of the non-ordained," are clergymen and seminary faculty, not laypeople. However, this represents a significant call for the mobilization of all of God's people wherever they are located.

**HUMPHREYS, KENT, & DAVIDENE HUMPHREYS,** CEO; HOMEMAKER ■ *Show and Then Tell: Presenting the Gospel Through Daily Encounters.* Moody Press, 2000. *204 pages.*

The central thesis of this book is to daily live worthy of Christ and carefully share God's love when the opportunity arises. Each chapter begins with Scripture and an inspirational bit of wisdom to provoke thought, then it covers a skill or characteristic that can help make an individual's witness more vital, compelling and true. Chapters end with a brief reflection on a character from the Bible who illustrates the skill. The writing is clear and easy to understand, incorporating true-life stories to illustrate important points. Enjoyable, helpful, challenging and reassuring, it's a good book from which to launch a group discussion.

**HUNSBERGER, GEORGE R.,** PROFESSOR OF MISSIOLOGY ■ *Bearing the Witness of the Spirit.* Eerdmans, 1998. *341 pages.*

In this scholarly work Hunsberger assesses the theology of Lesslie Newbigin. Examining Newbigin's published and unpublished works, Hunsberger explores Newbigin's groundbreaking theology of multicultural pluralism. Newbigin calls the Western church to approach our culture with a missionary attitude. In addition to revealing the implications of Newbigin's missionary theology, the author also examines the limits of religion and the church in reaching across cultural boundaries. A dense but rewarding book.

**HUNTER, IAN,** ECONOMIST ■ *Robert Laidlaw: Man for Our Time.* Castle, 1999. *354 pages.*

Robert Laidlaw was the John D. Rockefeller of New Zealand. He was a self-made millionaire businessman who played a major role in establishing several major Christian initiatives in New Zealand. The author fails to provide insight into whether Laidlaw's faith went beyond verbal evangelism, personal integrity, philanthropy and church work. It appears that Laidlaw is one of those successful business leaders who equates profitability, integrity and generosity with the sum total of the gospel.

**HYBELS, BILL,** PASTOR ■ *Christians in the Marketplace.* Victor, 1986. *144 pages.*
Hybels writes with remarkable wisdom about the life of the workaday Christian in a materialistic America. Taken from his sermons, this foundational and practical counsel deals with a variety of marketplace issues such as the dangers of consumerism, the importance of giving, the value of diligent labor and the problem of workaholism. Other topics include attitudes toward those in authority, broken relationships on the job, dealing with anger, how to handle money and Satan's tactics in disarming the Christian witness. This is an easy read, excellent for group study; a leader's guide is available.

*Laws That Liberate: The Relevance of the Ten Commandments to Modern Living.*
Victor, 1985. *132 pages.*
The Ten Commandments weren't meant to be left on Mount Sinai, maintains Hybels. Here he not only brings them down to earth, but introduces them into the practical situations of our everyday lives. Devoting one chapter to each command, Hybels shows how these laws were meant to guide us into paths of free and fulfilled living before a holy God. A leader's guide and transparencies are available for group study of this book.

*Who You Are When No One's Looking: Choosing Consistency, Resisting*
*Compromise.* InterVarsity Press, 1987. *113 pages.*
This is a book about character: courage, discipline, vision, endurance and love. Hybels offers immensely practical guidance that is work (and relationship) oriented. Hybels is well-practiced in communicating biblical truths with up-to-date realism. Great casual reading. An excellent gift for the Christian or non-Christian.

**INRIG, GARY,** PASTOR, TEACHER ■ *A Call to Excellence.* Victor, 1985.
*168 pages.*
Having been made in God's likeness, all human beings are implicitly called to excellence. Yet, writes Inrig, excellence in a biblical sense is neither achieving great things nor a matter of public conduct, for one can be a public success but a private failure. True excellence is consistent endeavor to grow into God's character in all areas of life. Inrig acknowledges that "none of us, however gifted, . . . will attain excellence in this life." However, the person intent on fulfilling God's purposes is headed in the right direction. This is no shallow study; Inrig's approach is thorough and unambiguous. He uses a broad range of sources and carefully distinguishes his biblical perspective from modern and classical theories. Deserves a wide audience.

**JACOB, W. M.,** PROFESSOR ■ *Lay People and Religion in the Early Eighteenth Century.* Cambridge University Press, 1996. *258 pages.*
This book investigates the part that Anglicanism played in the lives of laypeople in England and Wales between 1689 and 1750. It is concerned with what they did rather than what they believed, and explores their attitudes toward clergy; religious activities; personal morality and charitable giving, especially in relation to education and health care; and church building and improvement. Using evidence from diaries, letters, account books, newspapers and popular publications, and parish and diocesan records, Jacob demonstrates that Anglicanism held the allegiance of a significant proportion of people. Laypeople took the lead in managing the affairs of the parishes, which were the major focus of communal and social life, and supported the spiritual and moral discipline of the Church courts. The author shows that early-eighteenth-century England and Wales remained a largely traditional society and that Methodism emerged from a strong church.

**JACOBSEN, STEVE,** REALTOR, PROFESSOR, PASTOR ■ *Hearts to God, Hands to Work: Connecting Spirituality and Work.* Alban Institute, 1997. *88 pages.*
Written primarily for pastors, Jacobsen seeks to provide a framework for a thorough integration of "spiritual" and "work" worlds. The work of preaching, pastoral care, education and leadership is examined. See particularly the chapter on preaching and also appendix A, "Twenty-Five Ways to Serve People Who Work."

**JAMES, KAY COLES,** GOVERNMENT LEADER ■ *Transforming America from the Inside Out.* Zondervan, 1995. *166 pages.*
After decades of watching Christians politicize faith, James has written a book that challenges them to make a cultural difference through personal revival, not via political machinery. James knows government from the inside out and writes clearly and insightfully about both it and faith. Intelligent, articulate and unafraid, she does not hesitate to swim against the evangelical political tide to make her points on poverty, homosexuality, abortion and racism. Her approach to homosexuality is typically up front. She advocates love, not judgment. James has written a refreshing examination of issues that Christians must deal with in order to make a lasting impact on American culture today.

**JAMES, KAY COLES, WITH JAQUELLINE COBB FULLER,** GOVERNMENT LEADER; PROFESSOR ■ *Never Forget.* Zondervan, 1992. *182 pages.*
This is a very personal and gripping story of an African American female born to a troubled family in public housing and her rise to public service in the first Bush White House. She tells of the pain and delights of poor black families in modern

America as well as her struggle with the Christian faith which was resolved during her college days at Hampton Institute through involvement with InterVarsity Christian Fellowship. It is candidly written and very educational about a black woman's experience in government as a conservative, national prolife advocate and evangelical Christian.

**JANNEY, REBECCA PRICE,** WRITER, PROFESSOR ■ *Great Women in American History.* Horizon, 1996. *283 pages.*
Here are candid profiles of twenty-three women of faith. Janney's profiles include first ladies, a runaway slave, political leaders, famous authors, native Americans and educators. Each profile has an anecdote, "Facts at a Glance," a pencil sketch and a bibliography. This is a good addition for American history, the women's movement and the marketplace-faith movement.

**JENSEN, MARK,** HOSPITAL CHAPLAIN ■ *Shattered Vocations.* Broadman, 1990. *167 pages.*
Several years of serving as a chaplain in the cancer unit of a hospital has led Mark Jensen to think critically about how Christians view vocation. His experiences have taught him the uselessness of narrow, occupation-based definitions of vocation, and this book seeks to recapture a biblical view of Christian vocation.

**JOHN PAUL II,** POPE ■ *On Human Work (Laborem Exercens).* United States Catholic Conference, 1981. *64 pages.*
This impressive treatise explores biblical, historical and sociological dimensions of work. This brief but historic document is important reading for both Catholics and non-Catholics. Stylistically cumbersome in places.

**JOHNSON, PAUL G.,** PASTOR ■ *Grace—God's Work Ethic: Making Connections Between the Gospel and Weekday Work.* Judson Press, 1985. *143 pages.*
Lutheran clergyman Paul Johnson was troubled that the grace preached on Sunday did not seem to translate to the work ethic employed on Monday. In this book he calls pastors and laity to help the church become a natural place to connect the gospel and weekday work. He includes practical ideas for developing support groups with both employed and unemployed workers and for promoting dialogue between pastor and congregation. The illustrations are a bit dated, but there's still plenty of value here.

**JONES, DAVID CLYDE,** PROFESSOR ■ *Biblical Christian Ethics.* Baker, 1994. *224 pages.*

Every chapter of this book is outstanding, but the chapter on telling and not telling the truth is stunning in its clarity. Jones is a stellar lecturer, but his writing moves past the pedantic nature of most such texts and into a realm that makes it accessible to every reader. He leaves us little room for argument or to make excuses when faced with difficult choices. (See Phillip Haille's *Lest Innocent Blood Be Shed.*)

**JONES, G. BRIAN, & LINDA PHILLIP-JONES,** DOCTORS OF PSYCHOLOGY ■ *Men Have Feelings, Too! A Book for Men (and the Women That Love Them).* Victor, 1988. *232 pages.*

A husband-and-wife counseling team analyze the widespread problem of men who struggle to understand and express their feelings. In themselves emotions are neither good nor bad, say the authors. What matters is how we use and emphasize them. The authors discuss how faith, external circumstances and our internal feelings should interact. They also suggest ways to help ease the common male-female conflict over the communication of feelings. Questions in the form of personal experiments follow each of twelve chapters. The book offers beginner-level insight on an important subject, but it may disappoint those in search of theological or psychological depth.

**KANE, MARGARET,** INDUSTRIAL CHAPLAIN ■ *Theology in an Industrial Society.* SCM Press, 1966. *151 pages.*

Margaret Kane is a person involved in industrial mission (also see Simon Phipps) who pleads for a theology grounded in praxis more than in a particular theological tradition: "Theology must . . . start in the present and is in principle the concern of every person. This is contrary to the common view which sees theology as having its beginning and ending in a study of the Bible and other documents of the past, and of interest only to those who have special training." According to Kane, if such an approach were taken seriously, it would require "a revolution in the role of the lay people in order that theology might truly become something we 'do' together, . . . which learns from lay experience . . . and which issues in provisional formulation of faith rather than providing prescriptive answers."

**KARMIRIS, JOHN N.,** PROFESSOR ■ *The Status and Ministry of the Laity in the Orthodox Church.* Trans. Evie Zachariades-Holmberg. Holy Cross Press, 1992. *52 pages.*

This book examines the role of the laity in teaching, missionary, devotional, social and administrative ministries. "Orthodox theology does not acknowledge any ontological difference between the 'clergy' and 'laity' other than that of ordination, contrary to what Western theology professed at the Council of Trent" (p. 8).

**KAUFFMAN, DANIEL,** COLLEGE ADMINISTRATOR ■ *Managers with God: Continuing the Work Christ Began.* Herald, 1990. *196 pages.*
When Kauffman looks at a dollar he sees a drama that the rest of us would miss. Why isn't the offering the high point of the worship service? Why aren't the church's financial officers frontline heroes? Stewardship is not a necessary evil, it's high theology—a matter of people using all their gifts (time, talents and money) to help the church continue Christ's mission. No matter how hard we try, he says, we cannot isolate our wealth (and the way we earn it) from the larger purposes of God.

**KELBA, GERALD J.,** PRIEST ■ *The People Parish.* Ave Maria, 1986. *131 pages.*
Kelba, a white priest in a black church, faced his prejudice and fears and, with only a mustard seed of faith, turned to his parish and asked for their help. He listened to their suggestions, uncovered their talents and led them as their servant. Their vision statement reads, "to become the heart and center of the community." They became just that, spawning a child development center, a community credit union and other social services.

**KELLER, W. PHILLIP,** WRITER ■ *Salt for Society.* Word, 1981. *151 pages.*
Keller attributes the illness of Western society to the arrogance and hedonistic goals of its ideologies and institutions. Not success but meekness, not machismo but self-abandonment, not self-fulfillment but ministry—qualities found in Christ—are what transform humans and their cultures. This book is written for Christians who identify more with those goals of success than with the distinctives of a life after Christ. Keller is the author of eighteen other insightful devotional studies.

**KENNY, J. P.,** PRIEST ■ *Roman Catholicism, Christianity and Anonymous Christianity: The Role of the Christian Today.* Clergy Book Service, 1973. *124 pages.*
Kenny deals with three large questions: (1) Can people reach Christ and have his Spirit without the structures and paraphernalia of organized Christianity; and if so, "why require [them] to submit to the Catholic Church, and what is the point of being a Christian at all?" (2) What is the aim and meaning of church-sponsored missions, and are they the exclusive vehicle of Christ's work? (3) What is the role and what are the components of the modern Christian witness? Kenny arrives at his answers through a biblical and theological scrutiny of faith both within and outside the Roman Catholic Church. He examines theological issues with broad implications for the Christian in the marketplace.

**KERR, HUGH T., & JOHN M. MULDER,** CHURCH PROFESSIONALS ■
*Conversions.* Eerdmans, 1983. *265 pages.*
These fifty sketches include several key marketplace Christians alongside many religious professionals. A brief description of the person's significance and their work is followed by their own description of encountering God. The sketches include Blaise Pascal, Charles Colson, Dag Hammarskjold, Malcolm Muggeridge, John Newton, Albert Schweitzer, Tolstoy, Sojourner Truth and Ethel Waters. This work provides a wonderful window into faith in the lives of some people of fame who worked it out in the public eye.

**KIDNER, DEREK,** PROFESSOR ■ *The Christian and the Arts.* InterVarsity
Fellowship, 1959. *32 pages.*
Kidner deals with the apparent absence or seemingly negative treatment of the arts in the Scripture. He probes beneath the narrative into principles that call for excellence, integrity and morality to affirm the work of artists. His major appeal is rooted in the artistic quality that characterizes the writings in Scripture. This is the justification for good art according to Kidner.

**KINAST, ROBERT L.,** PRIEST ■ *Caring for Society: A Theological Interpretation of Lay Ministry.* Thomas More Press, 1985. *165 pages.*
This theology of the Roman Catholic laity is comprehensive. Kinast helps synthesize post-Vatican II developments in the American Catholic lay movement through 1985, while at the same time mediating lay-clergy communication. His approach is to "assume that lay Catholics are acting out a ministry experientially. [The] task is to discover the key elements in that experience and help people to articulate them within a framework consonant with the Christian tradition." Kinast finally offers "caring for society" as a paradigm to organize and open new avenues for church growth.

**KING, CORETTA SCOTT,** SOCIAL ACTIVIST ■ *My Life with Martin Luther King Jr.* Hodder & Stoughton, 1970. *304 pages.*
This is King's story of moving from her poor roots in Marion, Alabama, through education at Antioch College in Ohio and on to the Boston Conservatory of Music and marriage to Martin. It is clear that Coretta and Martin loved one another deeply, but they both knew that they were called by God to give themselves to others trapped by racism, poverty and violence. Mrs. King tells the story of her family life amid the chaotic demands of national and international leadership of her husband. This book adds insight into Martin Luther King Jr. as a Christian leader, daddy, pastor, scholar and companion.

**KING, DAVID S.**, PASTOR ■ *No Church Is an Island.* Pilgrim, 1980.
*133 pages.*
King tells how he has seen many churches, including his own, grow through active
outreach into their local communities. He maintains that a church succeeds to the
degree that it becomes a vehicle of service and Christ's healing to its neighbors. The
book is based on the premise that "the heart of the Christian faith is relationship" (foreword). It includes an extensive directory with the names and addresses of community
ministries nationwide, including food banks, art centers and home repair ministries.

**KLINGAMAN, PATRICK,** CONSULTANT, SPEAKER, WRITER ■ *Thank God It's
Monday: Making Business Your Ministry.* Victor, 1996. *204 pages.*
Klingaman first lays out a case for seeing business as a form of ministry, then
moves to "Godly Principles That Make Business Sense" (such as providing good
service, behaving with integrity and loving coworkers). The final section addresses
issues business executives face, like handling tough business decisions, avoiding
work addiction and seeing success through biblical eyes.

**KNAACK, TWILA,** SUPPORT STAFF ■ *Ethel Waters: I Touched a Sparrow.* World
Wide Publications, 1978. *156 pages.*
Knaack, a rural Minnesota woman, was working as a clerical staff when she was
introduced to Waters, a southern-born, internationally famous entertainer. Knaack
was assigned to assist Waters after she became a regular at Billy Graham crusades.
A whole new world opened up for Knaack, and a very intense relationship developed between them. They became more than coworkers—they became family to
each other. Knaack tells the story with obvious love and admiration (including
Waters's painful and lonely death in 1976). The book is a thoughtful description of
the loneliness at the top.

**KOBOBEL, JANET L.,** MANAGER ■ *"But Can She Type?" Overcoming Stereotypes
in the Workplace.* InterVarsity Press, 1986. *177 pages.*
Women in the workplace face stress, job insecurity and office politics. But, says
Kobobel, the greatest battle they face may be stereotyping. She offers examples of
how we view men and women at work: "He's a go-getter; she's pushy." "He can
make quick decisions; she's impulsive." Many men and women question whether a
woman can be an effective manager. But Kobobel, a manager herself, believes a
woman's distinct traits make her especially suited for the task. Topics include fear,
success, male and female differences, and flexibility for new challenges. A well-
researched Christian perspective employing twenty years of predominantly female
studies in sociology and psychology.

**KOHN, MELVIN L., & CARMI SCHOOLER,** SOCIOLOGISTS ■ *Work and Personality.* Ablex, 1983. *389 pages.*
This sociology textbook is the product of two decades of research exploring the impact of social stratification, job conditions and occupational self-direction on the worker's personality, values and psychological functioning. The authors assess more than fifty job conditions and interpret surveys issued in 1964 and 1974. They also discuss the reciprocal effects of work complexity and intellectual flexibility. The book includes chapters on housework and work as experienced in Japan and Poland. The authors also briefly consider the intergenerational transmission of religious and ethnic values and orientations. A scientific study from a limited, secular perspective.

**KOMISAR, LUCY,** JOURNALIST ■ *Corazon Aquino: The Story of a Revolution.* George Barziller, 1987. *290 pages.*
Aquino became the president of the Philippines after Ferdinand Marcos was toppled from his reign of abuse and greed. Komisar captures the complicated intrigue, the groundswell of opposition to Marcos and Aquino's rise to national prominence. A repeated theme is the depth of faith and values that make Aquino a great leader. Her faith also committed her to improving the lot of the masses of poverty-bound Filipinos. Komisar concludes, "She proved to her countrymen and to an astonished world that a political neophyte with little besides courage, tenacity and an innate good sense could embark on a moral crusade." This is a story of quiet, deep faith in national leadership triumphing over evil.

**KONIECZNY, STANLEY, & GREGORY F. AUGUSTINE PIERCE,** PRIEST; PUBLISHING EXECUTIVE ■ *For Those Who Work: Stations of the Cross, Ordinary Mysteries of the Rosary.* ACTA, 1991. *95 pages.*
Here is an attempt to connect two historical Catholic prayer and worship practices to the emerging focus on spirituality and work or job and family life. A very brief reflection on each stage of the fourteen Stations is coupled with a quote from one of the popes. Then five brief reflections are given for praying the rosary in light of daily work and family responsibilities. This is a very useable contribution with well-crafted insights and connections between personal worship and daily life.

**KOOP, C. EVERETT,** MEDICAL DOCTOR ■ *Koop: Memoirs of America's Family Doctor.* Random House, 1991. *342 pages.*
As Surgeon General under president Ronald Reagan, Koop surprised a lot of opposing leaders with his forthright, candid and sometimes unexpected positions on AIDS, smoking, abortion, euthanasia and safe sex. Not a few of his Christian friends

were offended when he did not always toe the party line. Koop also tells of his life-long journey as a man, husband, parent, churchgoer and professional. This is the way Christians should function in the marketplace.

**KOWALSKI, JUDITH A., & DEAN J. COLLINS,** PROFESSOR; DEPUTY INSPECTOR, MILWAUKEE POLICE ■ *To Serve and Protect: Law Enforcement Officers Reflect on Their Faith and Work.* Augsburg, 1992. *125 pages.*
The authors invite readers into the world of the criminal justice system, helping them identify with some of the ethical/spiritual dilemmas that they face daily. There are frank discussions on the home life of police officers, contextualization and how protection is a spiritual role. A must-read for those who want to understand and make sense of the world of the law officer.

**KRAEMER, HENDRIK,** PROFESSOR ■ *A Theology of the Laity.* Westminster Press, 1958. *192 pages.*
If you're looking for the starting point of and a single basic text on the modern lay movement, this is it. Kraemer restores biblical and Reformation understandings of the priesthood of believers without undervaluing the important role of the clergy. The church needs to be a fellowship or worship and training for the very purpose of being dispersed into society. Very highly recommended.

**KRAYBILL, DONALD B., & PHYLLIS PELLMAN GOOD,** EDS., PROFESSOR; EDITOR ■ *Perils of Professionalism: Essays on Christian Faith and Professionalism.* Herald, 1982. *240 pages.*
What does it mean to be a trained professional, and how does that affect relationships with clients, the public and the church? In this book, various Mennonite professionals in education, business, social sciences and health care talk about issues like "social power" and how their career affects their identity, values, social relationships, church life and Christian faith. Though a bit dated, this book faces the issues squarely.

**KREEFT, PETER,** PROFESSOR ■ *Making Choices: Finding Black and White in a World of Grays—Practical Wisdom for Everyday Moral Decisions.* Servant, 1990. *218 pages.*
This is not a marketplace–specific text. Read it anyway. Kreeft's works on apologetics are marvelous. This book focuses narrowly on what society likes to term "gray areas." He sees less gray and more clarity than our society sees, and he challenges much of our culture's self-taught wisdom on matters like sex, abortion and telling the truth. Kreeft discusses of the problems of morality, the principles

of morality and the possibilities of morality before diving into the particulars and the practice of morality.

**KREIDER, CARL,** PROFESSOR ■ *The Christian Entrepreneur.* Herald, 1980. *221 pages.*
Integrating religious and business thinking is second nature for Kreider. He includes brief yet pungent biblical guidance on numerous ethical issues, including wages and hiring practices, payment of interest, illegitimate business endeavors, sales promotion techniques and pricing, and environmental responsibility.

*The Rich and the Poor.* Herald, 1987. *168 pages.*
The purpose of this book is to heighten people's awareness and concern for the differences in standard of living between rich and poor countries. Someone once said, "You can't lift yourselves by your own bootstraps if you don't have boots." Kreider's position is, "Rich countries must supply the boots, but poor countries must do the lifting." This is a thoughtful treatment reflecting years of thinking, researching and teaching.

**KRESGE, STALEY S., & STEVE SPILOS,** BUSINESSMAN; JOURNALIST ■ *The S. S. Kresge Story.* Western Publishing, 1979. *373 pages.*
A son tells the story of his father who was the founder of the Kresge Company, now known as K-mart. Kresge's tenacity is admirable, but this book is a little too laudatory. More insight into the man and his struggles would have been helpful. The book is also filled with too much company related material, including pictures of every major executive (all males). The faith factor is not very evident.

**KROEKER, WALLY,** JOURNALIST ■ *God's Week Has Seven Days: Monday Musings for Marketplace Christians.* Herald, 1998. *298 pages.*
Here is a wonderful collection of 52 reflections from a veteran marketplace Christian and excellent writer. Kroeker combines realism, intriguing humor, lively candor and probing insight for everyday believers in the workplace. Here we find wisdom, vision and practical help to function in a broken world. Kroeker also provides material for congregations to use in bridging the painful gap between worship and work. This is a great gift book for coworkers, pastors and family members.

**LAPHAM, LEWIS H.,** JOURNALIST ■ *Money and Class in America.* Weidenfeld & Nicolson, 1988. *243 pages.*
Lapham ponders the dynamics of money in the American imagination as well as its effect on class structure, culture, celebrity, politics and crime. He wonders at Amer-

ica's contrary impulses: charitable yet self-aggrandizing. Lapham analyzes the virtues and vices of money. He points out the contradictions inherent in wealth: leisure often breeds petty anxieties, many of the freest and best-provisioned people on earth seem most in need of therapy. This is a speculative essay which is cosmopolitan, keen and disturbing.

**LARSEN, DALE, & SANDY LARSEN,** WRITERS ■ *Patching Your Parachute.* InterVarsity Press, 1993. *138 pages.*

In extremely realistic terms, the authors use real people to describe the various shocks, hurts and pains that accompany losing a job, and (worse) facing the rejections necessary to find another one. The encouragement they offer is best handled in a group setting. The suggestions are pragmatic and biblical. But the Larsens fail to adequately address disastrous long-term unemployment and catastrophic financial situations in an encouraging manner.

**LAUGHLIN, RODNEY S.,** REALTOR ■ *The Job Hunter's Handbook: A Christian Guide.* Word, 1985. *279 pages.*

Combining inspirational counsel and hard-nosed practicality, Laughlin helps the Christian "1) discover what you can do best, 2) identify and understand what organizations will benefit from your presence, 3) establish contact with those organizations, and 4) get hired." This book also includes chapters on writing a résumé, interviewing and the psychology of hiring. Woven throughout are lessons in discerning God's leading in one's life.

**LAUSANNE COMMITTEE** ■ *Evangelism and Social Responsibility.* Lausanne Committee for World Evangelism, 1982. *64 pages.*

This book summarizes the consensus which emerged among fifty evangelical leaders from twenty-seven countries after one week of lecture, discussion and prayer. Editor John Stott called it a "dramatic demonstration of the value of international conferences," as culturally and economically influenced prejudices were owned and disagreements faced "with charity." This was an attempt to define more clearly the content of "social responsibility" as well as its interrelationship with evangelism.

*The Willowbank Report: Gospel and Culture.* Lausanne Committee for World Evangelism, 1978. *36 pages.*

Thirty-three evangelical theologians, anthropologists, linguists, missionaries and pastors from six continents discuss how the process of communicating the gospel is influenced by the culture from which it comes and that in which it is proclaimed. Topics include the cultural context of Scriptural revelation, the nature of conver-

122 ——————————————————————— The Marketplace Annotated Bibliography

sion, the relationship between church and culture, and the transformation of life-style and culture.

**LAY COMMISSION ON SOCIAL TEACHING** ■ *Liberty and Justice for All.*
Brownson Institute, 1986. *26 pages.*
This booklet, written by respected Roman Catholic laity, is a response to the 1986 U.S. bishops' letter *Economic Justice for All* (see entry, p. 141). While generally supportive, the authors fault the bishops where they ventured into areas of partisan or ideological opinion, since the authors feel those areas belong more properly to lay authorities. They criticize the bishops' failure to grasp what makes poor nations into developed nations; their inadequate grasp of concepts such as enterprise, markets and profits; their excessive trust in the state; and their preference for solidarity over pluralism.

**LEAN, GARTH,** POLITICAL COLUMNIST ■ *God's Politician: William Wilberforce's Struggle.* Darton, Longman & Todd, 1980. *180 pages.*
"The object of this little book," writes Lean, "is to draw out the qualities and methods which made Wilberforce and his friends so uniquely effective in altering the spirit of their age. . . . 'Wilberforce proved that one man can change his times, but he cannot do it alone.' " Wilberforce stands as a model change agent for God. More people need to know his story and take similar risks with their faith.

**LECKEY, DOLORES R.,** CHURCH WORKER ■ *Laity Stirring the Church.*
Fortress, 1987. *119 pages.*
This is a uniquely valuable marketplace book. Leckey, executive director of the U.S. Bishop's Committee on the Laity, is an enthusiastic believer. Using an anecdotal writing style, Leckey addresses six lay-centered issues she considers of prophetic importance to the future of the church: spiritual hunger, marriage and family, the changing status and role of women, work, ministry and mission, and community. Recommended.

*Practical Spirituality for Lay People.* Sheed & Ward, 1987. *112 pages.*
Collected stories about laypeople and favorite saints and writers make up this collection of reflective pieces on everyday Christianity. "Where and how do you experience God in your everydayness?" Leckey asks. She encourages readers to allow the answers of others to stimulate their own in seven areas: spirituality, family, work, community, change, church and the world. Highly recommended to both Protestant and Catholic readers.

**LEE, PHILLIP,** CLERGYMAN ∎ *Against the Protestant Gnostics.* Oxford University Press, 1987. *288 pages.*

Lee locates classical Gnostic tendencies—belief in a secret knowledge revealed to the few, rejection of the physical world and escape into the self—in the thinking of modern Protestantism. He distinguishes between *gnosis* and faith, between escape and pilgrimage, between the exclusive and the inclusive, and between the nebulous and the concrete. Lee shows how the lack of these distinctions has proved detrimental to our understanding of issues like politics, feminism, ecology and parenthood. Lee then calls for reform, including a renewal of obedience to the Scriptures; a restoration of a dialectical faith and practice; and an affirmation of life, creation, sexuality and extended family/community. His examination is thorough and convincing.

**LEININGER, B. JOSEPH, WITH W. TERRY WHALIN,** COMMODITIES TRADER, INVESTOR ∎ *Lessons from the Pit.* Broadman & Holman, 1999. *201 pages.*

Leininger pictures life on the high-paced trading floor of the Chicago Mercantile Exchange, where he was a successful trader for over fourteen years. Eighteen chapters offer nicely-transferable insights—live in your strengths; hit singles, not home runs; learn from experts; live clean and lean; give to others—textured with a steady stream of true stories and lively illustrations. A Christian perspective, though light on Scriptural applications, candid and confessional in tone. (See also Mark A. Ritchie, *God in the Pits.*)

**LEMAN, DR. KEVIN,** PSYCHOLOGIST ∎ *Winning the Rat Race Without Becoming a Rat.* Thomas Nelson, 1996. *246 pages.*

Our culture actively promotes hard work, sometimes to the exclusion of all else. While Leman doesn't question this basic societal given, he does lay down some parameters on doing it wisely by using his own particular method he calls "birth order." The book seems manipulative, a guide for getting to know people's personality types through their birth order with the end design of getting them to perform as you want them to. It seems few people would want to be so "handled" by their employers or coworkers! The book title may be clever, but the concept is not.

**LENTZ, HAROLD, & ELEANOR LENTZ,** PASTOR; TEACHER ∎ *Twenty-Two Who Changed the World.* CSS Publishing, 1988. *134 pages.*

Taking us as far back as the ninth century (Alfred the Great), the authors offer twenty-two biographical sketches of people who have shaped world history. Each comes from vastly different social, economic, religious and historical contexts. Nevertheless, the authors set out to show that "one element in particular [unites] many of the lives of great distinction . . . that element is 'religion,' 'spirituality,' 'morality,' or 'faith.'" It is this reliance on a higher power that inspires human beings to courage, wisdom and commitment. Of the twenty-two sketches, twenty-one are laypersons and twenty are men.

**LEO XIII,** POPE ■ *On the Condition of Workers.* United States Catholic Conference, 1890.
This landmark encyclical was reissued in 1990 on the 100th anniversary of its publication. It addresses the demoralizing effects of both technological change and the shift of economic wealth on the relationship between workers and their employers. It also defines the functions of the church, state, employer and employee in the social order. A document of timeless appeal.

**LeTOURNEAU, R. G.,** CONSTRUCTION EXECUTIVE ■ *R. G. LeTourneau: Mover of Men and Mountains.* Moody Press, 1967, 1972. *296 pages.*
Here is the personal tale of an early twentieth-century rough-hewn man who became the builder of the world's largest earthmoving machinery. The journey was filled with frustrations and failures, which he candidly describes. He also loved Jesus and tells his story of faith and work in an honest, personal style. This story reflects the times when fundamentalist Christians were barely beginning to take the work-world seriously as a place of service. But LeTourneau rose above the idea that only pastors and missionaries could serve God. He saw his business success and wealth as a gift from God.

**LEWIS, DIANE, WITH JOE CARROLL,** OWNER OF EXECUTIVE PLACEMENT FIRM; WRITER ■ *Insider's Guide to Finding the Right Job.* Thomas Nelson, 1987. *190 pages.*
An excellent career guidance book written from an evangelical perspective. Lewis covers all the standard ground: what employers are looking for, what you should know about the job market, the importance of attitude and appearance, writing a résumé, preparing for interviews, and job hunting while employed. But Lewis uses a down-to-earth approach, giving commonsense tips with the ring of authority. She scales her advice down to twenty essential and easy-to-follow rules.

**LIEBIG, JAMES E.,** BUSINESS WRITER ■ *Business Ethics: Profiles in Civic Virtue.* Fulcrum, 1990. *241 pages.*
This book includes profiles of twenty-four American business leaders who value employee involvement, corporate social responsibility and ethical management.

Liebig first highlights an American tradition of virtuous business leaders and then shows that the virtuous leader is still alive and well today. He includes representatives from Control Data, Hammermill Paper, Hanover Insurance and Republic Airlines. These inspiring models include five women. Highly recommended.

**LIFE@WORK JOURNAL** ■ *The Life@Work Book.* Word, 2000. *163 pages.*
This workbook-size volume includes fourteen essays on how faith or spirituality can be integrated into the workplace. The essays, by Christian leaders such as Larry Burkett, Charles Colson, Max De Pree, Bill Hybels and Charles Swindoll, teach that work is good and a calling from God, that faith requires a minimum level of morality and ethics, and that coworkers deserve respect. This is a true marketplace book from Christian leaders. The quality of writing, ideas and insights is high, making it a great book to launch discussions in Bible studies or work discussion groups.

**LINDGREN, ALVIN J., & NORMAN SHAWCHUCK,** PROFESSORS ■ *Let My People Go: Empowering Laity for Ministry.* Abingdon, 1980. *129 pages.*
"This book is written for those who believe that the increased involvement and empowerment of lay persons in the church is sorely needed today." The authors discuss appropriate leadership style, the making of decisions and goal setting. Especially helpful is their second chapter where they expose three inherent hindrances in the church for lay involvement.

**LOWERY, JAMES L., ED.** ■ *Case Histories of Tentmakers.* Morehouse-Barlow, 1976. *83 pages.*
This book is a collection of case histories of several self-supporting clergy (mostly Anglican). These accounts are personal examples of how tentmakers find secular employment affecting their ministry. Both the benefits and struggles are dealt with.

**LULIC, MARGARET A.,** BUSINESS CONSULTANT ■ *Who We Could Be at Work.* Blue Edge, 1994. *261 pages.*
Lulic has done a good job of pulling together this collection of forty "war" stories from ordinary, frontline folks, and sets each story in philosophical and principled framework that advocates one or more of Lulic's ten guiding principles of business. A good book that sets principles in the context of real life, it's a bit lengthy, but her ten principles are certainly based in the reality of marketplace veterans. Not inherently Christian in its viewpoint, this book raises the big questions of life purpose, integration and systemically ethical approaches to business and life.

**LUNDEN, ROLF,** PROFESSOR ■ *Business and Religion in the American 1920s.* Greenwood Press, 1988. *220 pages.*
Lunden persuasively argues that since colonial times business has been America's dominant institution, wielding its influence in every sector of society. He shows how Protestant religion fully employed business ideology, organization and methods in the 1920s. This unique convergence, says Lunden, explains how "Robert Schuller's gospel of success or the business methods of Jerry Falwell's Moral Majority" have arisen in America, while such would be unimaginable in Europe. The second half of the book turns the tables and shows how religion lent "an idealistic and spiritual dimension to entrepreneurial activities" in the 1920s. Exhaustively researched; trustworthy by sheer weight of evidence.

**LUNDIN, ROGER,** PROFESSOR ■ *Emily Dickinson and the Art of Unbelief.* Eerdmans, 1998. *305 pages.*
Lundin traces Dickinson's New England Christian roots carefully and with some enlightening analysis that rises above the all-to-popular bashing of her family's Puritan heritage. He has done his homework on the times (eighteenth and nineteenth centuries) and has obviously read and reread her poetry along with the scores of other literary analysts and biographers. He wrestles with the faith presented to her by the family and the church.

**LUPTON, ROBERT D., & BARABRA R. THOMPSON,** DEVELOPMENT LEADER; EDITOR ■ *Theirs Is the Kingdom: Celebrating the Gospel in Urban America.* Harper & Row, 1989. *121 pages.*
In this insightful and moving series of vignettes Lupton shows how his experiences in a high crime area of Atlanta shattered many of his assumptions about himself and the nature of poverty in America. He found that his mission was as much about his own salvation as it was about that of the urban poor. He was surprised to learn that a spiritual life had already taken root in the urban soil, exposing his own patronizing attitudes, materialism and biases. Refreshingly lucid, well written, biblically sensitive. Highly recommended.

**LUTHER, JOE THOMPSON,** PASTOR ■ *Monday Morning Religion.* Broadman, 1961. *96 pages.*
Here is a pastor wrestling with his growing awareness that Sunday worship and Monday responsibilities are tragically separated. Luther declares, "Religion may be learned on Sunday, but it must be lived on Monday!" (p. 7). He acknowledges that the book is a personal confession. The twelve chapters are designed to be read with a recommended Scripture text, lending it to personal or group Bible study.

**MACDONALD, GORDON, PASTOR** ■ *Forging a Real World Faith.* Oliver Nelson, 1989. *222 pages.*

This book follows three seasons of growth MacDonald has discovered in his own spiritual journey, which he relates with candor: (1) learning about the person of God and what it means to worship him, (2) growing in self-knowledge and owning one's capacity for both beauty and wickedness, and (3) facing the rugged reality of work and the struggle inherent in human relationships. Written "for the men and women who have to pound out a living on those streets [and] in the marketplace."

*Ordering Your Private World.* Oliver Nelson, 1985. *181 pages.*

MacDonald addresses the lack of attention that the Western culture gives to internal or spiritual organization. Although many people 'appear to have the public dimension of their life well-regulated, their private world may be in disarray. MacDonald helps us bring order and control to our private world.

**MACKENZIE, ALISTAIR, PASTOR, MARKETPLACE MINISTER** ■ Review of "Dogmatic Constitution on the Church" *(Lumen Gentium)*, in *Faith at Work: Vocation, the Theology of Work and the Pastoral Implications*, thesis, 1997. *213 pages.*

Section 34 of the *Lumen Gentium* goes far beyond any previous papal document to explain how the laity participate in the prophetic, priestly and royal offices of Christ in their daily occupation. According the *Lumen Gentium*, the laity discharge these functions not only by contributing to the moral improvement of humankind through their involvement in secular affairs but also by assisting the advance of culture and civilization. This represents a significant change of emphasis in Catholic thinking. "The laity, by their very vocation, seek the kingdom of God by engaging in temporal affairs and by ordering them according to the plan of God. They live in the world, that is, in each and in all of the secular professions and occupations. . . . They are called there by God so that by exercising their proper function . . . they can work for the sanctification of the world from within, in the manner of leaven."

Review of "Gaudium et Spes Pastoral Constitution on the Church in the Modern World," in *Faith at Work: Vocation, the Theology of Work and the Pastoral Implications*, thesis, 1997. *213 pages.*

In this document the Second Vatican Council affirmed God's blessing on humanity's technological and economic achievements. It represents a significant change in Catholic thinking about human work. This call to humanize the world in the name of the coming kingdom encourages believers to take their daily work seriously as a spiritual exercise. It is a sign of Catholicism developing a work ethic of its own.

While recognizing the oppressive and dehumanizing effects of much work this document optimistically embraces human achievement, technological progress and economic growth.

**MACQUARRIE, JOHN,** THEOLOGIAN ■ *The Faith of the People of God: A Lay Theology.* Charles Scribner & Sons, 1972. *191 pages.*
This is a systematic theology organized around the principle "the people of God." In contrast to other theologians who have chosen starting points such as the Word of God or justification, Macquarrie writes from the perspective of the people of God.

**MAHEDY, WILLIAM, & CHRISTOPHER CARSTENS,** PASTOR; PSYCHOLOGIST ■ *Starting on Monday: Christian Living in the Workplace.* Ballantine, 1987. *165 pages.*
Mahedy and Carstens offer advice on how to be a proactive instead of a passive Christian. Their approach is to help readers help themselves rather than simply to dispense wisdom. In respective chapters, the authors provide seven principles of guidance in "learning to think like a Christian." These include remembering Jesus is with you on the job, respecting coworkers, applying reason and experience, and reading Scripture. This book offers tangible, step-by-step counsel in an easy-to-read style.

**MANWARING, RANDLE,** BUSINESSMAN ■ *A Christian's Guide to Daily Work.* Hodder & Stoughton, 1963. *63 pages.*
This is a tightly written and well-crafted book. Manwaring blends biblical truth and models with a realism about the daily grind. His topics range from guidance to interviews, from finances to witness, from ambition to sacrifice, and from managers to employees. He ends with a survey of the phases of a career, with some reflection on retirement. This is a treasure from the early days of the marketplace-faith movement.

**MARCINIAK, ED, ET AL.,** CONSULTANT, LABOR WORKER ■ *Challenge to the Laity.* Our Sunday Visitor, 1980. *135 pages.*
This is a collection of addresses given by four prominent Catholics at the National Assembly for the Laity in 1977. The authors challenge the laity "to discover how the Kingdom of God is fashioned out of the common-place events of everyday life." Also included is the complete text of "The Chicago Declaration of Christian Concern," which was the founding document of the National Center for the Laity in 1975.

**MARSHALL, PAUL,** PROFESSOR ■ *Labour of Love: Essays on Work.* Wedge, 1980. *123 pages.*
According to Marshall, the Bible portrays a very different view of work compared with other ancient sources: "The biblical authors stand out starkly in their praise of even the humblest honest labor. The Bible was a radical document in respect to work." Marshall looks for a way of reinterpreting vocation that draws together threads from the Reformed, cocreationist and "rest" traditions. He develops the apostle Paul's teaching most.

*Thine Is the Kingdom: A Biblical Perspective on the Nature of Government and Politics Today.* Marshall, Morgan & Scott, 1984. *153 pages.*
Marshall challenges evangelical Christians to move beyond personal morality to seeing the world from a political perspective. He develops guidelines for Christian political action today. Two particular issues that he addresses are the welfare state and the nuclear arms race.

**MARTIN, LINETTE,** ACTRESS, DANCER, JOURNALIST ■ *Hans Rookmaaker: A Biography.* InterVarsity Press, 1979. *187 pages.*
"Hans Rookmaaker was an enigma to many people. He was a devout Christian—Reformed in theology, intense in his study of Scripture. Yet he was also a man of high culture—an art historian [and] a lover of jazz" (back cover). On meeting Francis Schaeffer in 1948, Rookmaaker took on the mission of convincing evangelicals that art is not worldly and sinful.

**MATTHEWS, VICTOR H., & DON C. BENJAMIN,** PROFESSORS ■ *Social World of Ancient Israel: 1250-587 BCE.* Hendrickson, 1993. *327 pages.*
Two anthropologists bring their skills to study of ancient Israel and its times. The preface includes an excellent overview of "politics, economies, diplomacy, law and education" as systems of a people. This book helps recover the work-a-day realities of biblical people. A much needed addition.

**MATTOX, ROBERT,** EMPLOYEE ■ *The Christian Employee.* Bridge Publishing, 1978. *220 pages.*
Mattox believes Christians need to believe that God controls kingdoms and companies. They are employed by Christ, not by their company, their future depends on God and their response to him; their circumstances are designed by God; their superiors are worthy of honor; the Lord will direct their career; and their only status symbol is the cross. Mattox's single-mindedness and lack of sophistication should not be mistaken for naiveté. He poses a stiff challenge to take seriously the implica-

tions of Christian faith in a secular culture. This very readable book is packed with Scripture and anecdotes.

**MATTSON, RALPH, & ARTHUR MILLER,** EXECUTIVE PLACEMENT LEADERS AND MANAGERS ■ *Finding a Job You Can Love.* Thomas Nelson, 1986. *192 pages.*
This book is a readable and well-written discussion of the centrality of work in God's design for humans. Unusually warm and insightful, the book provides a framework within which to evaluate vocational goals and sense of calling. The authors' "System for Identifying Motivated Abilities" provides tangible assistance. Colorful and optimistic; an excellent resource. (A more thorough system is R. N. Bolles's *What Color Is Your Parachute?*)

**MCCLOUGHRY, ROY,** WRITER, SPEAKER ■ *The Eye of the Needle.* Inter-Varsity Press, 1990. *189 pages.*
A British layman seeks to erase the sacred-secular split and help Christians forge a robust integration of spirituality and action. He lays bare various idolatries, from narcissism to "the tyranny of economics," and calls for a lived-out faith that will infuse contemporary culture with kingdom values and give direction to a society at sea.

**MCCONNELL, FRANCIS J.,** CLERGY ■ *Christian Materialsm: Inquiries into the Getting, Spending, and Giving of Money.* Friendship Press, 1936. *167 pages.*
McConnell alerts his readers to the subtle but powerful nature of wealth. He states, "Material forces have a way of taking deadly revenge on anyone who would ignore them" (introduction, p. xi). He weaves between philosophical analysis, biblical thought, modern realities and practical matters. This work is an example of a churchman trying to be helpful outside the church context, but doing so in a manner that adds to the gap between the average work-a-day parishioner and the need for help in the area of wealth.

**MCCONNELL, WILLIAM T.,** MISSIONARY ■ *The Gift of Time.* InterVarsity Press, 1983. *120 pages.*
This book is the product of McConnell's years of crosscultural missionary experience. At issue is not the clash between cultures but the task of discerning from Scripture what time-ethic should govern a life surrendered to God and his kingdom. He asks whether the measures of time-efficiency dominating North America are biblically justifiable. Was time made for humans or were humans made for time? Clear, concise and enjoyable to read, this book is well-researched and contains an excellent bibliography.

**MCCULLOUGH, DONALD W.**, PASTOR, SEMINARY PRESIDENT ■ *Waking from the American Dream: Growing Through Your Disappointments.* InterVarsity Press, 1988. *210 pages.*

When the bubble of trouble-free living bursts, American Christians struggle to reconcile theologies of hope with the reality of despair. McCullough helps us accept that "Christ didn't die to deliver us from the harsh realities of life." He contends that wholeness through brokenness is more than an irony; it is a paradigm of ultimate reality established in Christ's death and resurrection. McCullough's writing is pastoral, wise and hopeful.

**MCKENNA, DAVID**, SEMINARY PRESIDENT ■ *Love Your Work!* Victor, 1990. *156 pages.*

McKenna asks, "If we believe that our spiritual development encompasses the whole of life, why is our daily work so often [considered] an eight-hour interruption in our growth?" Without ignoring limited work opportunities and dismal working conditions of many people, McKenna believes work should be prayerful, vocational, relational, developmental, rhythmical and meaningful. The book offers substantive and helpful insights. A reflection, question, application and prayer section follows each chapter. For individuals or groups; leader's guide available.

**MCLELLAN, VERN**, MUSICIAN, BROADCASTER ■ *Christians in the Political Arena: Positive Strategies for Twentieth Century Patriots!* Associate Press, 1986. *179 pages.*

McLellan outlines a series of conservative strategies for dealing with every political-cultural issue from abortion to nuclear weapons. The text is peppered with political cartoons and quotes from famous Christian conservatives. The book concludes with a call to action and a detailed plan of how to take steps to influence the political arena. McLellan naively assumes Christians will agree with his conservative agenda. Complex issues are handled simplistically.

**MCLELLAND, JOSEPH C.**, PROFESSOR ■ *A New Look at Vocation.* Ryerson Press, 1964. *30 pages.*

McLelland surveys the understanding of vocation in the New Testament, the early church, the Reformation and the present. He argues that in order to speak relevantly to the present situation we need to move beyond Calvin and Marx by rediscovering the ministry of the laity.

**McMAKIN, JACQUELINE, WITH SONYA DYER,** THEOLOGIAN, PASTOR; SOCIAL WORKER ■ *Working from the Heart.* LuraMedia, 1989. *184 pages.*
This insightful career guidance book places more emphasis on self-evaluation and emotional and spiritual support than on hard information or advice. Its exercises and tools help readers articulate a life direction and develop a career that honors their whole life. The book includes chapters on gifts, meaning, the practical parameters of my present life, vocational focus and finding an environment conducive to working from the heart. The authors recommend the book for use in groups. Not from an overtly Christian perspective.

**McNAIR, NIMROD,** MANAGEMENT CONSULTANT ■ *Absolute Ethics:A Proven System for True Profitability.* Executive Leadership, 1987. *46 pages.*
Writing from a capitalist perspective, McNair analyzes America's history of economic productivity and the loss of guiding morals and purpose. He suggests areas in which Americans have paid a great price for success and calls for a renewal of biblically based ethical leadership. The booklet ends with a blueprint for decision making in the business world based on the Ten Commandments. McNair makes a much needed call to an ethic that can bring genuine reform. Some will find this booklet too brief and simplistic.

*Executive Guide to Ethical Decision-Making.* Executive Leadership, 1987. *33 pages.*
This wallet-sized handbook is organized around the Ten Commandments. McNair, a staunch conservative, interprets each command and apples it to the business world. The booklet includes space for recording personal applications and goals. A handy marketplace resource.

**McNAMARA, PATRICK H.,** SOCIAL SCIENTIST ■ *More Than Money.* Alban Institute, 1999. *180 pages.*
McNamara portrays eleven congregations across the United States that have several things in common: taking the biblical mandate to minister seriously, a willingness to move out of their cultural box in response and an understanding that stewardship is not merely a type of fundraising. The portrayals exhibit both positives and negatives. The book is not an instructional guide; rather, its value lies in its ability to inspire, motivate and challenge other congregations to move into unknown territory and to share the abundance God has blessed them with.

**MEAD, LOREN B.,** CHURCH CONSULTANT, EPISCOPAL PRIEST ■ *The Once and Future Church.* Alban Institute, 1991. *92 pages.*
Mead, a practitioner of congregational health and vitality, reflects on his years of

experience and predicts where the local congregation is headed in a post-Christian era. "Congregations are living in a time in which landmarks have been erased and old ways have stopped working. . . . We have awakened to a world where the mission frontier has changed. The organization and the structures of church life, formed for that one mission, now need to be reoriented to face the new frontier." Mead's insights on where we've been and where we are going make this book a worthwhile read.

**MEEKS, M. DOUGLAS**, PROFESSOR ■ *God the Economist: The Doctrine of God and the Political Economy.* Augsburg Fortress, 1989. *208 pages.*
This book relates "the doctrine of God to reigning assumptions behind our market economy and society. . . . Meeks retrieves the biblical and theological history of God's 'economy' or household. . . . Meeks demonstrates the possibility of making new creative connections between the worlds of theology and work and ethics when a particular doctrine is investigated using a new set of questions raised by the practical concerns of people's existence. The result is a . . . creative theological revisioning of the place and purposes of economic activity—work, property, consumption—and the human relationships they entail" (publisher).

**MEILAENDER, GILBERT C., ED.,** PROFESSOR ■ *Working: Its Meaning and Its Limits.* University of Notre Dame Press, 2000. *271 pages.*
This fascinating collection of essays provides a wonderful, mind-stretching look at what work means to human beings. Meilaender has organized pieces from diverse people—Karl Marx, Anna Morrow Lindbergh, Peter Drucker, the apostle Paul and Mark Twain—around themes such as rest, work limitations and the meaning of work. By juxtaposing specific texts, he causes the student to think outside the box. Not only would this make a wonderful textbook for a class, it would make a great devotional book. It's a delightful and provocative work. Recommended.

**MEIER, PAUL, & LINDA BURNETT,** PSYCHIATRIST; MOTHER ■ *Mother's Choice: Day Care or Home Care?* Baker, 1990. *144 pages.*
The authors assist mothers in making one of life's most heart-wrenching decisions: day care or home care? This is one of the few books available that addresses day care from a Christian perspective.

**MELLICHAMP, JOSEPH MCRAE,** PROFESSOR ■ *Ministering in the Secular University.* Lewis & Stanley, 1997. *149 pages.*
This is a technique oriented how-to book that focuses on ministry by university fac-

ulty. Mellichamp covers how to write an ad for the campus newspaper, how to organize a meeting, how to prepare a talk and even to how to set up a room for a meeting. The book is practical, but it sorely lacks in two areas. Basic foundations of marketplace ministry such as calling, ideological conflict and the integration of faith and discipline are not addressed. It also lacks sufficient references to other people and resources in this particular calling.

**MENCONI, PETER, RICHARD PEACE, & LYMAN COLEMAN,** DENTIST; PROFESSOR; PUBLISHER ■ *Career: Take This Job and Love It.* NavPress, 1989. *61 pages, booklet.*
An attractive, well-organized and substantive small group guide to biblical study of career-related themes. Sections deal with career choice, planning, advancement, change, preoccupation and meaning. Each offers an opening question, Scripture to study, reflection and application. Versatile, it contains both entry- and advanced-level options. Thorough, this is an excellent marketplace resource.

*Money: Handling the Bucks.* NavPress, 1989. *58 pages.*
This is a well-organized and substantive small group guide to a biblical study of money. Sections deal with high and low finance, debt, the love of money and investment. Each offers opening thoughts, Scripture with discussion questions, reflection and application. This versatile book contains both entry- and advanced-level options. A good discussion starter. An excellent marketplace resource.

**MENKING, STANLEY J.,** PASTOR, THEOLOGIAN ■ *Helping Laity Help Others: The Pastor's Handbook.* Westminster Press, 1984. *114 pages.*
Menking urges fellow pastors to develop service projects shared by both congregation and clergy. Ideally these should spring from the lay efforts to meet local community needs. Menking offers counsel and tangible service ideas. The book begins with a discussion of the spiritual preparation and role of the pastor and proceeds to a discussion of lay training. The last third is logistical and discusses recruitment, organization and financial support for the ministries. Strong informationally; weak stylistically.

**MENKING, STANLEY J., & BARBARA WENDLAND,** PASTOR, THEOLOGIAN; LAY VOLUNTEER, HOMEMAKER, WRITER ■ *God's Partners (Lay Christians at Work).* Judson Press, 1993. *164 pages.*
This book takes the form of a lay-clergy dialogue on questions of self-understanding. They move through six questions, beginning with Who am I? The aim is to inform as to how Christians are God's partners in his work in the world.

**MIDDLEMAN, UDO,** PHILOSOPHER ■ *Pro-Existence.* InterVarsity Press, 1974. *126 pages.*
Starting from the premise that the world and all that is in it is the Lord's, Middleman affirms existence as a whole: the material world (property), spirituality, work, community and the civic order. Since God created earthly reality, meaning will be discovered only when we learn who he is and what he has communicated through Scripture. Middleman examines the value of human labor in terms of creativity, a fundamental characteristic of humans as God's image-bearer. Identity is theoretical and prone to collapse unless it is externalized or manifested through work.

**MILLER, ARTHUR F., WITH WILLIAM HENDRICKS,** MANAGEMENT CONSULTANT; WRITER ■ *Why You Can't Be Anything You Want to Be.* Zondervan, 1999. *255 pages.*
Miller suggests that if you're unhappy in your work, maybe the problem is that you're not designed for the job you're in. In three parts the book outlines Miller's idea of what he terms "giftedness," finding and following God's plan for your life and transforming the world around you through application of that plan. By mapping your own particular giftedness, Miller suggests, a revolution will occur not only in your life but in the lives of those around you. (See Richard Bolles, and Ralph Mattson.)

**MILLER, BASIL** ■ *William Carey: The Father of Modern Missions.* Bethany House, 1980. *152 pages.*
Miller tells of Carey's days as a plantation manager, school pioneer, translator, college professor, lobbyist and minority advocate, and educator. After being a cobbler, small-business owner and pastor, Carey was moved by a vision for unreached people in India. He moved his family to India and pioneered in many ways while his wife's mental and physical well-being declined. Carey wasn't just a missionary; he was a crosscultural entrepreneur and tentmaker.

**MILLER, CALVIN,** PROFESSOR ■ *Marketplace Preaching: How to Return the Sermon to Where It Belongs.* Baker, 1995. *188 pages.*
Miller looks at the changing face of church, making valuable suggestions on where it is going and how pastors can help. He makes a plea to pastors and seminary students to prepare sermons relevant to daily life. Quick and easy reading, with practical, implementable suggestions. Though Miller does not go far enough, this provides insight into his sermon preparation.

**MILLER, NORM, WITH H. K. HOSIER,** BUSINESSMAN; WRITER ■ *Beyond the Norm.* Thomas Nelson, 1996. *210 pages.*
Miller rose from route salesman to CEO and chairman of Interstate Battery. Along the way he drank as hard as he worked. For Miller, this is a before-and-after story describing the hard work of getting ahold of himself spiritually. His candor is refreshing. Then he takes us into the inner works of the growth of the company. The third section is focused on lessons of faith in leadership.

**MILLER-MCLEMORE, BONNIE J.,** PROFESSOR ■ *Also a Mother: Work and Family as Theological Dilemma.* Abingdon, 1994. *215 pages.*
Miller-McLemore examines the dilemma facing most women: working outside the home while continuing to carry a heavy load of "caring" tasks centered around that home. She points out that "caring labor" is not without value. Rather, it is the bedrock on which society is built. The dilemma most women face daily is actually a religious crisis for them and their families. The book suggests recasting the church's traditional views in light of the Scriptural values of caring love and work for both women and men.

**MITCHELL, JOHN E.,** MACHINE MANUFACTURER ■ *The Christian in Business.* Revell, 1962. *156 pages.*
"Is God interested in a lathe operator and in the quantity and quality of his output? or a stenographer and the way she types? or a salesman and what he says to a prospect?" Yes, says Mitchell. He details how biblical wisdom guided every aspect of the Mitchell family business for over sixty years. He touches on issues of management, personnel, organization, ethics, bureaucracy, competition and servanthood. Mitchell develops a biblically rich theology of work useful to Christians in any field. A historical perspective from a valuable mentor. Highly recommended.

**MITROFF, IAN I., & ELIZABETH A. DENTON,** CONSULTANTS ■ *A Spiritual Audit of Corporate America.* Jossey-Bass, 1999. *259 pages.*
The book examines the state of spiritual life in corporate America. Perhaps the most surprising discovery is that business managers do not want to dichotomize their lives but are confused about spiritual matters in the workplace. Many business leaders realize the need for a spiritual dimension in the workplace but lack a model to make it a practical (and inoffensive) reality. The authors outline several different models to help managers and CEOs think about workplace spirituality. A must-read for anyone in business leadership.

**MOGIL, CHRISTOPHER, & ANNE SLEPIAN, WITH PETER WOODROW,** WRITERS ■ *We Gave Away a Fortune.* New Society, 1992. *182 pages.*
This book talks about sixteen real-life individuals who have decided to share their wealth. They include well-known people such as Millard Fuller of Habitat for Humanity and Ben Cohen of Ben and Jerry's Homemade Ice Cream. The book is part minibiography, part inspirational testimony and part practical how-to manual. In between the bios, the authors examine topics such as spiritual economics, meaningful work, sharing power and liberating the rich.

**MOLTMANN, JÜRGEN,** THEOLOGIAN ■ *The Power of the Powerless.* SCM Press, 1983. *166 pages.*
In a series of sermons Moltmann addresses the experiences of limitation, bondage and powerlessness that characterize various marginalized groups in the world. He shows that the power of God is not found in worldly systems of authority but in the crucified Christ. To defeat the evils of our time we need the creative and redemptive love of God that forgives, accepts and suffers with us.

**MOORE, SAM, WITH PETE GILCHRIST,** BUSINESS EXECUTIVE; WRITER ■ *American by Choice: An Autobiography by Sam Moore.* Thomas Nelson, 1998. *214 pages.*
This is the tale of a Lebanese immigrant who attended a Christian college, developed a passion to sell and rose to the top of the Christian book and Bible publishing industry. It is a refreshingly open and honest description of someone who has been blessed by America but is not uncritical of its dark sides of racism, greed and politics. He vividly describes family life, immigration stress, schooling in English as a second language, dating and marriage, selling, and growing a small venture into a major corporate system. Sam Moore is passionate about faith, business commitment and success.

**MORGAN, EDMUND S.,** PROFESSOR ■ *The Puritan Dilemma: The Story of John Winthrop.* Scott Foresman, 1962. *224 pages.*
Puritanism faced a problem that affects society today. Morgan asks, "What responsibility does a righteous man owe his society? If society follows a course he considers morally wrong, should he withdraw and keep his principles intact, or should he stay?" Morgan points out that the Puritans were the rebels in English society. They withdrew and established a new society. But ironically, various Puritan visionaries threatened to upset the new society. America faces the dilemma of preserving individual freedom while maintaining social order. Good college text.

**MORLEY, PATRICK,** CONSULTANT ■ *The Man in the Mirror: Solving the 24 Problems Men Face.* Zondervan, 1989. *379 pages.*
Morley divides the twenty-four problems into six basic problem areas: identity, relationship, money, time, temperament and integrity. He devotes one section to each of these areas, examining common problems in such corners of life as church, job, finances, choices, family, friends and thoughts. The book is written in a style that most men will find very accessible and understandable, not touchy-feely or preachy but practical and oriented toward everyday experience. The book is well written, practical and honest.

**MORRIS, CHARLES R.,** WRITER ■ *American Catholic: The Saints and Sinners Who Built America's Most Powerful Church.* Times Books, 1997. *511 pages.*
This is a major work with some very helpful analysis about the history, difficulties and current struggles of American Catholicism. His analysis of the major social, economic and cultural changes that followed the post-World War II years is very helpful for discerning why marketplace faith issues began to crawl back into the psyche of congregants and some institutional gatekeepers of establishment American Catholicism (and mainline and evangelical Protestants). Andrew Greely said, "Morris has written the best one volume history of the last one hundred years of American Catholicism."

**MOTT, JOHN R.,** EVANGELIST, ENTREPRENEUR ■ *Liberating the Lay Forces of Christianity.* Student Christian Movement, 1932. *83 pages.*
Mott was the most influential evangelical Christian of the early twentieth century. His ability to rally the church, and especially Christian youth, was unparalleled. Here he exhorts Christian laity not to underestimate their value as ambassadors for Christ. The layperson's calling is just as important as the minister's or missionary's. Though out of print, it can be found in major U.S. libraries. (See also entry for *John R. Mott* by C. H. Hopkins.)

**MOTT, STEPHEN CHARLES,** PROFESSOR OF ETHICS ■ *Biblical Ethics and Social Change.* Oxford University Press, 1982. *254 pages.*
This book is a scholarly synthesis of biblical studies and ethics. "Emphasizing the importance of change in both individual character and social order, Mott covers such classic ethical subjects as evil, grace, love, and justice, and evaluates methods of achieving social change, including evangelism, the church as counter community, civil disobedience and political reform" (back cover).

**MOUW, RICHARD J.**, SEMINARY PRESIDENT ■ *Called to Holy Worldliness*, Fortress, 1980. *144 pages.*
Mouw brings a biblical piety to this address of the social and corporate dimensions of the church's calling; he neither politicizes the gospel nor ignores its political implications. Mouw attempts to go beyond now-common discussions of clericalism and empowering the whole people of God, although these are not left untouched. He stresses the imperative of relating faith to the structure of the professional work world. But, as Mouw admits, "Those looking for very practical advice will find this book disappointing." Mouw urges laypersons everywhere to work out their own faith in holy worldliness.

*Politics and the Biblical Drama.* Baker, 1976. *139 pages.*
Mouw argues that human government has its basis in creation, not in the Fall. Although perverted by the Fall, God still uses human government to achieve his purposes. Christian involvement in politics should take three forms: (1) proclaiming God's word to the world, (2) serving those who are suffering and (3) changing unjust structures.

**MURPHY, ELSPETH CAMPBELL**, TEACHER ■ *Chalkdust.* Baker, 1979. *63 pages.*
In these prayer poems, "Elspeth Murphy shares her insights on the kinds of pupils that all teachers will recognize: the class clown, the quiet child, the gifted child, the unmotivated child, the handicapped child. Murphy has struggled to come to grips with impatience, helplessness and self-doubt. . . . Anyone who works with children will empathize with the cries for help, the pleas for patience, and the bursts of praise woven throughout this book" (publisher). Delightful, true-to-life meditations every elementary teacher or childcare worker should have.

**MUSSER, JOE**, FILM PRODUCER ■ *The Cereal Tycoon: Henry Parsons Crowell: Founder of Quaker Oats.* Moody Press, 1997. *160 pages.*
This book is about an intense executive who not only loves Christ but acts on it in exceptional ways. Musser chronicles Crowell's tenacious integrity even when corporate competitors vilified him. He rallied Chicago leaders in opposing crime while demonstrating concern for its victims: he helped establish the federal Mann Act. Without fanfare, he stabilized Moody Bible Institute. On the more personal side, we join him in deep grief on the death of his wife.

**MYRA, HAROLD**, CEO, *Christianity Today* ■ *Leaders.* Word, 1987. *208 pages.*
Each chapter of this book is a candid interview with a proven leader who has grappled with issues such as resolving board conflict, motivating apathetic volun-

teers, inspiring organizational unity, making tough decisions and maintaining personal health. In an age lacking in strong, wise and compassionate male role models, this book is valuable simply as a doorway into the lives of fifteen godly men. Interviewees include J. Richard Chase (Wheaton College), Ted Engstrom (World Vision), Mark Hatfield (U.S. Senate) and Richard Halverson (chaplain of the Senate).

**NASH, LAURA,** BUSINESS PROFESSOR, CONSULTANT ■ *Believers in Business.* Thomas Nelson, 1994. *302 pages.*
This is a sociological and philosophical study of sixty-five evangelicals who are in the senior ranks of business. Nash analyzes how believers view and operate within an ethical framework on the job. Nash synthesizes four basic perspectives and presents the reasoning behind each. She advocates following the most integrated approach in an "evangelical portrait" and then shows how such an individual is able to hold absolutes in tension. An excellent presentation of an insightful study.

*Good Intentions Aside: A Manager's Guide to Resolving Ethical Problems.* Harvard Business School Press, 1990. *259 pages.*
Nash proposes a covenantal ethic for managers that emphasizes (1) value creation, (2) profit as a byproduct, not a motive, and (3) relationships (customer, coworker and shareholder). She shows managers how to get back in touch with their commonsense standards of integrity. A text used in business ethics classes, it offers valuable insight into some of the problems in our modern business mentality, which is now creeping into other fields. Not from a religious perspective.

**NASH, RONALD H.,** PROFESSOR ■ *Poverty and Wealth: Why Socialism Doesn't Work.* Probe Books, 1992. *224 pages.*
Nash not only explains the basic flaws in socialism while supporting capitalism but also raises serious issues about certain aspects of American capitalism. For example, Nash sees Social Security as inherently inefficient and perhaps unethical. No study questions accompany the book, but the issues raised in each chapter are more than sufficient as discussion starters.

*Social Justice and the Christian Church.* Mott Media, 1983. *175 pages.*
Nash examines which economic theory is most conducive to social justice. A champion of the free market, he indicts socialism in all forms. Much of the book answers the arguments of political liberals and disentangles capitalism from caricatures. Nash argues that moral problems in a capitalistic society will not be improved

through new economic structures. (For an alternative thesis, see Stephen Mott's *Biblical Ethics and Social Change*.)

**NATIONAL CONFERENCE OF CATHOLIC BISHOPS**, CLERGY ■ *Economic Justice for All*. United States Catholic Conference, 1986. *192 pages*.

This often-quoted pastoral letter sprang out of a concern "to lift up the human and ethical dimensions of economic life." It stresses the roles of family, church and community, and the United States' obligation to the world's poor. The book discusses labor and unemployment, food and agriculture, domestic education, and international trade. According to the bishops, "Every economic decision and institution must be judged in light of whether it protects or undermines the dignity of the human person." (For a rebuttal, see the Lay Commission on Social Teaching, *Liberty and Justice for All*.)

**NEILL, STEPHEN, & HANS-RUEDI WEBER, EDS.**, CHURCH EXECUTIVES ■ *The Layman in Christian History.* Westminster Press, 1963. *394 pages*.

This collection of essays by fifteen different scholars covers the life of the lay person from the early church up to the twentieth century, and includes two chapters on the perspective from Orthodoxy and Roman Catholicism. A very valuable and unique resource.

**NELSON, JOHN OLIVER, ED.**, PROFESSOR ■ *Work and Vocation: A Christian Discussion*. Harper & Brothers, 1954. *224 pages*.

A scholarly and readable attempt to put work and vocation into Christian perspective. Although somewhat dated, the issues dealt with are still relevant. Arising from concerns of the first assembly of the World Council of Churches, this book is a collection of essays that look at work and vocation in the Bible, history and contemporary society.

**NEWBIGIN, LESSLIE,** MISSIONARY, CLERGY ■ *Foolishness to the Greeks: The Gospel and Western Culture*. Eerdmans, 1986. *156 pages*.

Newbigin asks, "What would it mean to confront Western culture with the gospel?" First, he identifies the secular rationale that undergirds Western scientific, political and economic thought. Then he concludes that the "wider rationale" embodied in Christianity explains Western culture better than Western culture can explain itself. This leads to the main thrust of the book—how biblical authority can be a reality for those shaped by the West. Finally, he encourages the church in the West to testify shamelessly to the all-embracing message of the Scriptures. For the thoughtful reader.

*Honest Religion for Secular Man.* Westminster Press, 1966. *159 pages.*
Newbigin sought to alert the church to what we now call globalization and its associated secularism. He was concerned about the silence or even absence of the church in this vacuum of faith. He declared, "The church must be where men are, speak the language they speak, inhabit the worlds they inhabit. This is the simplest of missionary principles. . . . But these missionary efforts have, until recently, left untouched the position of the local congregation as the definitive form of the church, the place where the word is preached, the sacraments dispensed and godly discipline administered" (p. 112). Here we have a well-informed world leader calling for a recovery of the church's mission through the life and work of every believer.

**NIEBUHR, H. RICHARD,** PROFESSOR ■ *Christ and Culture.* Harper & Row, 1951. *256 pages.*
This book discusses the five most typical answers to the problem of Christ and culture. These are "Christ against culture," "the Christ of culture," "Christ above culture," "Christ and culture in paradox," and "Christ the transformer of culture." Niebuhr concludes each section by raising the traditional objections to each view.

**NIX, WILLIAM,** BANKER ■ *Transforming Your Workplace for Christ.* Broadman & Holman, 1997. *212 pages.*
Nix starts out with ten basic values that Christians can bring into their workplace, including forgiveness, accountability, communication, promise-keeping and integrity. He points out how they make a positive impact on the workplace and how Christians can model them in very practical ways. Nix also delineates five ways to make Christ an everyday presence in the workplace: prayer, evaluation of needs, evaluation of the workforce, gathering resources and taking a stand. He uses real-life examples to illustrate his points. He talks clearly about what is appropriate insofar as witnessing goes in the work setting. A helpful how-to book.

**NOLL, MARK A., NATHAN O. HATCH, & GEORGE M. MARSDEN,** PROFESSORS ■ *The Search for Christian America.* Crossway, 1983. *188 pages.*
Is America a Christian nation? These scholars carefully engage this popular notion. In probing the American Revolution, they state, "[It] was not Christian, but it stood for many things compatible with the Christian faith. It was not biblical, though many of its leaders respected Scripture. It did not establish the United States on a Christian foundation, even if it created many commendable precedents" (p. 100). The book is based on the principle that no nation, including America, can rightly claim to be "New Israel." The book helpfully fills the gap between personal piety

and nationalism with reason, good scholarship and helpful analysis. Excellent resources throughout.

**NOUWEN, HENRI J. M.,** PRIEST ■ *Creative Ministry.* Image, 1971. *123 pages.*
Nouwen writes about "the relationship between professionalism and spirituality in the ministry." Specifically he looks at the areas of teaching, preaching, pastoral care, organizing and celebrating, and suggests a new approach to each that flows out of spirituality. Ministry and spirituality must never be separated, because ministry is "a way of life, which is for others to see and understand."

*Making All Things New:An Invitation to the Spiritual Life.* Harper & Row, 1981. *95 pages.*
"The spiritual life is not a life before, after, or beyond our everyday existence," writes Nouwen in this brief description of the spiritual life. Nouwen focuses on the Spirit's work in us to replace our "worry-filled existence" with a single commitment to putting God's kingdom first. He introduces the two disciplines of solitude and community as fundamental for the spiritual life.

*The Wounded Healer: Ministry in Contemporary Society.* Image, 1972. *100 pages.*
Nouwen examines the modern condition and draws out implications for pastoral ministry. He suggests the only way to reach despair-filled and suffering people with the hope of the gospel is to risk exposing one's self as a suffering person who knows how to make wounds the source of healing.

**NOVAK, MICHAEL,** THEOLOGIAN, AMBASSADOR ■ *Business as a Calling: Work and the Examined Life.* Free Press, 1996. *237 pages.*
Novak outlines the inherent values of business and issues a call to business for the common good. "Business is a profession worthy of a person's highest ideals, and aspirations, fraught with moral possibilities of both great good and great evil. . . . Our work connects people with one another. It also makes possible the universal advance out of poverty, and it is an essential prerequisite of democracy and the institutions of a civil society." One of the best treatments from a theological and ethical perspective to date.

*Toward a Theology of the Corporation.* American Enterprise Institute, 1981. *57 pages.*
In chapter one Novak focuses "on what the reality of corporations teaches us about

the nature of a free society. After [defining] corporate activity . . . Novak describes the political and moral-cultural systems on which corporations depend. He shows that the corporation has goals and requirements beyond those of the economic system alone." In chapter two "Novak traces the moral and religious values upon which viable corporations depend: cooperation, creativity, liberty, social service, insight, and risk. He argues that corporate life is related to high moral-cultural ideals, in the light of which the conduct of corporations may be held to scrupulous account" (back cover). (See also chapters one and two in "The Judeo-Christian Vision and the Modern Business Corp." Notre Dame,1981.)

**O'COLLINS, GERALD,** THEOLOGIAN ■ *The Theology of Secularity.* Fides, 1974. *90 pages.*
Are humans gradually losing their religious sense? "Is there any relationship between the Jewish-Christian belief in creation and the scientific advancement in the modern world? In answering these [and other] questions, O'Collins challenges many theses popularized by Harvey Cox and others. He bases his 'Theology of Secularity' on Christ's death and resurrection, and connects it to the themes developed in Jürgen Moltmann's 'Theology of Hope.' He sees the implications that a healthy view of secularity holds for the liturgy, Church government, ordination of women, Christian ethics and secular mission of the Church" (back cover). A sophisticated approach to an important but abstract topic.

**O'CONNELL, MARVIN,** PROFESSOR ■ *Blaise Pascal: Reasons of the Heart.* Eerdmans, 1997. *210 pages.*
This is a careful and enlightening biography of a famous French inventor. Pascal was a scientific prodigy that came to a vital personal faith during times when there were great hostilities toward it. Many marketplace Christians have been inspired by his life and work.

**O'CONNOR, ELIZABETH,** WRITER ■ *Eighth Day of Creation: Gifts and Creativity.* Word, 1971. *111 pages.*
Sharing much of her experience at the Church of the Savior in Washington, D.C., O'Connor emphasizes gift recognition for all Christians. The role of the Christian community is listening, confirming the gifts of people and providing a nonthreatening atmosphere where the gifts can be exercised. Only then can creativity take place. Exercises are included.

**OECHSLIN, R. L.** ■ *The Spirituality of the Layman.* Desclee, 1964. *140 pages.*
Oechslin develops a lay spirituality. His method is threefold: (1) to determine the

proper tasks of the layperson, (2) to determine the conditions of life in the world and (3) to determine how laypeople can use the means of grace at their disposal.

**OGDEN, GREG,** PASTOR, PROFESSOR ■ *The New Reformation: Returning the Ministry to the People of God.* Zondervan, 1990. *224 pages.*
Ogden discusses the foundations of the purpose and mission of the church: empowering the body of Christ for ministry. He models how churches become equipping bodies that emphasize a down-to-earth approach to clergy-laity team ministry. Great resource for pastors and other church leaders.

**OLASKY, MARVIN,** JOURNALIST, PROFESSOR ■ *Renewing America's Compassion.* Regnery, 1997. *208 pages.*
Olasky argues that government has no obligation to be caretaker of the poor but that business, charities and the church do. He uses examples of organizations having an impact on individual lives. Olasky argues in an intelligent fashion and engages the reader as he reviews generally accepted principles of our society. He indicts the citizens, corporations, government agencies and the church. (For another perspective, see entries for Ron Sider.)

**OLDHAM, J. H.,** CHURCH EXECUTIVE ■ *Work in Modern Society.* SCM Press, 1950. *50 pages.*
Oldham's booklet probably is the first formal theology of work. Believing that modernity is "one of the great turning points of history," he is concerned that science and technology have so influenced society that people think of themselves as objects. Rather than examining the biblical doctrine of work, we should commence with the Christian understanding of humanity and what it means to be a person in relation to God, other people and the world. Oldham pleads for a lay-developed doctrine of work that will enable the majority of people to experience a genuine vocation to do ordinary kinds of work.

**ORTEGA, BOB,** REPORTER ■ *In Sam We Trust: The Untold Story of Sam Walton and How Wal-Mart Is Devouring America.* Random House, 1998. *413 pages.*
This is a classic case of the American dream being a biblical nightmare. Walton viewed himself as a good Christian, but evidence that his faith affected his work is missing. Ortega's documentation of unethical corporate practices is well done. He also provides a helpful historical overview of America's economy, lifestyle and retailing. This is very good social and spiritual commentary on America's self-absorption and comfort rooted in deep spiritual emptiness.

**OSWALT, JOHN,** PROFESSOR ■ *The Leisure Crisis.* Victor, 1987. *167 pages.*
Oswalt asks, "If for the first time in history we don't have to work sixty or more hours a week to supply our basic necessities, why do we feel so frantically busy? Why do we feel guilty when we allow ourselves to relax? How should a Christian fill his or her non-working hours? . . . Seeking diversions to escape boredom or finding ways to become more truly human, more deeply Christian?" Oswalt theorizes about God's view of work and leisure. He attempts to sort cultural from the biblical views of leisure.

**OWEN, FREDERICK G.,** PROFESSOR ■ *Abraham Lincoln: The Man & His Faith.* Tyndale House, 1987. *232 pages.*
This book is short enough for busy folks to digest, and unlike many biographies of Lincoln it deals with his faith. His faith came alive under the pressures of leading a nation in crisis. Owen examines Lincoln's "Ten Guidelines," which include reflections on thrift, balance of rights, class and responsibility. The book overlooks Lincoln's weaknesses and errors but is a good contribution and enjoyable read.

**OWENS, SHERWOOD, III,** PARISH WORKER ■ *All Our Works Begun: Reflections on Being a Working Parent.* Living the Good News, 1998. *117 pages.*
This is a collection of real-life observations about the challenge of living reflectively as a Christian. Each page includes an insight about daily work or family life. Owens poses questions that probe below the surface of superficial living. He demonstrates his commitment to love, patience, humor, quality relationships and serenity that God offers.

**OWENSBY, WALTER L.,** PASTOR, DENOMINATIONAL LEADER ■ *Economics for Prophets: A Primer on Concepts, Realities, and Values in Our Economic System.* Eerdmans, 1988. *201 pages.*
Owensby explains basic economic concepts and identifies moral and biblical dimensions to help Christians better understand what their faith has to say about workplace life. Maybe now more than ever we need a reminder that *profits* and *prophets* often are incompatible.

**PALMER, PARKER,** EDUCATOR ■ *The Active Life: A Spirituality of Work, Creativity and Caring.* Jossey-Bass, 1990. *162 pages.*
Palmer spent three years in a contemplative community, and determined, "I'm not a monk but an activist." Seeing prayer as energizing and work as draining is wrong. For Palmer it is just the opposite. Nevertheless, the active life has a dark side: the illusion that we make life happen, rather than receive it from God. Palmer's work is timeless.

*Let Your Life Speak: Listening for the Voice of Vocation.* Jossey-Bass, 2000.
*117 pages.*
In this book Palmer helps people discover their truest calling. Discerning your call involves getting beneath the events, crises and experiences of life to grasp what really motivates you. Then those motives are matched with world needs. This treatment of career decision making is rooted in Palmer's Quaker beliefs as he states, "We listen for guidance everywhere except from within" (p. 5), and adds, "We arrive in this world with birthright gifts—then we spend half our lives abandoning them or letting others disabuse us of them" (p. 12). Palmer provides insight into the God-created motivational grid each person possesses.

**PARENT, RÉMI,** THEOLOGIAN ■*A Church of the Baptized: Overcoming Tension Between the Clergy and the Laity.* Paulist Press, 1989. *213 pages.*
Parent takes a careful and critical look at the structure and beliefs of the Roman Catholic Church and concludes, "our images of God, Christ, Church, priesthood and the Mass have rendered the laity passive and the world profane."

**PASCARELLA, PERRY,** PUBLISHING EXECUTIVE ■ *Christ-Centered Leadership: Thriving in Business by Putting God in Charge.* Primal, 1999. *288 pages.*
Pascarella studies Christian business leaders and highlights successful principles. He doesn't promote a health and wealth gospel. Rather, he identifies how Jesus Christ transforms people from self-focused success hounds to "great commandment, great commission" leaders. A very useful blueprint for managers and would-be managers in the workplace.

*The Ten Commandments of the Workplace and How to Break Them Every Day.*
Zondervan, 1996. *144 pages.*
After years as a business executive, Pascarella uses his insight and wit to connect deep faith and tough weekday realities. He addresses topics like passive submission to the management, wanting to be liked, executive detachment or superiority, the apparent absence of God at work, and hiding faith on the job. He builds his work around the Ten Commandments, connecting them with daily life. Each chapter ends with some practical suggestions for action.

**PATON, DAVID, ED.** ■ *The Ministry of the Spirit: Selected Writings of Roland Allen.* World Dominion, 1960. *197 pages.*
A selection of writings by mission pioneer and creative thinker Roland Allen, designed to accompany his works on missionary methods. (See entries under Roland Allen.)

**PATON, DAVID, & CHARLES H. LONG, EDS.** ■ *The Compulsion of the Spirit: A Roland Allen Reader.* Eerdmans, 1983. *147 pages.*
A collection of readings from four of Roland Allen's books dealing with missionary practices of the church. Though not popular in his own day, today Allen's criticism of church structures and his promotion of voluntary clergy are being listened to.

**PATTERSON, BEN,** PASTOR, COLLEGE CHAPLAIN ■ *The Grand Essentials.* Word, 1987. *154 pages.* Reissued as *Serving God.* InterVarsity Press, 1994. *178 pages.*
In this book Patterson examines work, worship and hope. He believes work is a blessing and vocation, not a curse, and he explains why. Then Patterson outlines the difference between work and vocation. While most people have many jobs, they have one vocation. This book doesn't break any new ground, but it is well-written and thoughtfully presented.

**PAWLIKOWSKI, JOHN T., & DAVID M. BYERS,** PRIEST, PROFESSOR; WRITER ■ *Justice in the Marketplace.* United States Catholic Conference, 1985. *521 pages.*
This collection of Vatican and U.S. Catholic Bishops' statements on economic policy includes Pope Leo XIII's *On the Condition of Workers* (1890) and the U.S. Catholic Bishops' twelve major statements on economic justice made between 1919 and 1975.

**PEABODY, LARRY,** PASTOR ■ *Secular Work Is Full-Time Service.* Christian Literature Crusade, 1974. *142 pages.*
"This book has an important message for the believer who feels that he is sentenced to being a second-class citizen in the kingdom of God simply because he finds his daily calling in the secular world. . . . It is transforming to discover that the secular is sacred when God puts it into your hand, and that in working for that demanding earthly employer one is serving the Lord Christ" (foreword). Peabody consciously made Scripture, not personal anecdotes and experiences, his reference point. A study guide is available.

**PEARCE, JOSEPH,** RESEARCHER ■ *Wisdom and Innocence: The Life of G. K. Chesterton.* Ignatius Press, 1996. *522 pages.*
Born of wealth, education and privilege, Chesterton excelled as a cultural critic, author and newspaper editor. This readable biography offers many insights into this gifted Christian man and his relationship with his devoted and cherished wife.

**PECK, GEORGE, & JOHN S. HOFFMAN**, EDS., PROFESSOR; RESEARCHER, ADMINISTRATOR ■ *The Laity in Ministry: The Whole People of God for the Whole World.* Judson Press, 1984. *171 pages.*

A valuable collection of essays by laypeople and theologians concerned with helping men and women fulfill their ministry in the workplace. The authors deal with both practical situations and theological questions. Serious thought is also given to the implications for the church if lay ministry is to become a reality.

**PEEL, DONALD** ■ *The Ministry of the Laity: Sharing the Leadership, Sharing the Task.* Anglican Book Centre, 1991. *158 pages.*

Peel aims to meet the needs of church cell groups by giving them step-by-step guidance to group relationships. "People need to know *how* to express their Christian love in concrete and effective ways within the faith community" (p. 8). First Peel details the nature of lay ministry (e.g., theology, biblical data, nature of Christian leadership, varieties of volunteer ministry), then he provides basic training for group development, planning and leadership.

**PERRY, JOHN**, WRITER ■ *Unshakable Faith: Booker T. Washington & George Washington Carver.* Multnomah Press, 1999. *387 pages.*

Here are biographical profiles of two Christian African American men who suffered from slavery's manifold abuses and were inextricably bound together in the launching of Tuskegee Institute in the late 1800s. Washington, founder of Tuskegee, recruited Carver to join him in its early days. Launching an educational institution for poor blacks in rural Alabama that challenged them daily, they broke racial and economic stereotypes, served a disenfranchised people, raised money from Northerners, grew the food needed by the school and tested each other's attitudes. Perry writes with compassion without hiding the rough edges of each man's personality and genius.

**PETERSON, EUGENE**, PROFESSOR ■ *Leap over a Wall: Earthly Spirituality for Everyday Christians.* HarperCollins, 1997. *238 pages.*

This veteran pastor and professor, a lifelong student of Scripture and daily life, walks us through the life of Israel's greatest leader, King David. Peterson empowers us to better do the hard work of worshiping God in all that we do and say. Peterson doesn't force good theology down our throats but rather connects it with the routines of family, community and workplace. Get this volume for your pastor.

**PHILIPS, FREDERIK,** INDUSTRIALIST ■ *45 Years with Philips:An Industrialist's Life.* Blanford Press, 1976. *280 pages.*
Philips recounts the story of a small light bulb company becoming a multinational corporation. He also invites the reader into his personal journey into faith and its application to business, including the struggles of his Dutch company to survive Nazism and his own experience in concentration camps. We also hear about labor and management relations, take-overs and relating his company to various nations. This is a good contribution to the development of faith among lay leaders.

**PHIPPS, SIMON,** CHAPLAIN ■ *God on Monday.* Hodder & Stoughton, 1966. *192 pages.*
Based on his eight years of experience as industrial chaplain, Phipps develops a "secular-based theology" instead of a "church-based theology." For Phipps, the secular world is the arena of dialogue with God. He wrestles with the loss of relevance by the church of the mid-twentieth century in the industrial world. Phipps sees God at work in the processes of industry, technology and wealth creation. Though dated, this book could help today's clergy develop a biblically driven ministry to everyday workers.

**PIEPER, JOSEF** ■ *Leisure: The Basis of Culture.* Faber & Faber, London, 1952.
At the time this book was written, work increasingly was being displaced by leisure. Many theologians opposed the "problem of leisure" via the divine requirement for work. Pieper maintains that leisure, not labor, is the basis of the Western cultural tradition. Leisure implies inner calm and celebration, according to Pieper. We need to reinstate divine worship at the center of leisure. More philosophical than theological, *Leisure* has influenced subsequent theologies of work, especially those seeking to resist and critique cocreationism.

**PIERCE, GREGORY F. AUGUSTINE,** PUBLISHER ■ *Activism That Makes Sense.* ACTA, 1984. *148 pages.*
"Pierce's book is a street-wise explanation of the principles of community organization as they apply to church and synagogue. . . . Pierce argues that no progressive change can be negotiated without power and that power is obtained only through organization. Pierce tenders a multitude of entertaining stories, many from his own life as an organizer, in support of these propositions" (C. DiSalvo, *America* Magazine). Ecumenical, biblical and well written.

*Beyond the Balance Sheet: The Integration of Work, Personal and Family Life.* ACTA, 1994. *39 pages.*
This is a very good introduction to a Catholic perspective on lay ministry and con-

necting work with "family values." The booklet integrates personal anecdotes, Catholic teaching and contemporary cultural context. Written mostly from a management perspective, this booklet is a useful introductory presentation on an ethic for all of life.

*The Buck Stops Here: Perspectives on Christian Stewardship from Business and Professional Managers.* ACTA, 1992. *27 pages.*
This stimulating booklet is a position paper on the stewardship of (1) people, (2) products and services, (3) community, (4) environment, and (5) the social fabric. Raising more questions than answers, the booklet offers broad nontraditional principles of stewardship from a business perspective.

*Spirituality@Work: 10 Ways to Balance Your Life On-the-Job.* Loyola Press, 2001. *168 pages.*
In this handbook, Pierce suggests that human work is a reflection of God's own good work. He covers topics such as congratulating coworkers, thanking others, realizing that imperfection is part of being human and building community at work. He asks questions that help readers make decisions about work, including How much money is enough? When do you say no to additional responsibility? and How can you make your work area a spiritual space?

**PIERCE, GREGORY F. AUGUSTINE, ED.,** PUBLISHER ■ *Of Human Hands: A Reader in the Spirituality of Work.* ACTA, 1989. *124 pages.*
Eighteen essays are grouped into three sections: "What Is the Spirituality of Work?" "What Is the Spirituality of My Work?" and "How Can the Church Support the Spirituality of My Work?" Section two, in particular, contains honest accounts of the difficulties of those seeking to follow Jesus in their workplaces.

**PIKE, THOMAS, & WILLIAM PROCTOR,** COUNSELOR, PRIEST; WRITER ■ *Is It Success or Is It Addiction?* Thomas Nelson, 1988. *222 pages.*
Sacrificing everything for the company in order to beat the competition is euphemistic language for selling your soul to the American success cult, say Pike and Proctor. They unmask the doctrines, rituals and lifestyle of the secular gospel of success. Citing cases from pastoral and counseling experience, they expose the hazards of upward mobility and define success from a biblical perspective. Razor-sharp on Christian truth and refreshingly free of Christian lingo, this well-written hardback remains compelling throughout.

**PIPPERT, WESLEY,** JOURNALIST, PROFESSOR ■ *Faith at the Top.* Cook, 1973. *187 pages.*
This book is a collection of interviews with ten well-known Christian men and women from the fields of diplomacy, politics, sports, television, the army, the Secret Service and one of America's most powerful church organizations. Besides influence, writes Pippert, "all that [they] have in common is belief in Jesus Christ. . . . They are as different in point of view, vocation, style, and mode of worship as night and day." Interviewees tell how the Christian faith has made a difference in their work.

**PITTENGER, NORMAN** ■ *The Ministry of all Christians: A Theology of Lay Ministry.* Morehouse-Barlow, 1983. *88 pages.*
Pittenger provides a definition of ministry applicable to all Christians, not just the ordained. He argues that ministry should be seen functionally rather than in terms of status. This ministry extends to every man and woman and child.

**POLLARD, C. WILLIAM,** COMPANY CHAIRMAN ■ *The Soul of the Firm.* HarperCollins, 1996. *176 pages.*
This is the inspiring story of the ServiceMaster Company and its employees. Bill Pollard helps us rethink the mission of American business. ServiceMaster is an example of how God can bless and use a company's employees when they follow biblical principles. A quick worthwhile read with interesting stories and anecdotes.

**POUNTNEY, MICHAEL,** RECTOR ■ *Getting a Job: A Guide for Choosing a Career.* InterVarsity Press, 1984. *161 pages.*
Based on the experiences of university students' searches for employment after graduation, this book helps Christians in a similar predicament. In a popular and witty style, Pountney offers sound advice to relieve the anxiety of those searching for a job.

**PULLEY, MARY LYNN,** BUSINESS CONSULTANT ■ *Losing Your Job— Reclaiming Your Soul.* Jossey-Bass, 1997. *239 pages.*
Pulley interviewed dozens of professionals who found themselves in career-change mode. The result is a book about the transformation that can come through career transitions. Pulley shows job seekers that they can learn valuable, enduring lessons on the way. Though not from a Christian perspective, this is a refreshing, approachable and hopeful book. Not a how-to manual.

**RADEMACHER, WILLIAM J.,** PROFESSOR ■ *Lay Ministry:A Theological, Spiritual, and Pastoral Handbook.* Crossroad, 1991. *274 pages.*
The author establishes a historical, biblical and theological understanding of vocation and ministry, particularly in the Roman Catholic Church. "Twenty-five years after Vatican II the church is still not praying publicly for vocations . . . to the common priesthood of the faithful" (p. 25). Chapters included are "Ministering in a Sinful Church," "The Ministry of Women" and "Finding Your Work and Your Place in the Vineyard."

**RAINES, JOHN C., & DONNA C. DAY-LOWER,** PROFESSORS ■ *Modern Work and Human Meaning.* Westminster Press, 1986. *150 pages.*
The authors conducted interviews with the underemployed in the working-class neighborhoods of Philadelphia, Boston and Johnstown. They address work and human meaning. Topics include social class domination, blue-collar blues, lost community values, American public philosophy and its emphasis on individual success and self-reliance, and the dehumanizing effects of "bad" work.

**REARDON, PATRICK T.,** NEWSPAPER REPORTER ■ *Daily Meditations (with Scripture) for Busy Dads.* ACTA, 1995. *365 pages.*
Here is a one-minute reflection for every day of a year. Each entry is a thoughtful look at a Scripture text connected to daily routines of work, family and citizenship. This well-written book works for Catholics and Protestants.

**REDEKOP, CALVIN W., & BENJAMIN W. REDEKOP,** PROFESSORS ■ *Entrepreneurs in the Faith Community: Profiles of Mennonites in Business.* Herald, 1996. *268 pages.*
The Redekops share the stories of eleven successful Mennonite entrepreneurs who struggled to harmonize the demands of business with the faith and norms of the Mennonite church.

**REDEKOP, CALVIN, STEPHEN AINLAY, & ROBERT SEIMENS,** PROFESSORS ■ *Mennonite Entrepreneurs.* Johns Hopkins University Press, 1995. *291 pages.*
The Mennonite community typically understands "calling" within the context of their tight-knit faith network and frowns on excess. This is a fascinating glimpse into the community pressures that successful Mennonite entrepreneurs face. This readable sociological study will challenge the reader's theology of work and basic assumptions about community.

**REDEKOP, CALVIN, & URIE A. BENDER,** PROFESSOR; COMMUNICATIONS
CONSULTANT ■ *Who Am I? What Am I? Searching for Meaning in Your Work.*
Zondervan, 1988. *316 pages.*
In terms of research, this may be the most comprehensive one-volume Christian
analysis of work. The authors have carefully integrated diverse historical, cultural
and sociological factors affecting the modern search for meaningful work. Topics
include the evolution of work, theologies of work, the organization, alienation,
work as commodity, professionalism, specialization, male-female roles, midlife crisis, unemployment and kingdom conflicts. These themes are followed by seven
essays from workers. The authors provide an excellent book list. Advanced reading.

**RICHARDS, LAWRENCE O., & CLYDE HOELDTKE,** CHRISTIAN
EDUCATOR; CHURCH LEADER ■ *A Theology of Church Leadership.* Zondervan,
1980. *399 pages.*
The authors picture the church as a living organism—as opposed to an institution—
with Jesus Christ as its active and ruling head—as opposed to a figurehead. From
this they develop a picture of the Christian leader as one who serves by teaching
and example, and who is a catalyst for the development of relationships within the
church.

**RICHARDS, LAWRENCE O., & GIB MARTIN,** CHRISTIAN EDUCATOR;
PASTOR ■ *A Theology of Personal Ministry: Spiritual Giftedness in the Local
Church.* Zondervan, 1981. *302 pages.*
An impressive theology of the laity. The authors first define the identity of the
Christian and then derive practical implications. Much of the second section sug-
gests how church leaders can equip the laity for ministry.

**RICHARDSON, ALAN,** PROFESSOR ■ *The Biblical Doctrine of Work.* SCM Press,
1952. *78 pages.*
Not strictly a theology of work, this book does not view work as human creativity
but as a divine ordinance. "When a man turns to Christ in repentance, and faith, his
whole life is sanctified, including his life as a worker. What had formerly been done
as sheer necessity, or perhaps, out of a sense of duty, or even as a means of self-
expression and fulfillment, is now done 'unto the Lord,' and becomes joyous and
free service and the source of deep satisfaction." Richardson warns, "Our secular
occupations are to be regarded not as ends in themselves but as means to the service of the Kingdom of God."

**RILEY, LAURA SABIN,** FORMER CORPORATE MANAGER, NOW STAY-AT-HOME MOM ■ *All Mothers Are Working Mothers.* Horizon, 1999. *Unnumbered pages.*

After a disappointing search for biblical materials for full-time mothers, Riley wrote a "devotional book for stay-at-home moms and those who would like to be" (cover). Each month focuses on a different theme, like "The Job Description," "On-the-job Networking," "Performance Reviews" and "The Boss." Each day has a Scripture text, a reflection and a brief prayer. This book has good insights about parenting, nurturing and managing a home. Not recommended for mothers working outside the home.

**RINGWALD, CHRISTOPHER,** JOURNALIST ■ *Faith in Words: Ten Writers Reflect on the Spirituality of Their Profession.* ACTA, 1997. *152 pages.*

Can writers, editors and reporters incorporate religious convictions into their professions? Absolutely, say the ten practitioners who contributed to this book. They are less interested in sneaking the gospel onto the news pages than in showing how a Christian outlook actually affects daily tasks.

**RITCHIE, MARK A.,** BUSINESS OWNER ■ *God in the Pits: Confessions of a Commodities Trader.* Macmillan, 1989. *271 pages.*

Ritchie recalls the long trail that he took to become a successful commodities trader. He recounts seven years of scrimping to get through college, a conscience-bending commodities career, job-induced marriage trials and sanctuary provisions for Cambodian refugees in the Ritchies' home. Throughout this well-written book, Ritchie wears his heart on his sleeve and unabashedly raises tough questions about ethics, purpose and truth. Highly recommended reading. (See also B. Joseph Leininger.)

**ROBINSON, J. A. T.,** ED., BISHOP ■ *Layman's Church.* Lutterworth, 1963. *99 pages.*

This book is a collection of addresses given at a weekend lay conference in London. There is equal representation by both clergy and laity, covering topics such as the ministry of the laity, relationships between laity and clergy, and training of the laity.

*The New Reformation?* SCM Press, 1965. *105 pages.*

Here Bishop Robinson outlines the path that he sees Christianity must take if it is to be relevant in the twentieth century. In the third chapter he calls for theology to move from the seminary to the world, for this is where God's people meet the most difficult questions and challenges.

**RODIN, R. SCOTT,** PROFESSOR ■ *Stewards in the Kingdom: A Theology of Life in All Its Fullness.* InterVarsity Press, 2000. 224 pages.
Rejecting the sacred-secular dualism of our time, Rodin asserts that God must inhabit and make an impact on all areas of life, not just our finances. He examines the philosophies that influence modern thought and then looks at Scripture's presentation of stewardship as all-encompassing. Rodin challenges believers to change their viewpoint, noting that they must align themselves with God in order to be effective stewards. He concludes with a theology of Christian fundraising.

**ROOKMAAKER, H. R.,** PROFESSOR ■ *Modern Art and the Death of a Culture.* InterVarsity Press, 1970. 256 pages.
Rookmaaker offers a history of art and the emergence of modern art as a commentary on culture. His critique is based on his commitment to a Christian worldview, a love of art and the desire to help people understand art. His final chapter focuses on how to live as a believer in a broken world.

**ROSNER, BRIAN,** PROFESSOR ■ *How to Get Really Rich: A Sharp Look at the Religion of Greed.* Inter-Varsity Press, 1999, *156 pages.*
Despite being an academic, Rosner writes in a clear and passionate style accessible to anyone. He believes greed is idolatry. Not only does he unmask greed and idolatry, but he also examines the personal and spiritual ramifications, and offers an antidote: contentment and recognition of our true riches in Christ. There is a whiff of zealotry about this book that can be off-putting for those not thoroughly convinced by all he says.

**ROSSI, SANNA BARLOW,** MISSIONARY ■ *Anthony T. Rossi: Christian and Entrepreneur: The Story of the Founder of Tropicana.* Inter-Varsity Press, 1986. *200 pages.*
Anthony Rossi's business success was born of entrepreneurial instinct and Christian faith. His wife tells how this Italian immigrant with no formal education became the founder of Tropicana Products. Here is a very personal look into the challenges an immigrant faces. A quick read.

**ROWE, DAVID JOHNSON,** PASTOR ■ *Faith at Work: A Celebration of All We Do.* Smyth & Helwys, 1994. *114 pages.*
Rowe wrote this book as "a spiritual rationale for considering every effort we make, paid or volunteer, as a fitting and proper offering to God." Rowe's storytelling and his portrayal of Jesus as a worker are valuable. That Rowe considers his "best

work" coaching his son's baseball team is revealing. Rowe includes a few unique experiences from his international travels.

**ROWTHORN, ANNE,** PROFESSOR ■ *The Liberation of the Laity.* Morehouse-Barlow, 1986. *141 pages.*
Seeing the laity as the "prime ministers" in the church, Rowthorn calls for a liberation of the laity from the bondage of the clerical system that has until now suppressed their gifts for ministry. She draws an analogy between this and the call many South American theologians are making for the liberation of the poor. Her emphasis on the need for models of lay spirituality is a helpful addition to the discussion of lay theology.

**ROXBURGH, ALAN J.,** PASTOR ■ *The Missionary Congregation, Leadership & Liminality.* Trinity Press, 1997. *71 pages.*
This piece comes from the Gospel & Our Culture Network, based on the thought of Lesslie Newbigin and developing new forms of being Christ's people in mission. Roxburgh is thoughtful and analytical. He understands postmodern roots and dynamics and does not avoid the painful realities. His discussion of "liminality" is heavy but deserves careful reading. He concludes with portraits of what a pastor needs to be: poet, prophet and apostle.

**RUDY, DORIS,** EDUCATOR, COMMUNITY LEADER ■ *Worship & Daily Life: A Resource for Worship Planners.* Discipleship Resources-UMC, 1999. *112 pages.*
Rudy teamed up with United Methodist leaders to produce a collection of worship helps that take the daily life of congregations seriously. It includes a wide variety of prayers, readings, music, dedication liturgies and seasonal helps. Buy a copy for your pastor and worship leader.

**RUDY, JOHN H.,** MANAGER ■ *Money Wise Meditations.* Herald, 1989. *160 pages.*
Rudy wants to help people move beyond the seduction, self-indulgence and addiction that often comes with money. He declares, "We need a stewardship revival . . . when we bring our money . . . under the rule and reign of God." Each of the hundred or so meditations is about a page long. Topics range from money acquisition to fair wages, giving and estate planning.

**RUSH, MYRON,** BUSINESS EXECUTIVE ■ *Lord of the Marketplace.* Victor, 1986. *192 pages.*
Rush presents the Bible as the only true guide for matters of ethics and motivation.

He writes, "once I discovered that biblical principles worked, I wanted to implement them so my business would be more profitable." But he found that this approach was pharisaic and a cheap use of God. Rush provides no pat answers; instead he tells true stories of absolute loyalty to and love for God as "senior business partner." The book includes questions for personal application.

**RUSSELL, JIM,** BUSINESS EXECUTIVE ■ *Awakening the Giant: Mobilizing and Equipping Christians to Reclaim Our Nation in This Generation.* Zondervan, 1996. *175 pages.*
Claiming that the church has successfully evangelized the current generation, Russell points out the failure to do the harder work of discipling them. This book is heavy on analysis but weak on implementing a solution. Writing from the perspective of a media insider, Russell's insight into how to disciple those around us is inspiring. Includes good suggestions on how to use the media.

**RYKEN, LELAND,** PROFESSOR ■ *Redeeming the Time: A Christian Approach to Work and Leisure.* Baker, 1995. *301 pages.*
A systematic and academic presentation of the theology of time, work and leisure, this book examines time, work and leisure from biblical, pragmatic, theological and historical perspectives. This is perhaps the best and most integrated approach to daily life to date. Not only does Ryken analyze the problem, but he lays down some very practical ways to conform our views to a consistent Christian approach. Highly recommended.

*Work and Leisure in Christian Perspective.* **Multnomah Press, 1987.** *255 pages.*
Ryken encourages us to reapply the essence of the Protestant and Puritan understandings of work to contemporary experience. His theology of work is built around five themes—human work as cooperation with God, work as a curse, the sanctity of daily work, work as a calling and work as stewardship. Progress in faith and holiness is more important than advancing in our career. Ryken also argues that work and leisure belong together. Together they make up our lives, and our well-being depends on our satisfaction of both. (This book has been revised as *Redeeming the Time: A Christian Approach to Work and Leisure.* Baker, 1995.)

**SALKIN, JEFFREY K.,** RABBI ■ *Being God's Partner: How to Find the Hidden Link Between Spirituality and Your Work.* Jewish Lights, 1994. *181 pages.*
An insightful perspective on how to integrate faith and daily life. Salkin speaks of imitating God and erecting figurative altars in our offices, dedicating to him what

we spend most of our time doing. He calls us to integrate the Decalogue into all of our human interactions. Salkin includes examples from many different vocations and discussion questions at the end of each chapter. This book is an excellent introduction from a Jewish perspective.

**SARKISIAN, RICK,** VOCATIONAL CONSULTANT ■ *LifeWork: Finding Your Purpose in Life.* St. Ignatius Press, 1997. *123 pages.*
Sarkisian examines how work can give life meaning and purpose. God's presence can be found through our work. A workbook of self-discovery, the book takes readers through a step-by-step self-examination to find what vocations best suit them. Sarkisian's use of historical characters, questions and easy-to-understand examples makes the book practical and useful. (Protestants may be troubled with Catholic emphases like prayers to saints.)

**SAYERS, DOROTHY L.,** WRITER ■ *Are Women Human?* Eerdmans and InterVarsity Press, 1971. *47 pages.*
This collection of essays is a Christian classic. Sayers enjoys upending unthinking assumptions about gender and work. While many people would consider Sayers a feminist, she rejects such labels in favor of a no-nonsense, commonsense approach to the issue of women's roles in society.

*Creed or Chaos?* Sophia Institute Press, 1949, 1974. *116 pages.*
Sayers speaks forcefully and bluntly to those who would soften the claims of Christ, the Bible or the church's credal declarations. To "it doesn't matter what you believe, so long as you are sincere," she responds with "Balderdash!" She contends that "the reason why churches are discredited today is not that they are too bigoted about theology, but that they have run away from theology" (p. vi). To reinforce the point, she includes the Apostles', Nicene and Athanasian creeds.

*The Mind of the Maker.* Harper & Row, 1987 (originally 1941). *229 pages.*
Sayers sheds new light on the image of God, the Trinity, free will and evil. She strives to help her readers to understand that she is presenting historical church beliefs, not her opinions or personal convictions. An added treasure in this edition is the lengthy introduction by Madeleine L'Engle.

**SCANZONI, JOHN,** PROFESSOR ■ "The Christian View of Work," in Carl F. H. Henry et al., *Quest for Reality: Christianity and the Counter Culture.* InterVarsity Press, 1967. *161 pages.*
Scanzoni was disturbed by the diminishing respect for work he perceived among

college students. The problem stems from confusion between the outcomes of work and the work itself. When work becomes only a means for increasing material wealth, other dimensions of meaning are ignored. When work is done in light of God's purposes, it can be fulfilling and satisfying.

**SCHAEF, ANNE WILSON**, WRITER ■ *Meditations for Women Who Do Too Much.* Harper & Row, 1990.
This is a devotional for every day of the year. Each day includes a choice quote along with a carefully written reflection and declaration. It is not specifically Christian. A thematic index is included.

**SCHAEFFER, FRANKY**, ARTIST, WRITER, FILM MAKER ■ *Addicted to Mediocrity: 20th-Century Christians and the Arts.* Crossway, 1981. *127 pages.*
This book is a critique of art in our current age. It includes questions and answers for individuals who want to understand art or who are thinking about art as a vocation. A quick read. "Schaeffer shows how Christians who care can begin to reverse the slide toward mediocrity: by demanding excellence in the arts and media" (back cover). A good overview of the Christian view of the arts.

**SCHULTZE, QUENTIN J.**, PROFESSOR ■ *Internet for Christians.* Gospel Films, 1995. *159 pages.*
This was one of the first books to look at the Internet through eyes of faith and to help surfers be salt and light in this new medium. "I would like to propose," writes Schultze, "that instead of more Internet geeks, the church needs more Internet saints—believers who purposely and prayerfully use the new medium selflessly in service of the Kingdom of God."

**SCHUMACHER, CHRISTIAN**, ORGANIZATIONAL CONSULTANT ■ *God in Work.* Lion, 1998. *255 pages.*
This nonprofessional theologian applies faith to the modern work world. Schumacher makes significant and effective connections between the Trinity, creation and industry. This book reflects his career in organizational redesign, a career that is humane, understandable to nonreligious leaders and workers, and profitable in the long run.

**SCHUMACHER, E. F.**, ECONOMIST ■ *Good Work.* Harper & Row 1979. *223 pages.*
Work, Schumacher says, is one of the most decisive formative influences on character and performance. He argues that the purpose of work is threefold: (1) to pro-

vide necessary and useful goods and services, (2) to enable everyone to be good stewards by using and perfecting their gifts, and (3) to do so in service to and cooperation with others, which liberates people from inborn egocentricity. This is good work. Bad work is mechanical, artificial, restrictive, offers no challenge, no change or growth and must be rejected. Bad work is the result of the way we have used technology and allowed it to dominate workers.

*Small Is Beautiful.* Harper & Row, 1973. *324 pages.*
Schumacher examines small-scale economics, sometimes termed "Buddhist economics." This, he posits, will enable government to function "as if people mattered." Schumacher shows how making economics "small" can positively benefit everyone. He focuses on land use, nuclear energy, technology and even education as well as Third World development and problems. The last part of his book examines the concept of ownership, touching on socialism, the realignment of large-scale organizations and how the current pattern of economics can be changed. This book is a wonderful starting place for discussions of questions centering on economic justice.

**SEIBERT, DONALD V., & WILLIAM PROCTOR,** CEO; WRITER ■ *The Ethical Executive: A Top CEO's Program for Success with Integrity in the Corporate World.* Simon & Schuster, 1984. *208 pages.*
This book outlines a "program for success with integrity in the corporate world." Letting his approach speak for itself, Seibert makes sparing reference to his Christian convictions. A good look into the dynamics of the rough and tumble world of retailing.

**SHAFFER, THOMAS L.,** PROFESSOR ■ *On Being a Christian and a Lawyer.* Brigham Young University Press, 1981. *271 pages.*
Shaffer brings an extensive collection of legal, literary and biblical references to bear on the moral, philosophical and theological problems inherent in the practice of law. Provocative issues are introduced through the stories of well-known authors and through lawyers in history. Shaffer discusses modern legal ethics cases and traces the historical development of legal ethics to recent American Bar Association code. An important book by a man of impressive legal credentials.

**SHAMES, LAURENCE,** COLUMNIST ■ *The Hunger for More: Searching for Values in an Age of Greed.* Times Books, 1989. *291 pages.*
Shames takes on the daunting task of examining America's love affair with success, meaning more and more money. This is part history, part ethical commentary and

part political journey. Shames suggests America has gotten as rich as it is going to get. Greed must yield to a discovery of values and purpose. Consumption is not enough. A useful and discussion-provoking tool for individuals or groups.

**SHELLY, JUDITH ALLEN,** NURSE ■ *Not Just a Job: Serving Christ in Your Work.* InterVarsity Press, 1985. *139 pages.*

This is a good introductory-level book for individuals who are struggling with decisions regarding vocation, marriage, family, priorities and so on, and who want a biblical rather than cultural view of these issues. Includes a helpful appendix and a list of resources available in different professions.

*Spiritual Care: A Guide for Caregivers.* InterVarsity Press, 2000. *180 pages.*

This is a practical, insightful guide for those who care for others. In three simple steps, Shelly, a nurse, explains what spiritual care is, how to apply it in practical settings and the importance of taking care of yourself if you are the one providing the care. Compared with much of the strange practices advocated by so many health professionals these days, Shelly's book is a breath of fresh air. Best of all, it gives caretakers permission to care for themselves and to see that self-care is an important part of providing good, consistent care. Shelly covers topics like prayer, self-assessment, the Bible and the power of touching others.

**SHERMAN, DOUG,** CONSULTANT ■ *Keeping Your Head Up When Your Job's Got You Down.* Wolgemuth & Hyatt, 1991. *227 pages.*

When you talk to marketplace Christians, you soon find that family financial security is a huge concern. Sherman wrote this book after experiencing a crisis in his own work, and his point is that the issue of security is in God's hands. He starts with the inevitability of pain and struggle, and then moves to how he thinks God would have us cope with it. On the big issues in this book Sherman strikes a responsive chord for most marketplace Christians. An excellent resource for small groups. (Note, the patronizing words of praise for leaders Sherman has met can be a little disquieting.)

**SHERMAN, DOUG, & WILLIAM HENDRICKS,** CONSULTANTS ■ *How to Balance Competing Time Demands.* NavPress, 1989. *223 pages.*

Early in the book the authors describe the three common enemies we have in managing time and stress in our lives: rebellion, procrastination and discouragement. An example of the practicality of this book is its "stand-up rule": when you arrive home from work, if your spouse is standing between 5:30-7:00 p.m., you should stand too. Sound corny? Read the book, and you will discover the personal logic behind it. The study guide may be the key to the book's usefulness.

*How to Succeed Where It Really Counts.* NavPress, 1989. *227 pages.*
This book is too brief and general to be considered an outstanding resource. The authors do a good job defining true success. They contend that life's priorities occur in a circular rather than a linear pattern. The book is an excellent launching point for group discussion. A study guide is provided.

*Your Work Matters to God.* NavPress, 1987. *286 pages.*
This book is one of the most comprehensive and accessible texts available on the theology of work. In part one Sherman and Hendricks address problems resulting from the lost connection between faith and work (e.g., purposelessness and the irrelevance of religion). In part two the authors argue from Scripture that work matters to God. In part three they discuss practical implications for job selection, income and lifestyle, conflict with coworkers, leisure, and relationship to the church. Extensive topical and Scripture indexes are included.

**SHOEMAKER, HELEN SMITH,** CLERGY SPOUSE ■ *I Stand by the Door:The Life of Sam Shoemaker.* Word, 1967. *220 pages.*
This is a good profile of Shoemaker, an active leader in the Episcopal Church, cofounder of Alcoholics Anonymous, founding leader of Faith at Work and the pioneer of the Pittsburgh Experiment. He came from a privileged Maryland family and became a passionate servant of people from all walks of life during his ministry to parishes in New York City and Pittsburgh. Insights into his personal life are provided with selections from his writings and diary.

**SHOEMAKER, SAM,** RECTOR ■ *The Experiment of Faith:A Handbook for Beginners.* Harper & Row, 1957. *64 pages.*
Shoemaker says, "Laymen can exercise spiritual influence in places where it is hard for clergy to penetrate" (introduction). He casts the spiritual life as a journey rather than a decision or a destination. He has chapters on religion, spirituality, witness and workplace faith.

*Under New Management.* Zondervan, 1966. *126 pages.*
Shoemaker stayed close to his parishioners and their needs, turning down at least two offers to become an Episcopalian bishop. He coaches believers and seekers on how the faith should work out in relationships, families, workplaces and communities. This collection of timeless wisdom lends itself to daily devotional use. The illustrations and advice ring with truth and love.

**SIDER, RONALD J.**, PROFESSOR, ACTIVIST ■ *Cup of Water, Bread of Life.* Zondervan, 1994. *186 pages*.
This volume chronicles the work of ten worldwide ministries that model faith and compassion in deeds of service. They combine witness and service in an integrated and balanced manner that Sider applauds. The ministries range from London to Bangalore to Eastern Europe and South Africa. Sider carefully describes the struggles, beliefs and impact of each ministry. Footnotes supply data, sources and access to the organizations and leaders.

*Rich Christians in an Age of Hunger.* InterVarsity Press, 1977, 1997. *249 pages*.
A must-read classic for Christians concerned with social justice issues. The book has three basic parts: a presentation of the unequal state of affairs between the rich and the poor; an examination of how God views wealth, the poor and structural evil; and practical implementation of biblical truth in these areas. Throughout the book Sider uses Bible passages, facts and figures to drive home the gravity of the situation faced by the world's poor. While not providing definitive answers, Sider challenges readers to take an active role in searching out those answers and acting out the implications of their faith in everyday life.

**SIDEY, KEN**, JOURNALIST, EDITOR ■ *The Blackboard Fumble.* Christianity Today, 1989. *165 pages*.
Ten Christian veterans of public education (all men) comment on school reform and the place of moral principles in education. Chapters include "The Myth of Neutrality," "A New Definition of 'Public' Education," "Who Pays the Price for School Reform?" "Moral Literacy and the Formation of Character," "Beyond the Lesson Plan: Curriculum and Values," "What is Legal? What is Not? Religion in Public Schools," and "Parents as Partners with Public Education." This book includes suggested readings.

**SIMEON J. THOLE**, MONK ■ *Take Five: Prayers for the Workplace.* Liturgical Press, 1989. *64 pages*.
This pocket-size booklet has twenty-five small group prayers for workplace gatherings. It is designed as a group liturgy (with leader's narrative): a reading, a Scripture text and a prayer. Topics range from worry to ambition, buying and selling, and profit. It reflects the Benedictine tradition.

**SIMON, CHARLIE MAY**, PROFESSIONAL WRITER ■ *A Seed Shall Serve: The Story of the Spiritual Leader of Modern Japan–Toyohiko Kagawa.* Hodder & Stoughton, 1959. *133 pages*.
Abandoned as a child and nurtured by an American missionary, young Kagawa

became alarmed by the terrible plight of Japan's poorest citizens. He voraciously read the Bible and Christian authors, and charted a path of living among and serving the poorest of the poor. Kagawa established dwellings, schools, health care, agricultural training, labor law improvements and education for the least around him. His fame spread through his poetry and novels about modern life. Eventually, Kagawa was sought out by national and international leaders for his wisdom about poverty and compassion.

*Dag Hammarskjöld.* E. P. Dutton, 1967. *192 pages.*
Hammarskjöld was General Secretary of the United Nations during the middle of the twentieth century. A child of privilege and excellent education in one of Sweden's leading families, he gave himself to national and international diplomacy. Simon provides insights into Hammarskjöld's personal habits, hopes and feelings while highlighting his extensive U.N. accomplishments. He was a peacemaker par excellence.

**SINETAR, MARSHA,** ORGANIZATIONAL PSYCHOLOGIST, MEDIATOR, VOCATIONAL COUNSELOR ■ *To Build the Life You Want, Create the Work You Love: The Spiritual Dimension of Entrepreneuring.* St. Martin's Press, 1995. *209 pages.*
The worth of this book lies in its insights into developmental theory and parallels to personal understanding of vocation, career and calling. Sinetar could have developed this parallel further but instead offers encounters, letters and stories from her seminars. Sinetar also offers some good exercises for evaluating personal and career strengths, weaknesses and passions. If you are interested in developmental theory, it may be worthwhile reading, but otherwise don't bother. The theology is fairly syncretistic.

**SIRE, JAMES W.,** LECTURER, WRITER ■ *Habits of the Mind: Intellectual Life as a Christian Calling.* InterVarsity Press, 2000. *263 pages.*
Sire argues persuasively that some Christians are called to intellectual pursuits. Sire's reasoning is clear, his prose is persuasive and his arguments are accessible to most readers. He covers the basic characteristics of the intellectual life, including some historical background and the moral dimension of intellectual thought. The chapters "Thinking by Reading" and "Jesus the Reasoner" are excellent.

**SLATTERY, PATRICK,** JOURNALIST, FARMER ■ *Caretakers of Creation: Farmers Reflect on Faith and Work.* Augsburg Fortress, 1991. *125 pages.*
Midwestern farmers and their spouses, representing several Christian denomina-

tions, were interviewed about the relevance of Christian faith to their daily work. They speak about their sense of responsibility as stewards of God's land, the ethics of various farming methods, the miracle of the soil's productivity and so forth. Slattery saw similar strands of character in those he interviewed. "They are hardworking, honest, persevering, resourceful, community-minded, family-centered, and—last but certainly not least—faithful to God." Heartily recommended.

**SLOCUM, ROBERT E.,** ENTREPRENEUR ■ *Maximize Your Ministry: How You as a Layperson Can Impact Your World for Jesus Christ.* NavPress, 1990. *295 pages.*
Slocum challenges Christian laypeople to reach people for Christ in this high-tech age, because "lay men and women . . . make up more than ninety-eight percent of the people of God." Slocum moves from issues of discipleship to maturation of the heart to external strategies for ministry in the world. The book is highly personal, fast-paced and nontechnical.

*Ordinary Christians in a High-Tech World.* Word, 1986. *252 pages.*
Slocum calls for a new strategy for laypeople: one that has both an interior dimension (the development of the heart) and an exterior dimension (serving Christ in church, work, government and family).

**SMARTO, DONALD,** DIRECTOR, INSTITUTE FOR PRISON MINISTRIES ■
*Justice and Mercy.* Tyndale House, 1987. *350 pages.*
Smarto takes a Christian approach to America's correctional crisis. He visited eighty American prisons and interviewed top prison and government officials, including retired Chief Justice Warren Burger (full text included). The book contains chapters on economic, ethical and medical issues, overcrowding, discrimination, alternatives to incarceration, and a theology of punishment.

**SMEDES, LEWIS B.,** PROFESSOR ■ *Choices: Making Right Decisions in a Complex World.* Harper & Row, 1986. *121 pages.*
When others moralize and alienate, Smedes reasons and persuades. "We need some clear thinking about moral standards and how to apply them to real life." He suggests four standards: face the facts, respect the rules, consider the consequences and be responsible.

**SMITH, CAROL COX,** WRITER ■ *Recovery at Work.* Hazelden Foundation, 1990. *228 pages.*
This book claims to be "the first book to focus on the needs of recovering persons

trying to rebuild their careers—with guidance on reentering the workforce, assessing a job environment, and making healthy career choices" (Hazelden). Not significantly religious.

**SMITH, DONALD P.,** DENOMINATIONAL ADMINISTRATOR ■ *Congregations Alive.* Westminster Press, 1981. *183 pages.*
How do people come alive to ministry? Smith attempts to answer this question by surveying ninety-seven active and growing American churches from a variety of traditions. He notes six common characteristics that deal with how people are encouraged to see value in themselves and to care for one another.

**SMITH, GRAEME,** PROFESSOR ■ *The Theology of Work in the Postwar Period.* Master's thesis. University of Sydney, 1990.
Smith has made a comprehensive and comparative study of postwar theologies of work up to and including the 1980s. He argues that the repercussions of industrialization have not been given sufficient attention. Industrialization brought with it fundamental changes in the relationship between work, family and local community; in the division of labor between the sexes; in the priority given to employment; in the attitudes to time, leisure and material advancement; and in the very definition of work. Smith concludes that the main casualty in this process has been the proper consideration of women's work. He also concludes that "the influence of Marxism on the theology of work has been substantial."

**SMITH, THOMAS,** AIRLINE MANAGER ■ *God on the Job: Finding God Who Waits at Work.* Paulist, 1995. *180 pages.*
An excellent introduction to a theology of work. Written from a Catholic perspective, the book includes discussions on the importance and struggle of living an integrated life and how all work is a reflection of God's character. Smith has great insights into the powers and principalities of work (or cultural forces and how they attempt to remake us in their image). Each chapter includes a thought-provoking study and discussion guide for individuals or groups.

**SMITH-MORAN, BARBARA,** SCIENTIST, PRIEST ■ *Soul at Work: Reflections on a Spirituality of Working.* St. Mary's Press, 1997. *111 pages.*
Smith-Moran presents six daily meditations for six weeks. Each week centers on a theme like "Vocation or Calling," "Success" and "Setbacks." This is rooted in clear-headed thinking about humans as being co-creators with God, which means work is sacred, holy and significant. She acknowledges inspiration from Teilhard de

Chardin and Ignatian spirituality. Designed for the working person, the meditations can be used by groups in retreat settings. Very helpful contribution.

**SNYDER, HOWARD A.**, PROFESSOR ■ *Liberating the Church: The Ecology of Church and Kingdom.* InterVarsity Press, 1983. *258 pages.*
Snyder spells out a program for liberating the church for the work of the kingdom. He contends that the church exists not for its own preservation but for kingdom ministry in the world. Therefore we need to critically examine a variety of issues: leadership, the role of the laity, lifestyle, the role of theology, concerns for justice and the poor.

**SOELLE, DOROTHEE, WITH SHIRLEY A. CLYES**, PROFESSORS ■ *To Work and to Love: A Theology of Creation.* Fortress, 1984. *165 pages.*
Soelle pulls together different streams of theology to develop a Christian perspective on work. She begins with a theology of creation. From this foundation she explores the themes of work and sexuality, applies liberationist perspectives to work realities in the First World, and provides an example of Protestant cocreationist categories. Soelle reflects a feminist perspective, values the insights of Marx and is indebted to process theology. She is comfortable borrowing traditions from other cultures, appearing to give them equal status to the Bible. She makes no attempt to explore the traditional Christian doctrine of vocation.

**SOJOURNERS** ■ *Who Is My Neighbor? Economics As If Values Matter.* Sojourners, 1994. *180 pages.*
This excellent book—in a magazine format—is a thorough examination of a wide variety of economic issues relating to faith. Sojourners is known for its justice issues positions, thus the study guide heavily emphasizes such subjects as changing personal attitudes toward money and possessions; applying biblical principles about money to everyday life; giving that visions legs and arms; and transforming politics, the community and the church through this new vision. Chapter articles are written by different people, which makes the book interesting and varied. Of special interest is the chapter "Reimaging Consumer Economics," an in-depth examination of American consumerism. The article called "A Consuming Wilderness: Attracted and Repelled by the Mall of America" is a revelation. Any one of these articles could consume a Sunday school class or small group for at least half a year, so don't expect to whip through it in an afternoon. This study guide is one to live by—or at least to be challenged by.

**SOLOMON, JERRY, ED.,** PASTOR ■ *Arts, Entertainment & Christian Values: Probing the Headlines That Impact Your Family.* Kregel, 2000. *191 pages.*

In a collection of short essays Solomon helps parents answer their kids' questions when culture clashes arise. It examines some current trends and explains postmodern culture. Written from a very conservative evangelical viewpoint, the book is extremely simplistic. Ultimately, instead of urging Christians to engage culture, it underscores their separation from it, a separation that must be maintained for the sake of "keeping the faith."

**SORENSEN, DAVID ALLEN, & BARBARA DEGROTE-SORENSEN,** RELIGIOUS EDUCATORS ■ *Kindling the Spark: A Dialog with Christian Teachers and Their Work.* Augsburg, 1992. *121 pages.*

Two Christian educators reflect on some of the hot topics where work and faith intersect in education. There are frank discussions on the home and private lives of educators, burnout, motivation and balance. It helps readers identify with some of the ethical-spiritual dilemmas that teachers face daily. A must read for those who want to understand the world of public education.

**SOUTHERN BAPTIST BROTHERHOOD COMMITTEE** ■ *Bold New Laity: A Churchwide Study.* Brotherhood Commission, 1978. *71 pages.*

This is a record of what happened when the priesthood of all believers was rediscovered by the Southern Baptist Church. The book provides a brief biblical and historical perspective on the laity, followed by practical implications for the involvement of laypersons in church life. It mentions but does not develop broader contexts of lay ministry, such as work in the marketplace. Includes discussion questions.

**SPROUL, R. C.,** THEOLOGIAN ■ *Stronger Than Steel: The Wayne Alderson Story.* Harper & Row, 1980. *208 pages.*

Alderson, founder of the Value of the Person movement, provided an important model for bringing labor-management disputes to constructive agreement. Applying biblical principles of reconciliation, he brought troubled Pittron Steel from near bankruptcy to profitability. Well-written and realistic. (See also Wayne T. Alderson.)

**SPRUNGER, BEN, CAROL J. SUTER, & WALLY KROEKER,** NPO EXECUTIVES; EDITOR ■ *Faith Dilemmas for Marketplace Christians.* Herald, 1997. *73 pages.*

This well-crafted collection of thirteen case studies helps readers engage the marketplace dilemmas, connect with Scripture and process the lessons within.

The focus is on individual employees and small business leaders from the Mennonite community, but the appeal is broad because of the realism and candor presented.

**STAUB, DICK,** RADIO HOST, SOCIAL CRITIC ■ *Too Christian, Too Pagan: How to Love the World Without Falling for It.* Zondervan, 2000. *206 pages.*
Staub, a nationally syndicated radio personality, paints a clear picture of how to reach out to our culture with the gospel by letting us peek into his own spiritual journey. Along the way, readers learn ways to show people how the truths of Christ are relevant to Western culture. Warm and engaging, this book is unpretentious and humble. The chapter "Tell Short Stories" is worth the price of the book itself.

**STEDMAN, RAY C.,** PASTOR ■ *Body Life.* Regal, 1972. *149 pages.*
Out of his own experience as pastor of a large thriving church, Stedman outlines principles for creating and maintaining a flourishing church, including identity, unity, giftedness, equipping, leadership and ministry.

**STEINBRON, MELVIN J.,** PASTOR ■ *Can the Pastor Do It Alone? A Model for Preparing Lay People for Lay Pastoring.* Regal, 1987. *209 pages.*
Steinborn offers a viable alternative to the problem of how to effectively pastor a large church. Not only does he offer material on how to equip lay people for ministry, but he also discusses necessary support structures.

*The Lay-Driven Church: How to Empower the People in Your Church to Share the Tasks of Ministry.* Regal, 1997. *220 pages.*
This book is for the layperson and the pastor. Steinbron gives practical advice on motivating the laity to take on the actual work of the church. The book is organized around three basic questions: What kind of church does it take? What kind of people does it take? and What kind of effort does it take? He takes a step-by-step approach that can be annoying, but his advice rings true. The basics of the book are solid.

**STEVENS, R. PAUL,** PROFESSOR ■ *The Equipper's Guide to Every-Member Ministry: 8 Ways Ordinary People Can Do the Work of the Church.* InterVarsity Press, 1992. *203 pages.*
Stevens provides a no-nonsense guide for putting together an every-member ministry program in the local church. The book includes chapters on how members can teach and learn the Bible, conduct small groups, provide pastoral care, lead worship, provide guidance in the marketplace, evangelize neighborhoods, help

wounded marriages and families, and work for justice in society. "For pastors and laypersons ready to 'graciously conspire' to find the best way to release the full potential of the church" (back cover). This is a must read for individuals responsible for lay ministry programs within the local church.

*Liberating the Laity: Equipping All the Saints for Ministry.* InterVarsity Press, 1985. *177 pages.*

"Every church has far more work than any one person can do," writes Stevens. "The New Testament solution was for every member to be a minister." This is more than a utilitarian solution; it is the essence of "the priesthood of all believers," a doctrine central to the Protestant Reformation. Stevens tells how it took a recent five-year experience as a carpenter for him to understand (1) the reality of the layperson's world, (2) the importance of the nine-to-five life and (3) the centrality of the "equipping" function of the church.

*The Other Six Days: Vocation, Work, and Ministry in Biblical Perspective.* Eerdmans/Regent, 1999. *289 pages.*

Stevens acquaints readers with a "people theology" that challenges the division of God's people into laity and clergy. He provides a theological foundation for each person's calling to do the Lord's work. He lays a solid biblical foundation for changing individual lives and the life of the church as a whole. Although the book has an academic feel, it is accessible. Each chapter ends with discussion and study questions.

**STEVENS, R. PAUL, & GERRY SCHOBERG,** PROFESSOR, LAY ADVOCATES
■ *Satisfying Work.* Harold Shaw, 1989. *79 pages.*

Few Bible studies on work are more comprehensive than this. The thirteen topics include "earth-keeping," "work: curse or blessing?" "workplace temptation," "kingdom consciousness," "enticed by riches," "entrepreneurial homemaking," "the search for satisfying work" and "heavenly work." The authors cite significant contemporary marketplace literature. Highly recommended for neighborhood, student and church groups.

*Servant Leadership.* ■ Harold Shaw, 1990. *48 pages.*

An excellent eight-part Bible study on leadership and servanthood. The authors use Moses (the struggle with inadequacy), Simon (the lust for power), Eli (a toxic mix of work, marriage and family) and Elijah (the peril of individualism) as examples. Other subjects include finding our identity in God, comparing ourselves with others, being salt and light in society, and the meaning of servanthood.

**STOTT, JOHN R. W.**, RECTOR, THEOLOGIAN, WRITER ■ *The Contemporary Christian.* InterVarsity Press, 1992. *432 pages.*

This tome challenges laypeople to take the gospel into contemporary life in order to show its relevance to today's world. The book, a kind of evangelism primer, has five parts: the gospel, the disciple, the Bible, the church and the world. Stott carefully examines each theme in the light of evangelism for today, asking questions such as "Did the resurrection really happen?" and "Why is the resurrection important?" The study guide makes this good for individuals or groups. Excellent from start to finish.

*One People.* Revell, 1986. *127 pages.*

Stott uses four New Testament words to promote a united ministry in the church: *ecclesia* (the church), *diakonia* (service), *martyria* (witness) and *koinonia* (fellowship). While others express clericalist or anticlericalist sentiments, Stott addresses "one people" under God. Though his allusions are British and Anglican, the principles he expounds apply universally.

**STRINGFELLOW, WILLIAM,** LAWYER ■ *A Private and Public Faith.* Eerdmans, 1962. *93 pages.*

This is a prophetic and articulate message of concern for the weakness of the Christian church amid the brokenness of modern America. Stringfellow perceives that the church has turned inward, is far too self-serving and has been seduced by the "separation of church and state." In the introduction he declares, "Religion has virtually nothing to do with God and has little to do with the practical lives of men in society" (p. 8). His critique of postwar success, economic wealth and American power is clear, strong and rooted in a passion for the church to be a people rooted in biblical faith, not cultural comfort and ease.

*An Ethic For Christians & Other Aliens in a Strange Land.* Word, 1973. *156 pages.*

Here is a combination of good biblical theology with candid social criticism. Stringfellow turns his attention to corporate and political America declaring, "America . . . enslaves human beings, exacts human sacrifices, captures and captivates Presidents as well as intimidating and dehumanizing ordinary citizens" (preface). Using the book of Revelation, he compares America to ancient Babylon, not Jerusalem—God's holy city. He names several national sicknesses and focuses on a central one—politics. He pleads for use of the charismatic gift of the discernment of signs and spirits, followed by naming evil and raising true hope. He declares, "It is profane, as well as grandiose, to manipulate the Bible in order to apologise for America" (p. 14). This book needs to be read by every generation of American Christians.

*Dissenter in a Great Society: An Indictment of Christian Complacency in American Life.* Abingdon, 1966. *164 pages.*

The *New York Times* said, "This book hurts. . . . His targets are many: the idolatry of money; the decadence of white, middle-class society; the implication of everybody in the subjugation of the Negro; the exaltation of property over human rights; the immorality of a society that permits the existence of poverty it has the technical skill to eradicate" (back cover). Stringfellow names leaders who epitomize worst examples of the problems he exposes. He builds each of the chapters (poverty, politics, race and orthodoxy) on a biblical text. This is a classic!

*The Politics of Spirituality.* Westminster Press, 1984. *90 pages.*

Stringfellow rejects any spirituality that remains private, whether focused on self-realization or self-denial. He argues that biblical spirituality has to do with the restoration of relationship and the reconciliation with the rest of creation. It therefore has to do with politics.

**SUTER, HANS, & MARCO GMUR,** MISSIONARY; MISSIOLOGIST ■ *Business Power for God's Purpose: Partnership with the Unreached.* Verlag fur kulturbezogenen Gemeindebau, 1997. *127 pages.*

The Swiss authors declare, "The premise of this publication is that, in order to reach unreached peoples of this world and re-evangelize the old Christian West, there needs to be a powerful unleashing of the dormant potential of Christian businesspeople" (p. 100). They deal with biblical foundations for work and some case studies from European mission history. Suter and Gmur are candid about tentmakers' foibles, errors and contradictory thinking. Sometimes this book is difficult to read because of its crosscultural, multiethnic and multigenerational scope, and its brevity makes for oversimplification and dangerous generalizations in some topics. The authors provide several scriptural references and excellent footnotes. Overall, a good contribution to the literature on globalization of Christian witness in and through the workplace.

**SUTHERLAND, JOHN R.,** PROFESSOR ■ *Going Broke: Bankruptcy, Business Ethics, and the Bible.* Herald, 1991. *176 pages.*

Sutherland courageously takes on the moral stigma of bankruptcy and tries to see it in Christian terms. Could it be that bankruptcy is the state's way to implement biblical Jubilee? He explores what Scripture really says about usury, forgiveness of debt, the ethics of bankruptcy and, perhaps best of all, how congregations can respond in a holistic and helpful way.

**SUTHERLAND, JOHN R., ED.,** PROFESSOR ■ *Us and Them: Building a Just Workplace Community.* Work Research Foundation, 1999. *182 pages.*
Published by an organization related to a Christian labor union in Canada, this book on labor-management relations seeks to fashion a Christian viewpoint on issues like the role of strikes, win-win bargaining, building trust in the workplace and new priorities for unions. Christians, like others in society, are polarized on the issue of unions. But as one writer in this collection says, "When labor relations are poor, generally both sides are at fault." Christians on both the labor and management sides will be enriched by this book

**SUTTON, WILLIAM R.,** TEACHER ■ *Journeymen for Jesus.* Pennsylvania State University Press, 1998. *351 pages.*
This prize-winning historical profile of early nineteenth-century artisans (tailors, coopers, butchers, bakers, cabinet makers, etc.) in Baltimore shows how skilled laborers drew on their evangelical Methodist faith to resist the sweep of industrialization and the demotion of their God-given skills. Without becoming socialists or even social democrats, these workers formed unions supported by a powerful biblical rationale to fight for fair pay, livable working conditions, limited advancement and input into production decisions. An ennobling portrait of marketplace Christians who fought to preserve the dignity of their labors, challenging revolutionary new concepts of economic progress.

**SWARR, SHARON BENTCH, & DWIGHT NORDSTROM,** BUSINESS MISSIONARIES ■ *Transform the World: Biblical Vision and Purpose for Business.* Center for Entrepreneurship and Economic Development, 1999. *104 pages.*
Swarr and Nordstrom aim to tear down the wall between "business" and "missions" (secular and sacred), and show in practical, step-by-step ways how to accomplish this by making business an opportunity to share Christ and fulfill the Great Commission. The case is based on both Scripture and practical considerations. The balance of the book examines a variety of issues inherent in this integration, including creating versus accumulating wealth, entrepreneurship and ways to share the gospel as a businessperson abroad. The tone is zealous, which may attract some readers and repel others.

**SWENSON, RICHARD A.,** PROFESSOR ■ *Margin: Restoring Emotional, Physical, Financial, and Time Reserves to Overloaded Lives.* NavPress, 1992. *275 pages.*
An exceptional book on restoring limits to frantic lives. Swenson focuses on how modern people are overloaded in four key areas—emotional energy, physical

energy, time and finances. He then provides a principle-centered prescription to restore contentment, simplicity, balance and rest to all these areas. A good systematic presentation of the roots of our problems and principles to restore balance. Great teaching or small group resource. Highly recommended.

**SWINDOLL, LUCI,** BUSINESS MANAGER, PROFESSIONAL SINGER, SPEAKER ■
*After You've Dressed for Success.* Word, 1988. *160 pages.*
After thirty years at the Mobil Oil Corporation and fifteen years of professional singing with the Dallas Opera, Swindoll is now vice president of public relations at Insight for Living. "Swindoll addresses the need for professionalism, maturity, perspective and character in the career game. She . . . show[s] women how courage, brains, heart, and faith—not just proper image—are the keys to a fulfilling career as well as a full and happy life" (publisher). Includes a helpful list of suggested reading.

**TAM, STANLEY,** BUSINESS FOUNDER ■ *God Owns My Business.* Horizon House, 1984. *158 pages.*
Originally published in 1969, this autobiography recounts Tam's career as a salesman and then founder of what became a very large company in the mid-twentieth century. He was as intense about obeying God as he was about selling and making money. Along the way he grew in his faith and displayed a willingness to change. Tam broke the mold of wealth for wealth's sake by establishing a charitable foundation that owned at first 51 and finally 100 percent of his company, paying himself and his wife as employees. This is an easy-to-read personal story rooted in intense personal integrity and personal evangelism.

**TAMASY, ROBERT J., ED.,** PUBLICATIONS DIRECTOR ■ *Jesus Works Here: Leading Christians in Business Talk About How You Can Walk with Christ Through Stress, Change, and Other Challenges of the Workplace.* Broadman & Holman, 1995. *262 pages.*
This is an almost overwhelming collection of articles from more than thirty authors. The book deals with the priorities, opportunities, concerns and stresses of marketplace Christians. The value of this volume is its comprehensiveness and conciseness on each subject, drawing from the best of the best in writers as well as topics that Christian businesspeople struggle with. Good source for quotes and as an inspirational or reference volume.

**TANNER, RICHARD C.,** PASTOR ■ *Jesus Nine to Five.* Welch, 1989. *168 pages.*
A pastor shares workplace-related insights from the Gospel of Luke, gleaned from several years of leading lunch-hour Bible studies with people from the Toronto

business community. He finds Gospel stories that relate to lawyers, investment brokers, tax collectors, farmers, managers, homemakers and government officials. He demonstrates how anyone who works for a living can get some form of professional help from Doctor Luke.

**TAYLOR, HERBERT J.**, BUSINESSMAN, ROTARY INTERNATIONAL PRESIDENT ■ *The Herbert J. Taylor Story.* InterVarsity Press, 1968. *129 pages.*
The story of a deeply religious leader who supported or cofounded Child Evangelism Fellowship, InterVarsity Christian Fellowship, Rotary International and Young Life. Perhaps best known as the author of The Four-Way Test (used worldwide by the Rotary). He saved Club Aluminum from failing and applied the four-way test to his people, product, advertising and leadership. (See also Paul Heidebrecht.)

**TERKEL, STUDS**, JOURNALIST ■ *Working.* Avon Books, 1974. *762 pages.*
In this modern classic, Terkel opens our eyes to the stark and sometimes violent reality of American people's day-to-day working lives. He covered America over three years, interviewing farmers and salespeople, waitresses and policemen, hotel clerks and secretaries. Terkel asked workers how they felt about their jobs and about themselves in relation to their jobs. Fascinating to read, the book is considered by some a masterpiece in biographical journalism.

**THOMAS, CAL**, NEWSPAPER COLUMNIST ■ *The Things That Matter Most.* Zondervan, 1994. *219 pages.*
In this book Thomas takes on a long litany of "promises" U.S. post-Christian society has made about family, sexuality, education, euthanasia and government. Thomas's overriding concern is twofold: that American society has lost its moral underpinnings, and that what it promises in return is empty, amoral and in some cases downright dangerous. This book is not for someone looking for an easy way to apply marketplace principles to everyday life. But it is interesting, thought-provoking and a good discussion starter, particularly for a group comprising liberals and conservatives.

**THOMAS, DAVE, & RON BEYMA**, EXECUTIVE; WRITER ■ *Well Done! The Common Guy's Guide to Success.* Zondervan, 1994. *224 pages.*
This is the story of the founder and CEO of Wendy's fast-food chain, Dave Thomas. Popularly written, it is more the story of an orphan who achieved corporate success, advertising popularity and wealth than about a serious Christian. Thomas affirms values like integrity, teamwork, generosity, creativity and honesty among other subjects, but they are not significantly rooted in faith.

**TILLAPAUGH, FRANK R.**, PASTOR, CONSULTANT ■ *The Church Unleashed.* Regal, 1982. *224 pages.*

Tillapaugh notes that over the last forty years the American church has been concerned predominantly with the middle class while parachurch organizations minister to other sectors of society. He includes several chapters on how to target particular kinds of people.

**TING, JOHN**, PROFESSOR ■ *Living Biblically at Work.* Landmark, 1995. *200 pages.*

Ting helps Christians develop a biblical worldview, particularly with respect to the workplace and occupational decision making. After first advancing a biblical view of work and vocation, Ting expounds general principles applicable to Christians. He then examines case studies. Particularly aimed at the Southeast Asian context.

**TOBIAS, CYNTHIA ULRICH**, TEACHER, CONSULTANT ■ *The Way We Work.* Focus on the Family, 1995. *154 pages.*

The author draws convincing portraits of workplace characters and then unravels the mystery of each in the hope of showing us clues for how to deal with them. Along the way we are sure to recognize many coworkers, and the tools she offers can be immensely helpful. But what might be more surprising is how we will recognize ourselves too, and in that we might also become aware of how others have to "work around" our own idiosyncrasies.

**TODD, JOHN**, EDITOR ■ *Work: Christian Thought and Practice.* Darton, Longman & Todd, 1960. *221 pages.*

A collection of essays by prominent priests and laymen on the theological foundations of work and the application to everyday problems. Included is a section on the historical roots of our thinking about work, several essays examining particular occupations and a section concerning structures for organizing work.

**TOLSTOY, LEO**, WRITER ■ *A Confession of What I Believe.* Trans. Aylmer Maude. Oxford University Press, 1921. Reprinted 1932. *239 pages.*

This is a well-known but underused classic about everyday faith and the problems of institutional forms of faith. The reader is immediately caught up in Tolstoy's candor about the simplicity and abandonment of his childhood religious training. He bears his heart and mind about shallowness, inconsistency and evil in his own heart and among his literary peers. He shares his journey into honesty and integrity of mind and belief.

**TORRELL, DOLORES LYNN,** EXECUTIVE ■ *Heart Business: Building a Kinder, Gentler Workplace.* Resurrection Press, 1991. *81 pages.*
This volume, written from a Catholic viewpoint, explores the human side of business. Who wins, she asks, when meanness is "in" and competition rules? Where will the never-ending work ethic lead? How do spirituality and compassion in business help the bottom line? The author shows that even in a huge, seemingly impersonal corporation, one person committed to ministry in daily life can make a difference.

**TRUEBLOOD, ELTON,** PROFESSOR ■ *Abraham Lincoln: A Spiritual Biography.* Harper & Row, 1986. *236 pages.*
In a thoughtful but easy-to-read way, Trueblood probes the development of biblical faith in Lincoln's life. We see how the Old Testament prophets and Jesus informed Lincoln's worldview, how belief in God shaped his commitment to the poor of every race and nation. This volume addresses the core of Lincoln's often misunderstood and ignored faith commitments.

*The Company of the Committed.* Harper & Row, 1961. *113 pages.*
Trueblood's vision of the church is a company of committed people whose goal is the preservation and redemption of the world. Using the image of an army, he stresses the involvement and discipline of every member: "What we seek is not a fellowship of the righteous or of the self-righteous, but rather a fellowship of men and women who . . . can be personally involved in the effort to make Christ's kingdom prevail" (introduction).

*The Incendiary Fellowship.* Harper & Row, 1967. *121 pages.*
Trueblood agonizes over the emerging paganism and lack of witness in the church's "mild religion." Jesus said, "I came to bring fire on the earth" (Luke 12:49), but Trueblood perceives a mere flicker. Pleading for renewal of the church's conviction and passion, Trueblood illustrates fiery faith through the work of Blaise Pascal, John Wesley, Dietrich Bonhoeffer, Sam Shoemaker and Billy Graham. The book is biblically rooted, concise, clear and practical.

*The New Man for Our Time.* Harper & Row, 1970. *126 pages.*
This book focuses on the connection between inner peace and outer service. Trueblood expresses his grief over "Christian witness . . . [being] fractured today because of the emergence of opposing parties, one of which may be called activist and the other pietist" (p. 17). "The pietist is one who stresses chiefly the roots; the activist stresses chiefly the fruits. Service without devotion is rootless; devotion

without service is fruitless" (p. 25). He reiterates the three foundations of devotion, rigorous intellectual work and service to humanity. As is his pattern, he lifts up some of the great practitioners of holistic faith down through the centuries. Trueblood is thoughtful, caring and prophetic.

*A Place to Stand.* Harper & Row, 1969. *128 pages.*
Of his many books, this is Trueblood's most theological. He calls the church back to biblical convictions and practices amidst rising anti-intellectualism and amoral living. The church's most basic convictions are an inner life of devotion, a rational intellectual life and an outer life of human service. He is concerned that Christians know what death really is and how to die in hope of eternal life.

*Signs of Hope in a Century of Despair.* Harper & Brothers, 1950. *125 pages.*
Trueblood speaks out about decline in Western society and the need for the people of God to address acute cultural needs. Even though candid about America's shortfalls, Trueblood is hope-filled because of the power of the gospel. Chapter four, "The Emergence of Lay Religion," is of particular interest and value to the ministry-in-daily-life movement. This chapter is loaded with ideas, dreams and possibilities for the growth of the ministry of every believer.

*Your Other Vocation.* Harper & Row, 1952. *125 pages.*
Trueblood bemoans the retreat Christianity has made from society over the last few hundred years, and he argues that the only way to reverse this trend is to have the laity fully involved in ministry. The seeds of much contemporary marketplace thought can be found in this book (e.g., lay ministry in the world, the pastor as equipper and educator, the vocation of the laity).

TSCHUY, THEO, HISTORIAN ■ *Dangerous Diplomacy: The Story of Carl Lutz, Rescuer of 62,000 Hungarian Jews.* Eerdmans, 2000. *265 pages.*
Tschuy was the Swiss Consul to Hungary from 1942 to 1945. He cunningly saved doomed Jews from deportation to Nazi concentration camps. He risked his own life by confronting Nazi leaders, opposing Hungarian killing squads and bypassing overly cautious superiors. This is a well-written story of Christian conviction applied in a dangerous and evil situation.

TUCKER, GRAHAM, CLERGY ■ *The Faith-Work Connection: A Practical Application of Christian Values in the Marketplace.* Anglican Book Centre, 1987. *223 pages.*
Those wishing to understand the dynamics of the marketplace from Christian per-

spectives will value this book. It approaches faith-work issues at a greater depth than most volumes. Tucker uses diagrams, charts, models and itemized lists, and includes a small but well-organized bibliography.

**TUCKER, RUTH, & WALTER L. LIEFELD,** PROFESSORS ■ *Daughters of the Church: Women and Ministry from New Testament Times to the Present.* Zondervan, 1987. *552 pages.*
In this survey of women of faith down through history, the authors cover women leaders and pioneers in religious work. Some key biblical texts used to subjugate women are also considered.

**TURPIN, JOANNE,** WRITER ■ *Women in Church History: 20 Stories for 20 Centuries.* St. Anthony Messenger, 1990. *173 pages.*
This is a breakthrough study of Christian history. Turpin begins with the New Testament Prisca and then singles out a key person for each of the succeeding centuries. (Each profile includes a helpful contextual overview for the century of the subject's time.) Although Turpin is committed to diversity, most entries are of famous Roman Catholic saints or "religious" women. Some are rescued from obscurity, including some viewed as "just" the wives of famous men.

**TUTU, DESMOND MPILO,** ARCHBISHOP ■ *No Future Without Forgiveness.* Doubleday, 1999. *290 pages.*
In this powerful and painful story, Tutu, retired Anglican archbishop of Cape Town, South Africa, recounts his lifelong struggle to apply the Christian faith to a nation torn by apartheid. He is one of the architects rebuilding a nation filled with racism, violence and hatred. This autobiography illustrates his commitment to and the power of forgiveness. The writing style is vivid, gripping and compelling.

**UNSWORTH, TIM, & JEAN UNSWORTH,** JOURNALIST; ARTIST ■ *Upon This Rock: The Church, Work, Money and You.* ACTA, 1991. *119 pages.*
This is a history of the Roman Catholic Church's response to work and economic issues. Using the Church's best documents (papal encyclicals), the Unsworths probe subjects like usury, capitalism, labor, child labor, working conditions and unemployment. Good insights are blended with very interesting historical pieces. Includes helpful ideas for further study and practical activities.

**VANDERKLOET, ED,** EDITOR ■ *In and Around the Workplace: Christian Directions in the World of Work.* Christian Labour Association of Canada, 1992. *137 pages.*
For almost twenty-seven years Vanderkloet toiled with the Christian Labour Association of Canada, an unusual Christian union run by biblical principles. As editor of the Association's periodical, Vanderkloet wrote many columns on thorny issues like strikes, profits, drudgery, dignity and workplace equality. This collection gives fascinating insights into how to bring Christian faith to bear in a conflict-ridden workplace.

**VEITH, GENE EDWARD, JR., & CHRISTOPHER L. STAMPLER** ■ *Christians in a .Com World: Getting Connected Without Being Consumed.* Crossway, 2000. *190 pages.*
This book is a nice primer for Christians who have embraced computer and Internet technology. Admittedly, techies will find it simplistic, but the rest of us won't. It argues for using the Internet as a tool for the kingdom rather than a venue for our own appetites and goals. It includes opportunities the Internet creates for Christians, and may be especially useful for those who work at home.

**VINCENT, JAMES,** EDITOR, PUBLISHER ■ *Parting the Waters: How Vision and Faith Make Good Business.* Moody Press, 1997. *192 pages.*
This book is a stirring story of a family who refused to sacrifice principles for prosperity, even though it very nearly destroyed their business. (They supplied Eisenhower's forces in World War II). Even though Christlike decisions can have disastrous consequences the underlying theme is that God honors faithfulness. Vincent defines faithfulness as a long-term process with no shortcuts and no guaranteed formulas. An easy read, this is an excellent guide for business owners and key leaders facing tough decisions.

**VINCENT, MARK,** EDUCATOR ■ *A Christian View of Money: Celebrating God's Generosity.* Herald, 1997. *135 pages.*
Organized around seven foundational beliefs, this book draws on Vincent's deep, scriptural understanding of financial stewardship and his concern for justice and giving. The book is packed with thorny dilemmas from every area of life. Using Scripture and open-ended questions about time, talents and treasures, Vincent teaches readers *how,* not *what,* to think about family, work, church and world community. He also suggests seven congregational initiatives to focus church stewardship. The book is a multifaceted resource refreshingly free of dogmatism, an ideal for discussion and reflection.

**VISION FOUNDATION, INC.** ■ *Why Go to Work?* Vision Foundation, 1987. *43 pages.*
This book identifies the often dramatic differences between secular and biblical views of work. It expounds nine principles, five relating to work, four to leisure, to help Christians develop a balanced view of work and leisure.

**VOLF, MIROSLAV,** PROFESSOR ■ *Work in the Spirit: Toward a Theology of Work.* Oxford University Press, 1991. *252 pages.*
This is Volf's attempt to articulate a broad contemporary theology of work. According to Volf, the purpose of a theology of work is to "interpret, evaluate, and facilitate the transformation of human work." Volf sees no future in trying to rehabilitate the understanding of work as vocation. Instead he emphasizes the significance of pneumatology and eschatology—the Spirit is the agent through whom the future new creation is anticipated in the present. Work today should be patterned according to the values of the new creation and criticized in the light of the eschatological judgment. Only work that corresponds to the new creation is ultimately meaningful.

**VOLZ, CARL A.,** PROFESSOR ■ *Pastoral Life and Practice in the Early Church.* Augsburg, 1990. *240 pages.*
A detailed book about the nature of the early church from the New Testament through to the fifth century. Volz divides his subject matter by era (New Testament, early church fathers, imperial church) and by topic (pastoral office, pastor and people, pastor and proclamation, care of souls, pastoral role of women).

**VON BALTHASAR, HANS URS,** PRIEST, THEOLOGIAN ■ *A Short Primer: For Unsettled Laymen.* Ignatius Press, 1985. *134 pages.*
This book analyzes the state of affairs within the Catholic Church since the Second Vatican Council. It also interprets some of the after effects of the Council's rulings and encourages disillusioned Catholic laity. The author affirms those who are childlike in faith and tells them not to be intimidated by the modern "scientific theologian" whose sophistication often obscures the essence of the Christian life.

**VOS, NELVIN,** PROFESSOR ■ *Seven Days a Week: Faith in Action.* Fortress, 1985. *127 pages.*
Building connections between faith and daily experience, Vos examines ministry in the contexts of family, work, leisure, community and church. He suggests that for us to see all of life in terms of a faith commitment we need to have a view of ministry that "is not something we go out and do, but rather something we do as we go."

**WAGNER, C. PETER,** PROFESSOR ■ *Leading Your Church to Growth:The Secret of Pastor/People Partnership in Dynamic Church Growth.* Regal, 1984. 218 pages.
Wagner promotes the equipper model as a combination of the authoritarian pastor and the enabler who helps others reach their goals. "An equiper is a leader who actively sets goals for a congregation . . . and sees that each church member is properly motivated and equipped to do his or her part in accomplishing the goals."

*Your Spiritual Gifts Can Help Your Church Grow.* Regal, 1979. *263 pages.*
A basic book on spiritual gifts focusing on how gifts are to be used to promote church growth rather than on how they help individual Christians. Wagner identifies twenty-seven spiritual gifts, but he gives a detailed look only at the pastor, evangelist and missionary in discussing church growth.

**WALSH, BRIAN J., & RICHARD J. MIDDLETON,** PROFESSORS ■ *The Transforming Vision: Shaping a Christian World View.* InterVarsity Press, 1984. *214 pages.*
After defining the biblical worldview, based on creation, fall and redemption, the authors contend that the root of our contemporary problems is dualism—dividing life into areas of sacred and secular. By applying the biblical worldview to all of life, Christians can transform society.

**WALTKE, BRUCE,** PROFESSOR ■ *Finding the Will of God:A Pagan Notion?* Vision House, 1995. *181 pages.*
Waltke looks carefully at Christian decision making and what it means for a Christian to discern God's will. Though not designed for occupational decision making, this book could help Christians making decisions about their occupational calling. Aimed at a general readership, this book is filled with insight and good teaching.

**WALTON, CLARENCE C.,** UNIVERSITY PRESIDENT ■ *The Moral Manager.* Ballinger, 1988. *364 pages.*
Widely recognized as a pioneer in the field of business ethics, Walton asks, "Do managers have the responsibility to provide moral leadership? What are the bedrock values upon which business professionals' decisions and actions are based? What is the relevance of moral character to managerial effectiveness?" This is an advanced and exquisitely researched study for those interested in exploring morality.

**WALTON, WILLIAM B., WITH MEL LORENTZEN,** BUSINESSMAN; WRITER ■ *The New Bottom Line.* Harper & Row, 1986. *242 pages.*
The cofounder of Holiday Inn describes what can happen when one puts people

and loyalty first in business. Walton reveals how the values in Holiday Inn changed (to include alcohol and gambling) and how he fought these changes. He contends that this "new bottom line" ruined the company as money replaced people in importance. A well-written and interesting commentary on corporate value shifts.

**WARKENTIN, MARJORIE** ■ *Ordination:A Biblical-Historical View.* Eerdmans, 1982. *188 pages.*
Warkentin looks at ordination from historical, exegetical and theological perspectives. She argues that ordination inappropriately puts a person into a mediatorial role already filled by Christ. Warkentin further argues that Jesus' lordship and the Spirit's presence define a distinctive authority structure for the church.

**WATSON, DAVID,** CLERGY ■ *Called and Committed:World Changing Discipleship.* Harold Shaw, 1982. *198 pages.*
"Christians in the West have largely neglected what it means to be disciples of Christ. . . . If we were willing to become disciples, the church in the West would be transformed, and the impact on society would be staggering" (publisher).

**WEBER, HANS-RUEDI,** CHURCH EXECUTIVE ■ *Living in the Image of Christ.* World Council of Churches Publications, 1986. *79 pages.*
Weber speaks of the ministry of the laity in terms of "human vocation, lived in the light of Christ." From three pictures of Christ he draws implications for the laity: (1) Christ the sage, whose wisdom can be seen in creation and the cross, (2) Christ the crucified, who reminds us of our task to seek justice, and (3) Christ the artist, who transforms us into his own image. A valuable perspective on lay theology.

**WENTZ, FREDERICK K.,** PROFESSOR ■ *The Layman's Role Today.* Abingdon, 1963. *226 pages.*
Wentz begins with an analysis of the problem facing the laity. There is a great chasm between Sunday and the rest of the week, and this is partly due to the church's retreat into a ghetto where it does not concern itself with the affairs of the world. Wentz calls for a new understanding of the laity, presenting four images of lay ministry in the world: servant, light, salt and soldier.

**WEST, ROSS,** CHURCH AND BUSINESS CONSULTANT ■ *Go to Work and Take Your Faith Too.* Peake Road, 1997. *164 pages.*
West starts by posing some questions: Is work a curse or a blessing? What does faith have to do with work? Can my faith really make a difference in my work life? He then answers those questions by relating faith directly to work and a person's

purpose in life. He concludes the book with a chapter on how churches can help. A simple, quick read, the book would make a good discussion starter.

**WHELCHEL, MARY,** BUSINESS OWNER ▪ *The Christian Working Woman. Revell, 1986. 224 pages.*
Whelchel is the leader of the Christian Working Woman organization. She discusses issues such as ambition, success, money, feminine assertiveness, loving people, the impossible boss, dealing with men on the job, working mothers (she is a single parent), and job hunting and unemployment. Whelchel encourages readers to view their job as the corner of the world God has sent them to share Jesus Christ and his love. Biblical references abound throughout.

*How to Thrive from 9 to 5.* Vine, 1999. *201 pages.*
This is an immensely practical book about taking charge of one's work life and relationships, avoiding office politics, setting personal goals and earning the respect even of irritable coworkers. Whelchel focuses on sound communication and key people skills: returning calls, keeping promises, handling criticism, defusing coworker anger, learning to say no, and avoiding gossip and self-pity. Each chapter is packed with self-assessment tools and tests for personal use or staff training and development. Equally useful to men and women.

**WHITE, JERRY,** MINISTRY EXECUTIVE ▪ *Honesty, Morality and Conscience.* NavPress, 1996. *256 pages.*
White gives us a crunching commentary on the importance of the conscience. He meticulously reviews the so-called gray areas of life and mercilessly strips away the excuses used to rationalize unethical behavior. Biblical and down-to-earth writing coupled with a solid study guide.

**WHITE, JERRY, & MARY WHITE,** EXECUTIVE; SECRETARY ▪ *On the Job: Survival or Satisfaction.* NavPress, 1988. *297 pages.*
This fairly comprehensive text covers the gamut of common issues facing the Christian in the workplace, such as the purposes of work; handling frustrating work conditions; career change; ambition and fulfillment; midlife crisis; women and work; and juggling work, family and other priorities. The advice is both pastoral and scriptural, and it reflects not only their strong emphasis on Christian discipleship but their own struggle through years of employment in military and government service.

**WHITE, JOHN,** PSYCHIATRIST, PASTOR ■ *The Golden Cow: Materialism in the Twentieth-Century Church.* InterVarsity Press, 1979. *175 pages.*
This is a broad-ranging work on mammon and how it controls us directly and through our societal structures. White first looks at the Bible and then draws out implications for the use of money in the church (and parachurch).

*Excellence in Leadership: Reaching Goals with Prayer, Courage and Determination.* InterVarsity Press, 1986. *132 pages.*
White analyzes of the life and work of Nehemiah in order to discover biblical principles for Christian leadership today.

**WILBERFORCE, ROBERT, & KEVIN BELMONTE,** PARLIAMENTARIAN; PROFESSOR ■ *The Family Prayers of William Wilberforce.* Riven Oak Press, 1999. *56 pages.*
Fourteen of William Wilberforce's morning and evening devotionals from his daily family gatherings were collected by his son Robert in 1834. These have been edited by Belmonte for the modern reader. Each day's entry ends with the Lord's Prayer and the same affirmation of the grace of God for every person.

**WILLARD, DALLAS,** PROFESSOR ■ *The Divine Conspiracy: Rediscovering Our Hidden Life in God.* HarperSanFrancisco, 1998. *428 pages.*
Using language, anecdotes and illustrations everyone can relate to, Willard challenges the notion that Jesus has little or no relevance to today's culture, and he lays responsibility for changing that perception right at the reader's doorstep. Willard encourages readers to know Jesus now, and let the precepts of God permeate their lives today. Workplace Christians will find something helpful in every chapter.

*The Spirit of the Disciplines.* HarperSanFrancisco, 1991. *276 pages.*
Christians struggling with spiritual discipline or with being overwhelmed by culture and busyness need to study this book. Willard's writing is warm, inviting and soothing without being patronizing. He understands the joys of the spiritual disciplines and provides new ways for Christians to engage in them. Most marketplace Christians will appreciate his writing on solitude, and nearly everyone will find advice for their spiritual lives.

**WILLIAMS, RON C.,** PASTOR ■ *The Worklife Inspiration Bible.* Worklife Inspiration, 1998.
This is a thematic edition of the Bible focused on the realities of the business world. It is self-published and marketed by the author, an assistant pastor of an African

American church. Several hundred reflections on work are scattered throughout, covering topics like characteristics of a believer, travel, advertising, children and work, the environment, office parties, power lunches, competition, and entrepreneurs. A topical index and a year's worth of daily readings are included. This is a refreshing contribution to the black community, where little material on work and faith issues has been developed.

**WILLIAMS, OLIVER F., & JOHN W. HOUCK,** PROFESSORS ∎ *Full Value: Cases in Christian Business Ethics.* Harper & Row, 1978. *236 pages.*
Williams and Houck bring ethical help to the rise of big business in the American economy. They present ten case studies accompanied by careful analysis, biblical helps, ideas about actions and good bibliographic resources. In this book real people struggle with tensions in economics, conflict over profit and human values, stock value demands, and ethics. Well crafted and thoughtful, this is an important contribution to the application of faith to modern business.

**WILSON, DOROTHY CLARKE,** WRITER ∎ *Ten Fingers for God: The Life and Work of Dr. Paul Brand.* Zondervan, 1989. *289 pages.*
This is the story of a skilled physician who dedicated his life, marriage and career to caring for lepers. Brand was born a child of missionaries in India, where he established a leprosy hospital. World acclaim could not draw him away from the people he was called to serve. Brand also became a dedicated environmentalist. The breadth and depth of his faith is a model for everyone.

**WILSON, J. CHRISTY, JR.,** MISSIONARY, PROFESSOR ∎ *Today's Tentmakers: Self-Support—An Alternative Model for Worldwide Witness.* Tyndale House, 1979. *165 pages.*
Wilson promotes the tentmaking model for overseas missions. He gives many examples of how this model provides opportunities that are closed to traditional models of missions. Practical issues on tentmaking are addressed, including the kinds of opportunities that exist, preparation, the role of mission boards and life overseas.

**WILSON, MARLENE,** EDUCATOR ∎ *How to Mobilize Church Volunteers.* Augsburg, 1983. *156 pages.*
Wilson writes, "The church does not exist to be served but to provide and equip servants." Beginning with a theology which states that all Christians are gifted to function as priests in the church and the world, Wilson employs management tools (i.e., planning, organizing, staffing, directing and controlling) to help solve the problem of a passive laity. This book is full of practical suggestions.

**WINGREN, GUSTAF,** PROFESSOR ■ *The Christian's Calling: Luther on Vocation.* Trans. C. C. Rasmussen. Oliver & Boyd, 1957. *251 pages.*
An in-depth analysis of Luther's understanding of vocation, which applies not simply to the clergy but to all Christians.

**WOLGEMUTH, ROBERT,** LITERARY AGENT ■ *Daddy@Work.* Zondervan, 1999. *211 pages.*
This book puts a new and different spin on being a marketplace Christian. Wolgemuth urges fathers to take their parenting skills to work. He actually advocates taking the tender and caring aspects of "daddyhood" into the office and applying them to the corporate world. He also advocates bringing a bit of management and planning home.

**WOLTERSTORFF, NICHOLAS,** PROFESSOR ■ *Art in Action: Toward a Christian Aesthetic.* Eerdmans, 1980. *240 pages.*
Wolterstorff finds the typical aesthetician's view of art (that is, "high art") remarkably provincial. Instead he proposes a multifunctional approach to art as instruments or objects of action, the critique of which is dependent on the "ultimate concerns" and context of both artist and audience. He shows the significance of art in non-elite settings of home, street and hotel lobby. Illustrations are drawn from classical and modern plays, movies, poems, dramas, paintings and sculptures. A distinctly Christian perspective.

**WOOD, JAN,** PASTOR ■ *Christians at Work: Not Business as Usual.* Herald, 1999. *147 pages.*
Fear, anger, ornery coworkers, seductive power games—the deck seems stacked against a Christian presence at work. Wood shines the light of the gospel on the workplace (where we show who we really are). With clarity, charity and penetrating insight she shows how the love of God can transform life in the office, boardroom or factory floor.

**WOODBRIDGE, JOHN, ED.,** PROFESSOR ■ *More Than Conquerors: Portraits of Believers from All Walks of Life.* Moody Press, 1992. *360 pages.*
Woodbridge and friends profile believers from the everyday world and workplace. Featured are sixty-eight people in ten nonreligious contexts (e.g., politics, industry and commerce, sports and entertainment, writers and social reformers) as well as preachers, missionaries and evangelists. Eleven women are featured. Helpful items include pictures, sidebars giving the historical context for each individual and a list of further works by or about the person. Although there are few international and non-Anglo entries this is a wonderful contribution to the marketplace movement.

**WORLD HOME BIBLE LEAGUE** ■ *The Road Map of Life: Christ in the World of Trucking.* World Home Bible League, n.d. *313 pages.*
This is a specialty New International Version (NIV) New Testament published in cooperation with the organization Transport for Christ, Intl. and is designed as a give-a-way for truckers. It is, or was, available through their regional offices across America and Canada, and in New South Wales. There is a one-page explanation of their version of conversion, and a few verses have been selected and underlined as special helps.

**WYSZYNSKI, STEFAN,** CARDINAL ■ *All You Who Labor: Work and the Sanctification of Daily Life.* Sophia Institute Press, 1995. *191 pages.*
Cardinal Wyszynski (1901-1981), head of the Catholic church in Poland for thirty-two years, explains Catholic perspectives on the nature, purposes and problems with work. This book contains a wealth of insight of particular benefit for those struggling to understand the place of work in the life of the Christian.

*The Deeds of Faith.* Harper & Row, 1966. *187 pages.*
This is a rich collection of addresses given by Wyszynski to Polish educators, physicians, soldiers, nurses, taxi drivers, lawyers and writers. The book is filled with insightful and challenging words for the application of faith.

**YOUNG, ANDREW,** SOCIAL ACTIVIST, BUSINESSMAN ■ *A Way Out of No Way: The Spiritual Memoirs of Andrew Young.* Thomas Nelson, 1994. *172 pages.*
Young joined Martin Luther King Jr. as his personal aide during the civil rights movement. He has been a pastor, congressman, the U.S. representative to the United Nations, mayor of Atlanta, chair of the 1996 Olympics and cochair, with Jimmy Carter, of the Billy Graham crusade in Atlanta. His vision and commitment to justice and peacemaking is rooted in his biblical understanding of the Christian faith.

*An Easy Burden.* HarperCollins, 1996. *550 pages.*
Young tells his story beginning with his childhood roots in New Orleans, including his own discovery of being black and despised, through the tumultuous 1961-1968 Civil Rights Movement days. The role of Negro spirituals and Scripture is described with obvious appreciation. Young clearly describes and affirms the deep Christian roots, beliefs and principles that Martin Luther King practiced. He honors his own parents and siblings, and lifts up many unseen or unacknowledged people who gave so much energy, strength and service to the movement.

**YUSUF, JOLLY TANKO, WITH LILLIAN V. GRISSEN,** DIPLOMAT, MISSIONARY ■ *That We May Be One: The Autobiography of Nigerian Ambassador Jolly Tanko Yusuf.* Eerdmans, 1995. *123 pages.*

Yusuf, who served as a government leader and diplomat for Nigeria, applied Christ's words about unity to tribalism, Muslim-Christian tensions, racism, denominationalism and imperialism throughout his career. Though he writes with candor and bluntness about Islam, Yusuf seeks to achieve full citizenship rights for all people. He speaks with deep love for English and American missionaries but strongly critiques their practice of discrimination and air of superiority. Yusuf understands that "God was particularly calling—and challenging—me to witness for him politically" (p. 60).

**ZABLOSKI, JIM,** BUSINESS MANAGER, EDITORIAL DIRECTOR ■ *The 25 Most Common Problems in Business (and How Jesus Solved Them).* Broadman & Holman, 1996. *272 pages.*

Zabloski asks what Jesus would do as a receptionist, financial or personnel manager, a marketing director and so on. Each chapter begins with a look at "the business philosophies and strategy of a man whose ideas and products have remained on the market for [thousands of] years." Zabloski covers the wide terrain of day-to-day business practices: training, delegating, goal-setting, leading, negotiating, failing, team-building, hiring and firing, and trouble-shooting. Well written with pithy, practical advice. Highly recommended.

**ZABRISKIE, STEWART C.,** PASTOR ■ *Total Ministry: Reclaiming the Ministry of All God's People.* Alban Institute, 1995. *107 pages.*

Zabriskie, an Episcopalian bishop, relates new ways of seeing church organization and ministry: "the Holy Spirit living in and working through persons (not self-perpetuating organizations, institutions, and systems), ministry that comes alive in personal gifts offered in and as community" (publisher). Zabriskie describes the successes and difficulties he experienced in seeing ministry in this way.

**ZIGARELLI, MICHAEL A.,** PROFESSOR ■ *Christianity 9 to 5: Living Your Faith at Work.* Beacon Hill, 1998. *152 pages.*

This helpful book uses vignettes from the life of Mark, who begins his career as an earnest Christian and faces difficult faith challenges along his twenty-five-year journey. Zigarelli provides biblical guidance for workplace problems (coworkers, challenges to beliefs, office evangelism land mines, understanding a biblical rationale for work, misuses of anger, work and family tensions, and how to be a godly boss).

The theology of work presented is basic. An easy read that lends itself to small group discussion.

*Management by Proverbs.* **Moody Press, 1999.** *286 pages.*

In this book Zigarelli lifts nineteen management principles from Proverbs, which has an abundance of wisdom for everyday living. Through these principles he addresses workplace issues such as laying a foundation for personal success, building a competitive workforce, cultivating a culture of commitment, evaluating performance and controlling conflict. The counsel is practical and road-tested.

# Indexes

## Theme Indexes

### Case Studies

Coddington, Dean, *Christianity in the Workplace*

De Vries, Paul, *The Taming of the Shrewd*

Donaldson, Thomas, *Ethical Issues in Business*

Field, David, *Just the Job*

Fish, Sharon, *Spiritual Care*, 3rd ed.

Goetz, Joseph W., *Mirrors of God*

Goosen, Gideon, *The Theology of Work*

Greene, Mark, *Thank God It's Monday*

Guinness, Os, ed., *Character Counts*

Hill, Alexander, *Just Business*

Lindgren, Alvin, J., *Let My People Go*

Lowery, James L., ed., *Case Histories of Tentmakers*

Pierce, Gregory F. Augustine, *Of Human Hands*

Redekop, Calvin W., *Entrepreneurs in the Faith Community*

Sprunger, Ben, *Faith Dilemmas for Marketplace Christians*

Vincent, James. *Parting the Waters*

Williams, Oliver F., & John W. Houck, *Full Value*

### Congregational Studies

Allen, Tom, *The Face of My Parish*

Carey, George, *The Church in the Marketplace*

Crabtree, Davida Foy, *The Empowering Church*

Diehl, William E., *Ministry in Daily Life*

Geaney, Dennis, *Full Church, Empty Rectory*

Fenhagen, James C., *More Than Wanderers*

————, *Mutual Ministry*

Hahn, Celica A., *Learning to Share the Ministry*

Haille, Philip P., *Lest Innocent Blood Be Shed*

Johnson, Paul G., *Grace—God's Work Ethic*

McNamara, Patrick H., *More Than Money*

Mead, Loren B., *The Once and Future Church*

Melba, Gerald J., *The People Parish*

Menking, Stanley J., *Helping Laity Help Others*

Miller, Calvin, *Marketplace Preaching*

Smith, Donald P., *Congregations Alive*

Stevens, R. Paul, *Liberating the Laity*

Zabriskie, Stewart C., *Total Ministry*

### Especially for Pastors

Allan, Tom, *The Face of My Parish*

Allen, Roland, *The Case for Voluntary Clergy*

Armbruster, Wally, *Let Me Out!*

Anderson, James D., *Ministry of the Laity*

Ayres, Francis O., *The Ministry of the Laity*

Banks, Robert J., *All the Business of Life*

————, *The Complete Book of Everyday Christianity*

————, *God the Worker*

————, *Redeeming the Routines*

————, *Theology of, by and for the People*

Barnes, Craig M., *When God Interrupts*

Barnes, Geoffrey, *The Forgotten Factor*

Benjamin, Paul, *The Equipping Ministry*

Calian, Carnegie S., *Today's Pastor in Tomorrow's World*

Calkin, Jeffrey K., *Being God's Partner*

Carey, George, *The Church in the Marketplace*

Comfort, Earl V., *Living Stones*

Congar, Yves, *Lay People in the Church*

Cook, Jerry, *Love, Acceptance and Forgiveness*

### Leisure Studies

Banks, Robert J., *The Complete Book of Everyday Christianity*

Cook, Colleen, *All That Glitters*

Hansel, Tim, *When I Relax I Feel Guilty*

Heintzman, Paul, *Christianity and Leisure*

Helldorfer, Martin C., *The Work Trap*

Holmes, Arthur F., *Contours of a World View*

Lapham, Lewis H., *Money and Class in America*

Marshall, Paul, *Labor of Love*

Oswald, John, *The Leisure Crisis*

Pieper, Josef, *Leisure*

Ryken, Leland, *Redeeming the Time*

———, *Work and Leisure in Christian Perspective*

Sherman, Doug, *How to Balance Competing Time Demands*

Swenson, Richard, *Margin*

Solomon, Jerry, ed., *Arts, Entertainment & Christian Values*

Vision Foundation, *Why Go to Work?*

Vos, Nelvin, *Seven Days a Week*

Wolgemuth, Robert, *Daddy@Work*

### Multiethnic and International

Allen, Roland, *Missionary Methods*

———, *The Spontaneous Expansion of the Church*

Baker, James, *Brooks Hayes*

Bakke, Ray, *The Urban Christian*

Balda, Wesley D., ed., *Heirs of the Same Promise*

Barnette, Henlee H., *Clarence Jordan*

Beck, James R., *Dorothy Carey*

Cahill, Thomas, *How the Irish Saved Civilization*

Carson, Ben, *The Big Picture*

Carson, Clayborne, ed., *The Autobiography of Martin Luther King, Jr.*

Catherwood, Christopher, *Why the Nations Rage*

Guder, Darrell L., ed., *Missional Church*

Flood, Edmund, *The Laity Today and Tomorrow*

Haille, Philip P., *Lest Innocent Blood be Shed*

Halverson, Richard, *Relevance*

Hamilton, Don, *Tentmakers Speak*

Hammond, Pete, *The Word in Life Study Bible*

Hopler, Thom, *A World of Difference*

Hunsberger, George R., *Bearing the Witness of the Spirit*

James, Kay Coles, *Never Forget*

Karmiris, John N., *The Status and Ministry of the Laity in the Orthodox Church*

Kelba, Gerald J., *The People Parish*

Lausanne Committee, *The Willowbrook Report*

Lupton, Robert D., *Theirs Is the Kingdom*

McConnell, William, T., *The Gift of Time*

Miller, Basil, *William Carey*

Morgan, Edmund S., *The Puritan Dilemma*

Neill, Stephen, *The Layman in Christian History*

Newbigin, Lesslie, *Foolishness to the Greeks*

Paton, David, *The Compulsion of the Spirit*

———, ed., *The Ministry of the Spirit*

Perry, John, *Unshakable Faith*

Rowthorn, Anne, *The Liberation of the Laity*

Roxburgh, Alan J., *The Missionary Congregation*

Salkin, Jeffrey K., *Being God's Partner*

Scanzoni, John, *The Christian View of Work*

Sider, Ronald J., *Rich Christians in an Age of Hunger*

Sojourners, *Who Is My Neighbor?*

Suter, Hans, *Business Power for God's Purpose*

Swarr, Sharon Bentch, *Transform the World*

Ting, John, *Living Biblically at Work*

Williams, Ron C., *The Worklife Inspiration Bible*

Wilson, J. Christy, Jr., *Today's Tentmakers*

Wyszynski, Stefan, *All You Who Labor*

———, *The Deeds of Faith*

Young, Andrew, *An Easy Burden*

———, *A Way Out of No Way*

Yusuf, Jolly, *That We May Be One*

### Profiles, Autobiographies and Biographies

Alderson, Wayne. *Stronger Than Steel* by R. C. Sproul

Philips, Frederick. *45 Years with Philips*

Ritchie, Mark. *God in the Pits*

Rockefeller, John D., Sr. *TITAN, Sr.* by Ron Chernov

Rockefellers. *The Rockefeller Century* by John Ensor Harr

Rookmaaker, Hans. *Hans Rookmaaker* by Linette Martin

Rossi, Anthony T. *Anthony T. Rossi* by Sanna Barlow Rossi

Sayers, Dorothy L. *Maker & Craftsman* by Alzina Stone Dale

Schumacher, Christian. *God in Work* by Christian Schumacher

Shoemaker, Sam. *I Stand by the Door* by Helen Smith Shoemaker

Tam, Stanley. *God Owns My Business* by Stanley Tam

Taylor, Herbert J. *The Herbert J. Taylor Story*
———. *God's Man in the Marketplace* by Paul H. Heidebrecht

Thomas, Dave. *Well Done!* by Dave Thomas

Tocmé, Andre. *Lest Innocent Blood Be Shed* by Philip P. Haille

Tutu, Desmond Mpilo. *No Future Without Forgiveness* by Desmond Mpilo Tutu

Vereide, Abraham. *Modern Viking* by Norman Grubb

Walton, William B. *The New Bottom Line* by William B. Walton

Washington Carver, George. *George Washington Carver* by David R. Collins

Washington, Booker T., & George Washington Carver. *Unshakable Faith* by John Perry

Waters, Ethel. *Ethel Waters* by Twila Knaack

Wilberforce, William. *God's Politician* by Garth Lean

Winthrop, John. *The Puritan Dilemma* by Edmund S. Morgan

Young, Andrew. *A Way Out of No Way* by Andrew Young
———. *An Easy Burden* by Andrew Young

### Books with Several Profiles

Banks, Robert J., *Faith Goes to Work*

*Christian History* magazine, *131 Christians Everyone Should Know*

Clark, James Kelley, *Philosophers Who Believe*

Deen, Edith, *All the Women of the Bible*
———, *Great Women of the Christian Faith*

Diehl, William E., *Christianity and Real Life*

Goetz, Joseph W., *Mirrors of God*

Gosse, Joseph, *The Spirituality of Work*

Guinness, Os, ed., *Character Counts*

Harris, Irving, *He Touched Me*

Harrison, Patricia, ed., *America's New Women Entrepreneurs*

Janney, Rebecca Price, *Great Women in American History*

Kerr, Hugh T., *Conversions*

Leckey, Dolores R., *Practical Spirituality for Lay People*

Lentz, Harold, and Eleanor Lentz, *Twenty-Two Who Changed the World*

Lulic, Margaret, *Who We Could Be At Work*

Mitchell, John E., *The Christian in Business*

Mogil, Christopher, *We Gave Away a Fortune*

Mott, John R., *Liberating the Lay Forces of Christianity*

Nash, Laura L., *Believers in Business*

Neill, Stephen, *The Layman in Christian History*

Pippert, Wesley, *Faith at the Top*

Redekop, Calvin, *Mennonite Entrepreneurs*

Turpin, Joanne, *Women in Church History*

Woodbridge, John, *More Than Conquerors*

### Industry Specific
### Arts

Barber, Elizabeth Wayland, *Women's Work*

Briner, Bob, *Roaring Lambs*

Collins, David, *Francis Scott Key*

Dale, Alzina Stone, *Maker & Craftsman*

Dylong, John, *The Spirituality of Work*

Gallagher, Susan V., *Literature Through the Eyes of Faith*

Garlow, James L., *We "Laity" Are Ministers*

Hammond, Pete, *The Word In Life Study Bible*

Hind, James F., *The Heart and Soul of Effective Management*
Hopkins, C. Howard, *John R. Mott*
Hunter, Ian, *Robert Laidlaw*
Klingaman, Patrick, *Thank God It's Monday*
Kreider, Carl, *The Christian Entrepreneur*
Kresge, Staley S., *The S. S. Kresge Story*
Leininger, B. Joseph, *Lessons from the Pit*
Leman, Dr. Kevin, *Winning the Rat Race Without Becoming a Rat*
LeTourneau, R. G., *R. G. LeTourneau*
Liebig, James E., *Business Ethics*
Life@Work Journal, *The Life@Work Book*
Lulic, Margaret, *Who We Could Be at Work*
McNair, Nimrod, *Executive Guide to Ethical Decision-Making*
Miller, Norm, *Beyond the Norm*
Mitchell, John E., *The Christian in Business*
Mitroff, Ian I., *A Spiritual Audit of Corporate America*
Moore, Sam, *American by Choice*
Musser, Joe, *The Cereal Tycoon*
Nash, Laura L., *Believers in Business*
———, *Good Intentions Aside*
Nix, William, *Transforming Your Workplace for Christ*
Novak, Michael, *Toward a Theology of the Corporation*
Ortega, Bob, *In Sam We Trust*
Pascarella, Perry, *Christ-Centered Leadership*
———, *The Ten Commandments of the Workplace and How to Break Them Every Day*
Philips, Frederik, *45 Years with Philips*
Phipps, Simon, *God On Monday*
Pierce, Gregory F. Augustine, *The Buck Stops Here*
———, *Spirituality @ Work*
Pollard, C. William, *Soul of the Firm*
Redekop, Calvin W., *Entrepreneurs in the Faith Community*
Redekop, Calvin, *Mennonite Entrepreneurs*
Rossi, Sanna Barlow, *Anthony T. Rossi*
Rush, Myron, *Lord of the Marketplace*
Seibert, Donald V., *The Ethical Executive*

Sherman, Doug, *How to Succeed Where It Really Counts*
Smith, Thomas, *God on the Job*
Sproul, R. C., *Stronger Than Steel*
Sprunger, Ben, *Faith Dilemmas for Marketplace Christians*
Suter, Hans, *Business Power for God's Purpose*
Sutherland, John R., *Going Broke*
———, *Us and Them*
Swarr, Sharon Bentch, *Transform the World*
Swindoll, Luci, *After You've Dressed for Success*
Tam, Stanley, *God Owns My Business*
Tamasy, Robert J., ed., *Jesus Works Here*
Taylor, Herbert J., *The Herbert J. Taylor Story*
Thomas, Dave, *Well Done!*
Torrell, Dolores Lynn, *Heart Business*
Tucker, Graham, *The Faith-Work Connection*
Vincent, James, *Parting the Waters*
Walton, William B., *The New Bottom Line*
Whelchel, Mary, *The Christian Working Woman*
———, *How to Thrive From 9 to 5*
Williams, Oliver F., *Full Value*
Wolgemuth, Robert, *Daddy@Work*
Zabloski, Jim, *The 25 Most Common Problems in Business (and How Jesus Solved Them)*
Zigarelli, Michael A., *Christianity*
———, *Management by Proverbs*

### Calling, Career and Unemployment
Bolles, Richard Nelson, *The New Quick Job-Hunting Map*
———, *What Color Is Your Parachute?*
Bramlett, James, *Finding Work*
Buford, Bob, *Game Plan*
Congar, Yves, *Called to Life*
Ellis, Lee, *Your Career in Changing Times*
Gosse, Joseph, *The Spirituality of Work*
Larsen, Dale, & Sandy Larsen, *Patching Your Parachute*
Novak, Michael, *Business as a Calling*

Harper, Michael, *Let My People Grow*

Harrisville, Roy A., *Ministry in Crisis*

Hauerwas, Stanley, *Resident Aliens*

Henricksen, Walter, *Layman, Look Up!*

Humphreys, Fisher, *Laos*

Hunsberger, George R., *Bearing the Witness of the Spirit*

Jacob, W. M., *Lay People and Religion in the Early Eighteenth Century*

Kauffman, Daniel, *Managers with God*

Kelba, Gerald J., *The People Parish*

Keller, W. Phillip, *Salt for Society*

Kenny, J. P., *Roman Catholicism, Christianity and Anonymous Christianity*

Kinast, Robert L., *Caring for Society*

King, David S., *No Church Is an Island*

Kraemer, Hendrik, *A Theology of the Laity*

Leckey, Dolores R., *Laity Stirring the Church*

Lee, Phillip, *Against the Protestant Gnostics*

Lindgren, Alvin J., *Let My People Go*

Lunden, Rolf, *Business and Religion in the American 1920s*

Luther, Joe Thompson, *Monday Morning Religion*

Mackenzie, Alistair, review of *"Dogmatic Constitution on the Church,"* found in *The Documents of the Vatican II* by Walter M. Abbott

Macquarrie, John, *The Faith of the People of God*

Marciniak, Ed, et al., *Challenge to the Laity*

Mead, Loren B., *The Once and Future Church*

Menking, Stanley J., *God's Partners*

———, *Helping Laity Help Others*

Miller, Calvin, *Marketplace Preaching*

Morris, Charles R., *American Catholic*

Morris, Margie, *Volunteer Ministries*

Neill, Stephen, *The Layman in Christian History*

Newbigin, Lesslie, *Honest Religion for Secular Man*

Niebuhr, H. Richard, *Christ and Culture*

Nouwen, Henri J. M., *Creative Ministry*

———, *The Wounded Healer*

O'Connor, Elizabeth, *Eighth Day of Creation*

Oechslin, R. L., *The Spirituality of the Layman*

Ogden, Greg, *The New Reformation*

Parent, Remi, *A Church of the Baptized*

Paton, David, *The Compulsion of the Spirit*

Peabody, Larry, *Secular Work Is Full Time Service*

Pearce, Joseph, *Wisdom and Innocence*

Peck, George, *The Laity in Ministry*

Peel, Donald, *The Ministry of the Laity*

Pierce, Gregory F. Augustine, *Activism That Makes Sense*

Richards, Lawrence O., *A Theology of Church Leadership*

———, *A Theology of Personal Ministry*

Robinson, J. A. T., ed., *Layman's Church*

———, *The New Reformation?*

Rowthorn, Anne, *The Liberation of the Laity*

Rudy, Doris, *Worship & Daily Life*

Russell, Jim, *Awakening the Giant*

Sayers, Dorothy L., *Creed or Chaos?*

Shoemaker, Helen Smith, *I Stand by the Door*

Sider, Ronald J., *Cup of Water, Bread of Life*

Smith, Donald P., *Congregations Alive*

Snyder, Howard A., *Liberating the Church*

Sojourners, *Who Is My Neighbor?*

Southern Baptist Brotherhood Committee, *Bold New Laity*

Stedman, Ray C., *Body Life*

Steinbron, Melvin J., *Can the Pastor Do It Alone?*

———, *The Lay-Driven Church*

Stevens, R. Paul, *The Equipper's Guide to Every-Member Ministry*

———, *Liberating the Laity*

———, *The Other Six Days*

Stott, John R. W., *One People*

Stringfellow, William, *Dissenter in a Great Society*

———, *A Private and Public Faith*

Tillapaugh, Frank R., *The Church Unleashed*

Trueblood, D. Elton, *The Company of the Committed*

———, *The Incendiary Fellowship*

Gushee, David P., *Toward a Just and Caring Society*

Haas, Richard C., *We All Have a Share*

Halteman, James, *Clashing Worlds of Economics and Faith*

Hammond, Pete, et al., *Living in a World of Wealth and Poverty*

Haughey, John C., *The Holy Use of Money*

Hore-Lacy, Ian, *Creating Common Wealth*

Hybels, Bill, *Christians in the Marketplace*

Kreider, Carl, *The Rich and the Poor*

McCloughry, Roy, *The Eye of the Needle*

McConnell, Francis J., *Christian Materialism*

McCullough, Donald W., *Waking from the American Dream*

McNair, Nimrod, *Absolute Ethics*

Meeks, M. Douglas, *God the Economist*

Menconi, Peter, *Money*

Mogil, Christopher, *We Gave Away a Fortune*

Moltmann, Jürgen, *The Power of the Powerless*

Nash, Ronald H., *Poverty and Wealth*

—————, *Social Justice and the Christian Church*

National Conference of Catholic Bishops, *Economic Justice for All*

Owensby, Walter L., *Economics for Prophets*

Pike, Thomas, *Is It Success or Is It Addiction?*

Ritchie, Mark A., *God in the Pits*

Rodin, R. Scott, *Stewards in the Kingdom*

Rosner, Brian, *How to Get Really Rich*

Rudy, John H., *Money Wise Meditations*

Schumacher, E. F., *Small Is Beautiful*

Shames, Lawrence, *The Hunger for More*

Sider, Ronald J., *Rich Christians in an Age of Hunger*

Unsworth, Tim, *Upon This Rock*

Vincent, Mark, *A Christian View of Money*

Walton, William, *The New Bottom Line*

White, John, *The Golden Cow*

### Government

Ashcroft, John, *Lessons From a Father to His Son*

Beck, Roy Howard, *Prophets & Politics*

Belmonte, Kevin, *Choice Treasures*

—————, *Selected Spiritual Writings of William Wilberforce*

Brown, Robert McAffee, *Spirituality and Liberation*

Carson, Clayborne, ed., *The Autobiography of Martin Luther King, Jr.*

Carter, Jimmy, *Keeping Faith*

—————, *Sources of Strength*

Cassidy, Richard J., *Society and Politics in the Acts of the Apostles*

Catherwood, H. F. R., *The Christian Citizen*

Cerillo, Augustus, Jr., *Salt and Light*

Cunningham, Ginny, *The Spirituality of Work: Military Personnel*

Elliott, Charles, *Praying the Kingdom*

Ferguson, John, *O My People*

Grubb, Norman, *Modern Viking*

Harkness, Georgia, *John Calvin*

Hammond, Pete, *The Word In Life Study Bible*

Hatfield, Mark O., *Conflict and Conscience*

Hudnut, William, III, *Minister/Mayor*

James, Kay Coles, *Never Forget*

Komisar, Lucy, *Corazon Aquino*

Lay Commission on Social Teaching, *Liberty and Justice for All*

Lean, Garth, *God's Politician*

Marshall, Paul, *Thine Is the Kingdom*

McLellan, Vern, *Christians in the Political Arena*

Morgan, Edmund S., *The Puritan Dilemma*

Olasky, Marvin, *Renewing America's Compassion*

Owen, Frederick G., *Abraham Lincoln*

Pippert, Wesley, *Faith at the Top*

Simon, Charlie May, *Dag Hammarskjöld*

Trueblood, Elton D., *Abraham Lincoln*

Tschuy, Theo, *Dangerous Diplomacy*

Tutu, Desmond Mpilo, *No Future Without Forgiveness*

Vanderkloet, Ed, *In and Around the Workplace*

Young, Andrew, *An Easy Burden*

—————, *A Way Out of No Way*

Yusuf, Jolly, *That We May Be One*

## Title Index

*God the Economist,* M. Douglas Meeks

*God the Worker,* Robert J. Banks

*God's Frozen People,* Mark T. Gibbs & Ralph Morton

*God's Man in the Marketplace,* Paul H. Heidebrecht

*God's Partners,* Stanley J. Menking & Barbara Wendland

*God's People in God's World,* John Gladwin

*God's Politician,* Garth Lean

*God's Week Has Seven Days,* Wally Kroeker

*God's Work in Our Hands,* Committee on Social Witness Policy (PCUSA)

*Going Broke,* John R. Sutherland

*The Golden Cow,* John White

*Good Intentions Aside,* Laura L. Nash

*Good Work,* E. F. Schumacher

*Good Work,* Bruce Hiebert

*The Gospel According to Woman,* Karen Armstrong

*Grace—God's Work Ethic,* Paul G. Johnson

*The Grand Essentials,* Ben Patterson

*Great Women in American History,* Rebecca Price Janney

*Great Women of the Christian Faith,* Edith Deen

*Habits of the Mind,* James W. Sire

*Half Time,* Bob Buford

*Hans Rookmaaker,* Linette Martin

*He Touched Me,* Irving Harris

*Healing the Wounds,* David Hilfiker

*Health and Medicine in the Methodist Tradition,* Brooks E. Holifield

*The Heart and Soul of Effective Management,* James F. Hind

*Heart Business,* Dolores Lynn Torrell

*Hearts to God, Hands to Work,* Steve Jacobsen

*Heirs of the Same Promise,* ed. Wesley D. Balda

*Helping Laity Help Others,* Stanley J. Menking

*The Herbert J. Taylor Story,* Herbert J. Taylor

*A History of Women in America,* Carol Horowitz & Michelle Weissman

*The Holy Use of Money,* John C. Haughey

*Honest Religion for Secular Man,* Lesslie Newbigin

*Honesty, Morality, and Conscience,* Jerry White

*How I Changed My Mind About the Church,* Richard C. Halverson

*How Now Shall We Live?* Chuck Colson & Nancy Pearcey

*How the Irish Saved Civilization,* Thomas Cahill

*How to Balance Competing Time Demands,* Doug Sherman & William Hendricks

*How to Get Really Rich,* Brian Rosner

*How to Keep God Alive from 9 to 5,* John V. Chervokas

*How to Mobilize Church Volunteers,* Marlene Wilson

*How to Succeed Where It Really Counts,* Doug Sherman & William Hendricks

*How to Thrive From 9 to 5,* Mary Whelchel

*The Human Enterprise,* Richard W. Gillett

*The Hunger for More,* Laurence Shames

*I Believe in the Creator,* James M. Houston

*I Stand by the Door,* Helen Smith Shoemaker

*In and Around the Workplace,* Ed Vanderkloet

*In Sam We Trust,* Bob Ortega

*In Search of Faithfulness,* William E. Diehl

*The Incendiary Fellowship,* Elton Trueblood

*Insider's Guide to Finding the Right Job,* Diane Lewis & Joe Carroll

*Internet for Christians,* Quentin J. Schultze

*The Invasion of the Computer Culture,* Allen Emerson & Cheryl Forbes

*Is It Success or Is It Addiction?* Thomas Pike & William Proctor

*It's Easier to Succeed Than to Fail,* Truett Cathey

*Jesus Nine to Five,* Richard C. Tanner

*Jesus Works Here,* ed. Robert J. Tamasy

*The Job Hunter's Handbook,* Rodney S. Laughlin

*John Calvin,* Georgia Harkness

*John R. Mott,* C. Howard Hopkins

*Journeymen for Jesus,* William R. Sutton

*Just Business,* Alexander Hill

*The Long Loneliness,* Dorothy Day

*Lord of the Marketplace,* Myron Rush

*Lord, Where Are You?* Merle G. Franke

*Losing Your Job—Reclaiming Your Soul,* Mary Lynn Pulley

*Love, Acceptance and Forgiveness,* Jerry Cook & Stanley C. Baldwin

*Love Is the Measure,* Jim Forest

*Love Your Work!* David McKenna

*Loving and Working,* Rosemary Curran Barciauskas & Debra Hull

*Loving Monday,* John D. Beckett

*Lydia,* Lois T. Henderson

*Made in the U.S.A.,* Thomas V. DiBacco

*Maker & Craftsman,* Alzina Stone Dale

*Making All Things New,* Henri J. M. Nouwen

*Making Choices,* Peter Kreeft

*The Making of a Leader,* J. Robert Clinton

*Making the Church Work,* Edward H. Hammett

*Making Your Life a Ministry,* Jo Berry

*The Man in the Mirror,* Patrick Morley

*Management by Proverbs,* Michael A. Zigarelli

*The Management Methods of Jesus,* Bob Briner

*Managers with God,* Daniel Kauffman

*Margin,* Richard A. Swenson

*Marketplace Networks,* Pete Hammond & Brian Rust

*Marketplace Preaching,* Calvin Miller

*Marshall McLuhan,* Terrence W. Gordon

*Mary Kay,* Mary Kay Ash

*Master Your Money,* Ron Blue

*Maximize Your Ministry,* Robert E. Slocum

*Meditations for Women Who Do Too Much,* Anne Wilson Schaef

*Men Have Feelings Too!* Brain G. Jones & Linda Phillip-Jones

*Mennonite Entrepreneurs,* Calvin Redekop, Robert Seimens & Stephen Ainlay

*The Mind of the Maker,* Dorothy L. Sayers

*Minding God's Business,* Ray S. Anderson

*Ministering in the Secular University,* Joseph McRae Mellichamp

*Minister/Mayor,* William Hudnut III with Judy Keene

*Ministry and Solitude,* James C. Fenhagen

*Ministry in Crisis,* Roy A. Harrisville

*Ministry in Daily Life,* William E. Diehl

*The Ministry of All Christians,* Norman Pittenger

*The Ministry of All God's People,* Donna M. Costa

*Ministry of the Laity,* James D. Anderson with Ezra E. Jones

*The Ministry of the Laity,* Francis O. Ayres

*The Ministry of the Laity,* Donald Peel

*The Ministry of the Spirit,* ed. David Paton

*Mirrors of God,* Joseph W. Goetz

*Mission in the Marketplace,* Jeffrey W. Comment

*Missional Church,* ed. Darrell L. Guder

*The Missionary Congregation, Leadership & Liminality,* Alan J. Roxburgh

*Missionary Methods,* Roland Allen

*Modern Art and the Death of a Culture,* H. R. Rookmaaker

*Modern Viking,* Norman Grubb

*Modern Work and Human Meaning,* John C. Raines & Donna C. Day-Lower

*Molder of Dreams,* Guy Rice Doud

*The Monday Connection,* William E. Diehl

*Monday Morning Religion,* Joe Thompson Luther

*Money,* Peter Menconi, Lyman Coleman & Richard Peace

*Money and Class in America,* Lewis H. Lapham

*Money and Power,* Jacques Ellul

*Money, Sex and Power* (see *The Challenge of the Disciplined Life*), Richard J. Foster

*Money Wise Meditations,* John H. Rudy

*The Moral Manager,* Clarence C. Walton

*More Leadership Lessons of Jesus,* Bob Briner & Ray Pritchard

*More Than Conquerors,* John Woodbridge

*More Than Money,* Patrick H. McNamara

*More Than Wanderers,* James C. Fenhagen

*Mother's Choice,* Paul Meier & Linda Burnett

*Mutual Ministry,* James C. Fenhagen

# Marketplace Ministry Helps

### The Four-Way Test Association

This widely used ethics measurement was developed by Herbert J. Taylor. It is particularly shaped by his memorization of Jesus' Sermon on the Mount (Matthew 5—7).

By 1990 the Four-Way Test was used by approximately 800,000 business and community leaders in fifty-one countries. It is also found on monuments, billboards, the walls of schools, libraries, factories and business offices. It has been adopted by state legislatures and city councils, and has been the inspiration for several large civic and community-wide campaigns in Dallas, Texas; Daytona Beach, Florida; and Pittsburgh, Pennsylvania to name a few.

The Four-Way Test Association, a nonprofit organization, was founded in 1959 to promote the use of the Four-Way Test. The association works to provide resource materials, instruction, speakers and consultants to individuals and groups—introducing and encouraging its use in schools, governments, businesses and homes as a yardstick for building better communications and stronger, more effective relationships between people.

The Four-Way Test . . . of What We Think, Say or Do
1. Is It the TRUTH?
2. Is It FAIR to All Concerned?
3. Will It Build GOODWILL and Better Friendships?
4. Will It Be BENEFICIAL to All Concerned?

Contact the 4-Way Test Association Inc., 4211 Carmichael Rd., Montgomery, AL 36106

### The Mockler Center

The Mockler Center at Gordon-Conwell Theological Seminary was established in 1996 with the help of Mrs. Joanna Mockler in memory of her late husband, Coleman M. Mockler, former chairman of the board of the Gillette Company. Mockler was very interested in exploring how faith affected his work as an executive and industry leader, and he probed issues of faith, values and ethics in business.

Today the Mockler Center's mission is to equip the church and its members to bring the work of Christ into the activities of daily life, especially life in the business world. The Center engages in research, education and direct ministry to bring the resources of biblical interpretation, Christian theology and ethics, and practical ministry into the working world.

The mission is carried out in three arenas: the Gordon-Conwell community, churches and the workplace. Events include classes on practical faith in the marketplace, taught by retired Raytheon CEO Tom Phillips; workplace ministry mentoring groups, led by professor Gary Parrett; a pastor's forum on equipping parishioners for the workplace, featuring Gordon-Conwell trustee Caleb Loring and Dole & Bailey CEO Nancy Matheson Burns; and a lecture series featuring prominent marketplace leaders and scholars from around the country. Mockler Center

Director Will Messenger is also a leader in the seminary's doctor of ministry program in Marketplace Ministry.

For further information on the programs of the Mockler Center call 978-646-4072 or e-mail <mockler@gcts.edu>

## InterVarsity Graduate & Faculty Ministries

God is at work among graduate students and faculty at every college and university, drawing many to himself. Their goal is to see each Christian graduate student and every Christian faculty member share the following four ministry commitments:

*Spiritual formation.* They desire to be conformed to the image of Christ. To achieve this, they cultivate habits that deepen their spiritual lives such as regular prayer, rigorous Bible study and other foundational disciplines.

*Evangelism and service.* As a community they demonstrate and proclaim the gospel to the university so that Jesus Christ is esteemed over all else. Believing that God is at work to initiate people into his kingdom, they pray and work with expectation for their conversion. They also seek to authenticate this witness in their service, especially to the poor and the oppressed.

*Community.* They choose to gather regularly as a community of graduate students and faculty to learn and worship, to challenge and care for each other, and to serve as a welcoming place for both believers and seekers.

*Faith, learning and practice.* Because the God they worship is Creator of all, they seek a unity of truth and practice in the university and all institutions and believe that the integrity of this pursuit will be a witness to the university and professional world.

For more information, please contact director Cam Anderson at InterVarsity Christian Fellowship/USA or visit the GFM website at: <www.ivcf.org/grad>.

## InterVarsity's Business School Ministry

InterVarsity's MBA Ministry supports Christian fellowship groups in the nation's business schools and is a vital part of IVCF's growing ministry to professional students and faculty.

Each year 100,000 young men and women leave their jobs, communities and, in many cases, countries, to study at America's 320 accredited MBA programs. These students are the future entrepreneurs and leaders of American and international business. They will play a significant role in shaping global commerce, governments and culture. The desire is to see students and faculty come to faith in Jesus Christ and pursue a life of integration, in which their Christian faith penetrates and informs all activity, including work and business practice. The objectives are fourfold:

1. Develop MBA fellowships that embody strong personal friendships; hold effective group meetings for Bible study, prayer and worship; and challenge students to relevant and active witness.

2. Host conferences that advance thinking on business-faith integration and provide an effective setting for students, faculty and business professionals to form relationships that will be reinforcing, stimulating and vital for continuing faithfulness.

3. Encourage a continuing network of MBA students, faculty, alumni and mentors that extend well beyond the two years in business school.

4. Plan short-term missions opportunities for MBA students that utilize acquired skills, suggest alternatives to their professional routines, challenge spiritual complacency and motivate compassion and ambition for the needs of the world.

For more information, please contact director John Terrill at InterVarsity Christian Fellowship/USA or visit the MBA Ministry website at <www.ivmba.org>.

**InterVarsity's Ministry in Daily Life (formerly known as Marketplace)**
InterVarsity's Ministry in Daily Life Resource Group exists to help the church recover the biblical truth that God calls all Christians to minister daily in the places they live and work.

The mission of InterVarsity's Ministry in Daily Life Resource Group affirms the biblical truth that Jesus is Lord of all life—including our homes, campuses, neighborhoods, marketplaces and workplaces—and asserts the biblical teaching that God calls all Christians to these places of ministry.

Their mission originated in 1986 from the need to renew and reequip their campus staff to prepare Christian students for ministry in their future workplaces. Since then they have served as a resource center and consulting group for anyone interested in whole-life-discipleship.

For more information, please contact InterVarsity Christian Fellowship/USA or visit the MDL Ministry website at <www.ivmdl.org>.

**Nurses Christian Fellowship**
The good news of Jesus Christ is communicated through relationships. NCF aims to help nurses discover what it means to know God through a relationship with Jesus Christ and to live out that relationship in nursing, bringing hope to their colleagues and those in their care.

NCF provides local, regional, national and international networks for Christian nursing. Local groups meet for prayer, Bible study, mutual encouragement and outreach. NCF staff and volunteers provide mentoring, vision for ministry and help to establish campus and area-wide chapters. NCF enables Christian nurses to officially identify with NCF's vision and goals.

For more information, please contact InterVarsity Christian Fellowship/USA or visit the NCF Ministry website at: <www.ivcf.org/ncf>.

# Book Reviewers & Helpers

**Robert Alexander** reviewed over forty volumes while he was a student at Gordon-Conwell Theological Seminary in the mid-1990s. There he served as a GCTS Mockler Center Scholar after working in a variety of positions in the energy industry and receiving his MBA from Eastern College. He now resides in North Carolina with his wife Rebecca and daughter Katie.

**Georgia Beaverson** is a professional writer living in Madison, Wisconsin, with her husband, Bob, and their two children. Georgia reviewed many of the most recent books in this field and assisted in editing the introduction.

**Steve Cook** served as an associate director of InterVarsity's Marketplace Division and contributed several reviews. He is now executive pastor in Madison, Wisconsin, where he lives with his wife, Diann, and their two children.

**DeAnn Franklin** serves as the administrator of InterVarsity's Marketplace/Ministry in Daily Life group. She spent many hours fine-tuning this manuscript. She lives in Fitchburg, Wisconsin, with husband Larry.

**Pete Hammond,** a veteran InterVarsity leader who founded and directed its Marketplace Division, is the general editor and leader of this project. He is the creative developer of the *Word in Life Study Bible* and the founding director of the Mockler Center at Gordon-Conwell Theological Seminary. He and his wife, Shirley, live in Madison, Wisconsin.

**Wally Kroeker** is editor of *The Marketplace* magazine, published by Mennonite Economic Development Associates. He contributed several reviews and regular encouragement for this work. Wally and his wife, Millie, live in Winnipeg, Canada. They have two married children and three grandchildren.

**Alistair Mackenzie** and his wife, Alison, live in Christchurch, New Zealand, where he is a pastor and founding leader of the marketplace ministry Faith at Work. Several of our reviews come from his M.Th. thesis, which explored the theology of work and the equipping and support of Christians.

**Colman M. Mockler** was the president and CEO of the Gillette Company prior to his death. His widow **Joanna** established the Colman M. Mockler Center at Gordon-Conwell Theological Seminary in honor of his commitment to faith-based integrity as a marketplace leader. The Mockler Center gives seminary students and faculty the opportunity to explore ministry in daily life, and several of its scholarship students reviewed books for this project.

**R. Paul Stevens** has served as professor and academic dean at Regent College, Vancouver, British Columbia, where he is the David J. Brown Professor of Marketplace Theology. Many of the book reviews grew out of Paul's teaching and his students' research.

**Gerry Schoberg** has worked alongside Paul Stevens at Regent College on several marketplace-faith projects. Gerry developed several reviews for this book.

**Denyse Stoneman** was the administrator of InterVarsity's Marketplace Division in the early 1990s when we launched this project. She lives in Madison, Wisconsin, with her husband, Larry.

**Todd Svanoe** reviewed 240 volumes during a year of study in the early days of this project. He is a journalist covering urban faith-based initiatives, and lives in Minneapolis, Minnesota, with his wife, Vicki, and their children.

**Herbert J. Taylor** is the author of the Rotary International's *Four Way Test*. Herbert and Gloria's children—**Robert and Ramona Lockhart** and **Allen and Beverly Mathis**—and their families continue Herbert's legacy through the foundation today. They have helped fund this venture.

**Hunter Weimer** graduated from Gordon-Conwell Theological Seminary in 2000. During his studies he served as the administrator of the Mockler Center and was a Mockler scholar, and provided some book reviews through his study of marketplace ministry. He lives in Falls Church, Virginia, with his wife, Carolyn.

# How to Find Out-of-Print Books

If you can't find a book, here are a few steps you can take to locate the book you are looking for.

Abebooks
415 Dunedin Street, Suite 4
Victoria, BC Canada V8T 5G8
Phone: 250-475-6013
E-mail: <buyertech@abebooks.com>
Website: <www.abebooks.com>

Abooksearch.com
20 million out-of-print books
E-mail: <abook@redshift.com>
Website: <www.abooksearch.com>

Abracadabra Booksearch International
32 S. Broadway
Denver, CO 80209-1506
Phone: 800-545-2665 (toll free within
  USA)
Phone: 303-733-5700
Fax: 303-871-0172
E-mail: <abrabks@abrabks.com>
Website: <www.abrabks.com>

Alibris
1250 45th Street, Suite 100
Emeryville, CA 94608
Website: <www.alibris.com>

The Archives
1387 E. Washington Blvd.
Pasadena, CA 94608
Phone: 800-204-2063 (toll free within
  the USA)

Baker Book House Used/Out of Print
  Division
P.O. Box 6287
Grand Rapids, MI 49506
Phone: 616-957-3110
Fax: 616-676-9573
Website: <www.bakerbooks.com>

Bibliofind
E-mail: <admin@bibliofind.com>
Website: <www.bibliofind.com>

Bookfinder
Website: <www.bookfinder.com>

BookLook
Phone: 800-223-0540 (toll free within USA)
E-mail: <sales@booklook.com>
Website: <www.booklook.com>

Bookstreet, Ltd.
800 Park Avenue
Syracuse, NY 13204
Phone: 315-422-1564
Fax: 315-426-9620
E-mail: <info@rarebooks.com>
Website: <www.rarebooks.com>

Carol Butcher Books
3955 New Road
Youngstown, OH 44515
Phone: (1) 330-793-6832

Ex Libris Theological Books
1340 E. 55th Street
Chicago, IL 60615
Phone: 773-955-3456

Kregel Used Books
P.O. Box 2607
525 Eastern Ave. S.E.
Grand Rapids, MI 49501-2607
Phone: 616-459-9444
Fax: 888-USD-BOOK (toll free)
E-mail: <usedbooks@kregal.com>
Website: <www.kregal.com>

Lodowick Adams, Booksellers
2021 8th Street
Tuscaloosa, AL 35401
Phone: 205-345-9654
Fax: 205-345-9717
E-mail: <info@lodowickadamsbooks.com>
Website: <www.lodowickadams.com>

Loome Theological Booksellers
320 N. 4th Street
Stillwater, MN 55082
Phone: 651-430-1092
Fax: 651-439-8504
E-mail: <loomebooks@prodigy.net>
Website:
  <www.booktown.com/loome/loome.htm>

Steels Used Christian Books
214 East 18th Avenue
North Kansas City, MO 64116
Phone: 816-300-2665
E-mail: <steels@mwis.net>

Trinity Book Service
P.O. Box 395/160 Changebridge Road
Montville, NJ 07045
Phone: 800-722-3584 (from within
  USA only)
Fax: 973-402-2688
E-mail: <TrntyBkSvc@aol.com>
Website: <www.trinitybookservice.org>

Tuttle Antiquarian Books, Inc.
28 South Main Street
Rutland, VT 05701
Phone: 802-773-8229
Fax: 802-773-1493
E-mail: <tuttbooks@together.net>
Website: <Website: <www.tuttlebooks.com>

Windows Booksellers
150 W. Broadway
Eugene, OR 94701
Phone: 800-779-1701 (toll free within USA
  only)
Fax: 541-465-9694
E-mail:
  <WindowsBks@academicbooks.com>
Website: <www.academicbooks.com>

The Worn Bookworm
177 B Short Street
Bishop, CA 93514
Phone: 760-873-6074

Both Barnes and Noble <www.bn.com>
and Amazon <www.amazon.com> have
out-of-print book searches on their web-
sites.